Selected Poetry

VICTOR HUGO

Selected Poetry

translated by Steven Monte

CARCANET

This edition first published in Great Britain
in 2001 by
Carcanet Press Limited
4th Floor, Conavon Court
12–16 Blackfriars Street
Manchester M3 5BQ

A CIP catalogue record for this book
is available from the British Library

ISBN paper edition 1 85754 539 7
ISBN cased edition 1 85754 572 9

The publisher acknowledges financial assistance
from the Arts Council of England

Set in Monotype Garamond by XL Publishing Services, Tiverton
Printed and bound in England by SRP Ltd, Exeter

for my parents

Contents

Contents

from *Les Contemplations* (1856)

from *Contemplations*

Introduction

WHEN ASKED WHO the greatest French poet was, André Gide replied, 'Victor Hugo – alas!' This response sums up the attitude of more than a few modern readers. Yet Hugo's reputation as a poet, dramatist, and novelist was almost unassailable in his own time: for many of his contemporaries he was the most important literary figure of the nineteenth century. His life (1802–1885) almost spanned the century, and when he died at the age of eighty-three an estimated one million people visited his casket, which was placed for a day of viewing under the Arc de Triomphe. This sort of admiration and attention no doubt contributed something to the response of Gide's generation, and grudging praise has remained the staple of Hugo criticism to the present day – occasionally punctured by harsher assessments and the impassioned defences of a few champions.

But in spite of the lament-filled tone with which the French sometimes evoke Hugo, his stature as a poet has never really been questioned in France. French schoolchildren continue to learn by heart poems like 'Tomorrow, at dawn ...' and poets themselves recognize if nothing else his importance and influence. Even academic criticism of Hugo has undergone a resurgence since the 1950s. In English-speaking countries, however, Hugo is still almost unknown as a poet. The old film *The Hunchback of Notre Dame*, the more recent Disney cartoon *Notre-Dame de Paris*, and the Broadway musical based on *Les Misérables* have helped promote his novels perhaps, and there is a slight chance that the general reader has heard of Hugo's plays *Hernani* and *The King Takes his Amusement* through Verdi's operas *Ernani* and *Rigoletto*, or through the controversy *Hernani* sparked and the battle it helped wage on behalf of romanticism. But Hugo's poems? Most Anglophone readers would be hard-pressed to name even one title. This situation seems especially odd in view of the popularity of other nineteenth-century French poets. The poems of Charles Baudelaire and Arthur Rimbaud, for example, are widely available in translation and occupy a space in our poetic imagination. The last English-language poets to praise Hugo highly may be Swinburne and Tennyson, and translations of Hugo are mostly old and out of print.

Given the beauty and power of Hugo's poetry, there is no satisfactory explanation of why it has not received more attention in the English-speaking world. It is true that by the time Hugo had become wildly famous the literary movement and aesthetic he stood for was on the wane, if not in disrepute, in Britain and America. It is also true that some of his work, such as his political poetry, is directed toward a specifically French audience. And naturally there are some translation difficulties: Hugo's use of the alexandrine, for example, has a significance that is hard to grasp outside the context of French poetry. Nevertheless, much of Hugo's poetry seems well suited to a modern audience, in spite or because of its romantic features; meaningful and moving to readers of English whatever its French aspects; and more accessible, on the whole, than the poetry of Rimbaud, Mallarmé, and Valéry – all of whom owe a great deal to Hugo. An English-language audience for Hugo's poetry is an event waiting to happen.

Hugo's Life

The best introduction to Hugo is the poetry itself, though some initial biographical and stylistic remarks can be helpful. As he often pointed out after he became famous, Hugo was the son of an officer in Napoleon's army and a woman from the Vendée (a strongly monarchist region of France). This split background was made tangible to the young Hugo by his parents' estrangement, separation and eventual divorce. At first at least, Victor and his brothers sided with their mother, entering the literary scene in their teens by collaborating on a journal, *The Literary Conservative*. Hugo's early poems courted favour with the restored monarchy, and the King rewarded him with a pension for his 'Ode on the Death of the Duke de Berry', an elegy to an assassinated member of the royal family. After his mother died in 1821, Hugo began to have more contact with his father, and throughout the 1820s gradually adopted new political and aesthetic views. His first collection of verse, *Odes and Other Poems,* appeared in 1822, the same year as Alfred de Vigny's *Poèmes* and two years after Alphonse de Lamartine's *Méditations*. Over the next few years Hugo reworked and expanded this volume into *Odes* (1823) and *New Odes* (1824), then finally into *Odes and Ballads* (1826, 1828). Shortly after the publication of *Odes and Other Poems,* Victor married Adèle Foucher, a woman to whom his brother Eugène had also tendered some affections. Eugène went mad the night of the wedding, and afterwards was placed in an asylum, where he died in 1837. This instance of insanity was one of several in the Hugo family.

Victor Hugo's breakthrough volume of verse was *Orientalia* (1829), a tour de force of poetic forms, images, and diction inspired by contemporary views of the Middle East and literary examples such as Byron and Goethe. While the subject matter of these poems is largely conventional, the technical mastery of pieces like 'Djinns' and 'The

Captive' is astounding, and the poems toward the end of the volume look forward to his more personal lyrics of the next decade. By the 1830s, Hugo had established himself as the leader of the romantic movement in France, largely because of the uproar surrounding his play *Hernani*. At its first performance on 25 February 1930, bohemian romantics flocked to the Comédie Française to show their raucous support for Hugo in what became known as the Battle of Hernani. At this time, romanticism was closely linked with liberal politics: the aesthetic war over Hugo's plays continued in reviews after the première, pitted romanticism against classicism and liberalism against conservatism. Hugo then built on his literary success with his novel *Notre-Dame de Paris* (1831), increased involvement in the theatre, and four more collections of lyric poetry: *Autumn Leaves* (1831), *The Songs of Daybreak* (1835), *Inner Voices* (1837), and *Sunbeams and Shadows* (1840). The poems of this decade are mostly personal, sometimes domestic lyrics, though occasionally Hugo ventures into the political, especially in the first half of *The Songs of Daybreak* and in odes like 'To the Column', which show the poet growing more and more enamoured of the Napoleonic legend.

For all of the confident declarations and idyllic reflections in his poetry, Hugo's private life became increasingly complicated in the 1830s and 1840s. Several poems allude to a kind of ideal domestic life with his four children, wife, and friends gathering around the fire, playing games, and exchanging stories. Whatever domestic bliss existed, however, was punctured in the early 1830s by Madame Hugo's affair with Hugo's close friend, Charles-Augustin Sainte-Beuve. (Sainte-Beuve, France's most eminent nineteenth-century critic, later wrote an autobiographical novel, *Volupté,* that recalls this lovers' triangle.) Hugo in turn had an affair with an actress, Juliette Drouet, and she became his permanent mistress, leaving the theatre and devoting her life to him. Hugo often travelled with Drouet and many of his love poems are addressed to her, but he gradually began to have other affairs, including a scandalous one with a married woman, Léonie Biard, whose husband's detectives caught her and Hugo in bed with each other. In his later life, Hugo became notorious for his flings, which he recorded in code in order to keep them secret from his wife and mistress.

Ostensibly busy with political and social affairs, Hugo did not publish any collections of poetry between 1841 and 1853. In 1841, he was elected to the *Académie Française*. This mostly honorific post (83 francs a month for contributing to the dictionary of the French language) opened up new social and political doors for him. He became a regular visitor to the royal family and especially to Louis-

Philippe, conversing with the King late into the night. Hugo did not own land or pay enough taxes to stand for Parliament, but as a member of the Academy he could be elevated to the peerage and take his place in the upper chamber. (Louis-Philippe helped him to achieve this in 1845.) Meanwhile, tragedy had struck in Hugo's private life. His favourite child, Léopoldine, and her husband, Charles Vacquerie, had drowned at Villequier on 4 September 1843, just three months after their wedding. As evidenced in poems like 'To the One Who Stayed Behind in France', up until his exile Hugo marked this event with annual visits to Léopoldine's grave. He also wrote many poems about his daughter over the years and organized his collection of poems, *Les Contemplations* (1855), around her death, breaking it into two volumes, 'Former Times (1830–1843)' and 'Today (1843–1855)'.

Before Hugo could bring this collection and *Les Misérables,* the novel he had begun, to completion, he became more deeply involved with politics following the 1848 revolution. In 1849, he was elected to the legislative assembly, but, with the coup of Louis Napoleon in December 1851, was forced to flee Paris, going first to Belgium with the help of Juliette Drouet, then, in 1852, to Jersey, an island off the French coast, and finally to Guernsey, another Channel Island, in 1855. This forced exile did wonders for Hugo's creative output. After composing political invectives like *Napoleon the Little* (1852), he published a volume of poems directed against Louis Napoleon, *Punishments* (1853), before returning to the more personal lyrics of *Contemplations.* In 1859, Hugo published the first series of *The Legend of the Centuries,* a collection of mostly narrative poems ('little epics') beginning with the dawn of creation and continuing through the present day and even into the future. In 1862, Hugo published *Les Misérables*, his most famous novel.

Exile seemed to take a greater toll on Hugo's family than on Hugo himself. In 1863, his daughter Adèle stowed away on a ship bound for Canada in search of an English army officer with whom she was infatuated, and eventually went mad: (her story has been dramatized in the French film *Adèle H.*). Weary of island life, Madame Hugo moved what remained of the household to Brussels, leaving Hugo and Juliette Drouet alone on Guernsey for a time. Hugo went on writing, publishing a collection of poetry, *Songs of the Streets and the Woods* (1865), and a novel, *The Toilers of the Sea* (1867). *Songs of the Streets and the Woods* stands in direct contrast to *The Legend of the Centuries* in that it consists of short poems in short lines – mostly octosyllabic quatrains – on lyric subjects. This deliberately light collection may have been Hugo's response to the chiselled quatrains of Théophile Gautier's *Emaux et Camées* (*Enamels and Cameos,* 1852–72), a kind of challenge and nod of admiration to his old friend.

In 1868, Madame Hugo died. One might imagine that Hugo, by now a sixty-six-year-old grandfather with a host of successful novels, plays, and poems behind him, would settle into a quiet retirement with his lifelong mistress, but instead events took a turn that propelled him back to France and public life. When the Franco-Prussian war brought about the fall of Louis Napoleon and the Second Empire in 1870, Hugo returned to Paris, where he stayed through the Prussians' siege of the city. He commemorated these experiences in his next volume of verse, *The Horrific Year* (1872). With the help of his reputation as a man of the people, his long-standing opposition to the empire in exile, and, in general, his immense fame, Hugo was elected a national representative in 1871; in 1876 he was elected senator. As a politician Hugo was better at making thunderous speeches that at the practical implementation of programmes. As a representative of Paris, he opposed vigorously the surrender of any French land to the Prussians (in fact, he boasted that France would cross the Rhine and take German cities the way Napoleon's armies had done half a century earlier) and indignantly stormed out of the peace talks, resigning his position. Hugo's views might be best expressed as nationalistic with a strong show of moral support for the downtrodden. After the defeat of the Paris Commune, for example, he called for clemency, even though he did not support the aims of the Communards. He went so far as to harbour fugitives in Belgium, an activity that resulted in the Belgian government asking him to leave the country and an angry mob surrounding his house and calling for his head.

As before, Hugo's public notoriety was accompanied by private tragedy. Soon after he left the peace talks his son Charles died of a heart attack followed by a haemorrhage. The funeral took place on the same day that the Commune began. As the funeral train made its way through Paris's streets, it became something like the first public ceremony of the new state: people emptied out of cafés to follow the procession while barricades thrown up by revolutionaries forced the mourners to follow a circuitous course to the cemetery. Early in 1872, Hugo's daughter Adèle was finally brought back from the New World where she had fled a decade before; mentally ill, she failed to recognize her father and family and was placed in an asylum outside Paris. Hugo's only other remaining child, François-Victor, died of renal tuberculosis the following year.

Throughout all of the public and private travail, Hugo continued to write. In the 1870s he published several autobiographical commentaries and some travel literature. He also completed and published *Ninety-three* (1874), a historical novel centered on a pivotal year in the

French Revolution. His poetic output of this decade includes the second series of *The Legend of the Centuries* (1877) and *The Art of Being a Grandfather* (1877). The latter volume shows Hugo at his most domestic, a grandfather playing with, spoiling, and being spoiled by his two grandchildren, Georges and Jeanne ('George' and 'Jeannine' in my translations). After a stroke and congestion of the brain in June of 1878, Hugo wrote little poetry in the remaining years of his life. In part through the efforts of his editors, however, his published output continued uninterrupted, preserving his public image of vitality. Poetic works that had already been written, in some cases many years before, appeared one after the other: four long poems, *The Pope* (1878), *The Highest Pity* (1879), *Religions and Religion* (1880), and *The Ass* (1880); a volume of 'satiric, dramatic, lyric, and epic verse', *The Four Winds of the Spirit* (1881); a play, *Torquemada* (1882); and the third and final series of *The Legend of the Centuries* (1883).

The events of Hugo's last years include countless honours bestowed on the aging writer; a seventy-ninth birthday party in 1881 ('Victor Hugo entering his eightieth year') for which half a million people passed by Hugo's house, saluting him as he and his grandchildren waved from the balcony; and the death of Juliette Drouet from stomach cancer in 1883. To judge from the coded recordings in his diary, Hugo remained sexually active into the spring of 1885, almost to the end. In May, 1885 he contracted pneumonia, seemed to recover, then died in a little over a week. His decline was front-page news in many newspapers around the world. Obituaries compared Hugo's life with the history of the nineteenth century, and the day after his funeral was a national holiday.

Hugo's Poetry

Readers coming to Hugo after French symbolists like Baudelaire and Mallarmé, Anglophone modernists like T.S. Eliot and Wallace Stevens, or any poet who places a high value on poetic economy may initially find his work exasperating. Hugo thrives on expansiveness, believes strongly in human progress, and is unabashed by multiple exclamation points. At times his language seems overinflated, poetic in the pejorative sense, or padded to fill out the line. Conversely, readers coming from Hugo's older and younger contemporaries, William Wordsworth and Walt Whitman, may at first be reassured to find similarities in tone and gesture, including romantic themes and concerns, only to be upset by the combination of philosophical reflections and topical invectives, the sublime and the ridiculous, in his work. Further difficulties may arise due to Hugo's verse forms, especially his alexandrines, if only because most English speakers since romanticism have not been entirely able to disassociate rhyming couplets from artificiality. For readers of any stripe, of course, the sheer volume of his work can prove to be a stumbling block to enjoyment.

Most barriers to an appreciation of Hugo will fall given an appropriate selection of poems: if you like poetry, the odds are that you will enjoy something in Hugo the first time you read him. But as with all poetry, a closer look at the style and the context in which the poems have been received can deepen one's appreciation. Hugo's expansiveness, for example, is a relative trait: as 'Tomorrow, at dawn …', 'At Villequier', and 'To the One Who Stayed Behind in France' show, Hugo was capable of writing short, medium-sized, and long elegies; his poems range from brief lyrics like 'My Two Daughters' to sprawling poems in multiple parts like 'The Expiation'. More importantly, Hugo's poems tend toward a conversational style even at their most visionary moments and thus remain easy to peruse whatever their length. In spite, and to some extent because, of all the rhymes and start-and-stop rhythms in his poetry, Hugo's verse feels almost like prose with its unfragmented expressions of thought and forward-moving flow. Hugo furthers this effect by incorporating everyday words and phrases into passages that otherwise seem invested in a more grandiose rhetoric, such as the opening of 'The Parricide' ('Le Parricide'):

One day, Kanut, when twilight, soft and heaven-sent,
Was closing eyes everywhere beneath the firmament,
Having only one (blind and giant) witness, night,
Seeing his old and senile father under torchlight
Asleep, without a guard or guard dog – bending low,
Murdered him, remarking, 'Even he doesn't know.'
Then he was a great king.

[Un jour, Kanut, à l'heure où l'assoupissement
Ferme partout les yeux sous l'obscur firmament,
Ayant pour seul témoin la nuit, l'aveugle immense,
Vit son père Swéno, vieillard presque en démence,
Qui dormait, sans un garde à ses pieds, sans un chien;
Il le tua, disant: Lui-même n'en sait rien.
Puis il fut un grand roi.]

In this passage, the image of twilight 'closing eyes everywhere beneath the firmament', the metaphor of night as a 'blind and giant' witness, and other more overtly poetic details are framed by the pedestrian phrases 'One day', 'Even he doesn't know', and 'Then he was a great king'. What is more, the verse keeps advancing, refusing to pause too long on its lyric descriptions, surprising the reader with the sudden act of murder, and then summing up the consequences of everything in a pointedly short sentence that stops in the middle of the line. Hugo is playing the poetic and the prosaic off each other.

As can be glimpsed already, Hugo's simultaneously lyrical and conversational style owes something to the way he handles rhyme and rhythm. Understanding the full effect of Hugo's innovations in verse requires some literary-historical background. Hugo's favourite poetic line, the *alexandrin,* was the most common verse form in France from the seventeenth century to the twentieth. The French alexandrine couplet consists of a pair of rhymed, twelve-syllable lines. The rules for composing poems in alexandrines are more stringent than anything comparable in English: they develop gradually in the sixteenth century, are said to be fully present in the poetry of François de Malherbe (1555–1628), and are codified by the time of the classical dramatists Pierre Corneille (1606–84) and Jean Racine (1633–99). A suggestive, though somewhat misleading, English analogue is anapestic tetrametre:

> Twas the nìght| before Chrìst|mas and àll| through the hoùse,
> Not a creà|ture was stìr|ring, not è|ven a moùse.

The insistent rhythms of the English are virtually absent from the French alexandrine, where stress, if it exists at all, occurs at the end of the phrase when intonation rises. In the classical French alexandrine, there is also a break, or caesura, in the middle of the line, typically coinciding with the end of a clause or a phrase:

> You can see that from here. All ochres and chalk-whites. ('Letter')
> [Tu vois cela d'ici. Des ocres et des craies. ('Lettre')]

The break need not be as abrupt as in the above example, though Hugo often uses the caesura in this way. Hugo also dislocates the midline caesura by adding other breaks in the line:

> The water runs; a finch passes; 'Thank you!' I say,
> 'Thank you, my God!' I live this way. And in this way … ('Letter')

> [L'eau coule, un verdier passe; et, moi, je dis: Merci!
> Merci, Dieu tout-puissant! – Ainsi je vis; ainsi … ('Lettre')]

Another feature of Hugo's alexandrines is what might be called 'hard enjambment'. Enjambment is the carrying over of a clause or other grammatical unit from one line to the next, as in Shakespeare's 'Let me not to the marriage of true minds/ Admit impediments.' In classical French poetry, enjambment was rarely used in a way that called attention to itself. Hugo, however, influenced by some famous examples in the work of André Chénier (1762–94), set about exploring the expressive possibilities of meant-to-be-noticed enjambment:

An Aeginean hand sculpted there, on its base,
Europa ...   ('The Spinning Wheel of Omphale')

[Un ouvrier d'Égine a sculpté sur la plinthe
Europe ...   («Le Rouet d'Omphale»)]

A small chick runs, a child plays and dances; a lamb
Jumps ...   ('The clarity that fills ...')

[Le poussin court, l'enfant joue et danse, l'agneau
Saute ...   («Le firmament est plein ...»)]

While Hugo's opposition to Napoleon III, his innovations in the theatre, and his support for the downtrodden may account for his revolutionary reputation during his lifetime, his experiments in verse have arguably had a more lasting influence. These experiments go beyond the formal issues surrounding the alexandrine to such features as a vastly increased range of poetic vocabulary and subject matter, and a provocative blend of the lowbrow and the highbrow.

Readers have not signalled out for praise all features of Hugo's poetry. More than one critic has felt that his facility with rhyme, for example, leads him to ramble on occasion. The enumerations and lists of adjectives that mark his poetry may add to the prosaic feel and rhythmic drive of his verse, but they can also feel like padding. Some adjectives, like *sombre, sinistre, absolu, éternel,* and *ineffable,* are used frequently and in ways that suggest that Hugo did not care about their precise meanings. Although Hugo's poems raise issues that have far-reaching philosophical, religious, and political implications, his actual thoughts on these subjects often seem cliché-ridden, arising out of or moving toward simplistic morals and punchlines. (Hugo's poetic universe sometimes feels like a child's fantasy, a place in which giant and almost unnamable forces struggle, and where justice prevails as if in compensation for the real world's inevitable inadequacy.) Even or especially at their most intense moments, Hugo's poems risk bombast. Enjoying Hugo does not preclude acknowledging that there is some truth to these criticisms. For a modern reader, appreciation of Hugo's poetry may even require such an acknowledgement, an updated version of Gide's sigh. Nevertheless some of the criticisms levelled against the work are only half truths, stemming more from caricature than evenhanded appraisal, and many are misdirected, missing what is most important about the poems. Hugo's expansiveness, for example, may at times verge on longwindedness, but it is also fundamental to his voice, if not his subject matter, and often in its excess enacts or points to some of the poetry's concerns – the difficulty of expression, an overwhelming emotion, the immensity of a scene, the power of a vision. Hugo himself spoke of the need to understand his work as a whole, a consideration that takes some of the sting out of criticisms directed at local shortcomings in the verse, and that adds depth to his view of his œuvre as a monumental artistic accomplishment, like the epics of the ancients, in which the whole is greater than the sum of the parts. (In his writings and drawings, Hugo in fact represented his work in architectural terms, the most striking example of which may be his 'vision' of *The Legend of the Centuries:* a massive temple with a long, winding procession of people leading up to it.) Hugo's aesthetic views surface now and then in the poems, sometimes with a touch of humour:

> For God composes a long poem with variants,
> And like old Homer, he repeats himself now and then,
> Only it's with flowers, forests, waves, or a mountain!
>
> ('Shepherds and Flocks')

> [Car Dieu fait un poëme avec des variantes;
> Comme le vieil Homère, il rabâche parfois,
> Mais c'est avec les fleurs, les monts, l'onde et les bois!
>
> ('Pasteurs et troupeaux')]

As Hugo chides God, via a comparison to Homer, for repeating himself in his creations, he alludes to the famous adage which downplays flaws in works of genius, 'Even Homer nods'. Hugo is nodding toward his own work, placing himself on the same level as the author of the *Iliad* and the author of all creation, maybe even above them.

One way to approach Hugo's poetry is to allow it room to work its magic. 'To allow it room' should suggest not shutting down one's critical faculties so much as letting oneself be guided by the desire to experience something new, the way one allows a piece of music holding in suspension several motifs, or a piece of critical prose juggling several lines of argument, time to yield its full power or insight because the pleasure one feels in the meantime promises a more holistic satisfaction. Though hardly constructed like Bach fugues, Hugo's poems yield immediate pleasures that increase as one becomes more familiar with them and experiences surprising convergences in thought, image, sound. Hugo is not difficult in the ways that Mallarmé and Eliot can be, but he may require his own sort of acclimation.

For readers, like myself, apt to hold Hugo to the highest standards, out of admiration, mistrust, or a little of each, I offer some additional experiences as a translator. Time and time again, when I was stuck translating a phrase that I suspected Hugo had included to fill a line, or a word that seemed chosen because of its sonorous quality without regard to the register or sense of its context, or an image that had little to recommend it other than some vaguely 'poetic' quality, I would find upon closer inspection that my initial impression was either mistaken or misguided. Often my misjudgement stemmed from Hugo's use of familiar words in unexpected contexts or unusual senses. In 'The Infanta's Rose', for example, Hugo describes seeing a large palace 'comme au fond d'une gloire', a phrase that, taking 'gloire' in its usual and potentially grandiloquent sense, 'glory', one might render 'as at the bottom of a glory' or 'as though deep inside a glory'. The phrase feels awkward, though it makes a kind of sense: the poem has already described the sun setting behind the palace and 'glory' helps evoke the image of a bright light framing a comparatively dark building. Hugo is in fact employing 'gloire' in a technical sense. The word refers to the halo-like light emanating from behind saintly or supernatural figures in medieval paintings, where the figures appear to emerge from the canvas. For all the precision of this simile, Hugo is not comparing the appearance of a palace, backed by the setting sun and therefore seeming to jut out more, to a painterly phenomenon, the way John Donne compares two lovers to a draftsman's compass, in order to establish a series of logically consistent correspondences. Nor is Hugo primarily drawing on the recherché sense of a rhyming word, like Mallarmé, to unlock some secret within language, or to cause the reader to experience a *frisson* of momentary disequilibrium. 'Gloire' seems dictated mostly by Hugo's vision of the scene at hand and the poem's thematic concerns: his verbal portrait of the infanta is likely to have been inspired by a famous painting by Diego de Silva y Velázquez, the infanta is decidedly innocent and virginal (a mixture of those oft-haloed figures, the baby Jesus and Mary), and the background subject of the poem is Philip II and his would-be glorious military enterprise, the Armada. Consciously or not, Hugo has combined the painterly and everyday senses of 'gloire'.

Even when the logic behind Hugo's diction is not clear, his words are worth pondering. Reading through the poems with an eye to translation, I noticed that those infamously vague and repeated words of his were more precise than reputation had lead me to suppose and that they accrued suggestive senses through repetition. One such word, *sinistre,* appears frequently enough to make one wonder whether Hugo suffered from paranoia: must everything be sinister? But after one acquires some familiarity with his poetry, patterns in usage emerge. Hugo's syntax sometimes forces *sinistre,* an adjective, to become something like an adverb in that the word points to the verb it is near as much if not more than to the noun it modifies, as if to suggest that the action described by the verb is an event that ushers in ill:

> Then my hand would open and I'd say, 'Nothing lasts!'
> And the bouquet fell, sinister …
> > ('To the One Who Stayed Behind in France')

> [Puis ma main s'ouvrait triste, et je disais: Tout fuit!
> Et le bouquet tombait, sinistre …
> > («À Celle qui est restée en France»)]

This sense of foreboding also haunts the more typically adjectival usages of *sinistre:*

> The wool of all the sinister sheep of the sea.
> > ('Shepherds and Flocks')
> [La laine des moutons sinistres de la mer.
> > («Pasteurs et troupeaux»)]

> Nor the shrill insistence of the sinister gulls   ('Letter')
> [Ni l'importunité des sinistres oiseaux.   («Lettre»)]

The two lines cited above come at the end of their respective poems and thus suggest looming or present danger as much via their climactic position in a lyric meditation as through meanings latent or acquired in 'sinister'. Apparently Hugo is pushing *sinistre* toward its etymological roots: the Latin *sinister* means 'on the left'; it acquired the senses 'unlucky' and 'ominous' from the Roman augurs' practice of interpreting birds flying to the left as an evil omen. His sinister birds at the end of 'Letter' virtually revive this historical meaning. It is likely that Hugo, a good Latinist writing in a Romance language, is consciously playing on the etymology of *sinistre*. (In 'The Parricide' he describes someone walking 'vers la gauche sinistre', 'toward the left and sinister side'.) But even if this wordplay or like effects in his poetry are not entirely planned, his ear seldom fails him.

Translating Hugo

Translating a substantial selection of Hugo's poetry is a challenge different from that of translating many other poets' work, even poetry from the same period. In some respects, the task of Hugo's translator is easier than that of, say, Rimbaud's or Mallarmé's: Hugo's expansive style and aesthetic allow the translator more room, if not licence, to operate; the sense of his poems is largely straightforward; he is one of France's greatest poets yet remains woefully undertranslated; his audience is potentially large given the wide range of his poetic subjects; and his poems gain a great deal from being read together even as they thankfully demand selection (conservative estimates place his poetic production at over 155,000 lines). Some of these points in favour of the translator are at the same time disadvantages: unlike the difficult poetry of the symbolists, Hugo's poetry feels closer to everyday language and syntax and thus more brutally exposes any line which, as the saying goes, sounds like translation; his expansiveness, even or especially when rendered literally, can misleadingly come across as overblown or as the translator's embellishment; and selecting poems from such a large œuvre will inevitably force the translator to make painful choices, resulting nonetheless in a gargantuan enterprise (especially if one tries to keep to the Hugolian spirit), and raising thorny questions about what is included and what is left out, and about audience.

The translator of Hugo is immediately faced with one question: whether to render Hugo's rule-laden yet flexible French verse in English metre and rhyme. Given a clear sense of audience and purpose, this question turns out to be less difficult to answer than one might imagine. If the translator's aim is to help an Anglophone audience appreciate Hugo through English versions of the poems, prose translations are a mistake and free verse translations will at least need to gesture toward the effects of rhyme and metre. Prose translations, however useful as aids for reading the French, would leave readers wondering why anyone would declare (even with a sigh) that Hugo is the greatest French poet. Hugo's verse is like Robert Frost's in that the ways in which it plays the poetic and the prosaic off each other are fundamental to its power as poetry. Removing either element would short-circuit the poetry's energy and produce something that one would hesitate to call a poem. Consider the effects first of removing the line breaks and incidental capitals from the famous close of Frost's 'Stopping by Woods on a Snowy Evening' ('The woods are lovely, dark, and deep, but I have promises to keep, and miles to go before I sleep, and miles to go before I sleep') and then of undoing the rhymes, the more insistent rhythms, and the repetition of the final phrase ('The woods are beautiful and mysterious, but I have responsibilities and a long road to travel before I can rest'). Even a free verse translation is likely to be flaccid – mentally reinsert the line breaks into the de-rhymed version of Frost – especially considering that Hugo's favourite verse form requires a rhyme in every other line, and that he often exploits specific features of the alexandrine couplet in order to give his poetry its characteristic rhythmic drive. These formal concerns are even the poetry's subject matter on occasion:

> It's all true. Curse us. The measured line that wore
> A band of twelve feathers on its forehead before
> And jumped between rackets every time it was hit
> By what they call prosody and good etiquette,
> Breaks rules now, deceives the caesura by a word,
> And escapes, shuttlecock changing into a bird,
> From the cage of mid-line ...   ('Reply to an Act of Accusation')

> [C'est vrai, maudissez-nous. Le vers, qui sur son front
> Jadis portait toujours douze plumes en rond,
> Et sans cesse sautait sur la double raquette
> Qu'on nomme prosodie et qu'on nomme étiquette,
> Rompt désormais la règle et trompe le ciseau,
> Et s'échappe, volant qui se change en oiseau,
> De la cage césure ...   («Réponse à un acte d'accusation»)]

If, as is often claimed, syntax is a kind of metaphor in Mallarmé, rhyme and rhythm are virtually figures of thought in Hugo. A good translation must find ways to convey their effects.

A more prickly question facing the translator is what sort of English verse form suits Hugo's poetry best. Over the years many translators have felt that iambic pentameter is the closest English equivalent to the French alexandrine. Shakespeare, Milton, Wordsworth, Browning, Yeats, Frost, and many other poets writing during and beyond the centuries in which the alexandrine dominated French verse have accustomed our ears – so the argument runs – to a line generally ten syllables long and in a rhythm supposedly close to that of natural speech: five units, or feet, of alternating unstressed and stressed syllables, with varying allowances for alternative feet within the basic pattern. Established and perceived norms certainly affect how we read, and the strong tradition of blank verse and rhyming pentameter in English is a compelling rationale for rendering French alexandrines in iambic pentameter. Given its epic pedigree, blank verse may in fact be well suited to Hugo's long narrative poems. This logic of historically accrued associations, though, can just as easily be applied against iambic pentameter. Pairs of rhyming pentameter lines ('heroic couplets') may evoke the ghosts of Dryden and Pope, a neo-classical aesthetic of balance and proportion, and in doing so infuse the translation with associations at cross-purposes with the effects one is seeking to produce – a particular danger when translating romantic poetry. And if blank verse feels ordinary to an Anglophone ear, it risks domesticating Hugo's odd alexandrines. Perhaps a mildly alienating verse form is more fitting. When used to exclude all other possibilities, any rationale for translation can become a rationalization.

Iambic pentameter is not an inevitable substitute for the *alexandrin;* with Hugo's poetry an equally if not more compelling case can be made for an English alexandrine. Most obviously, the extra syllables of the alexandrine give the translator more room and thus more flexibility, a welcome situation even when rhyme is not a concern. To the objection that alexandrines 'just don't work' in English, one need only adduce the opening sonnet of Sir Philip Syndey's *Astrophil and Stella,* whose advice to the poet seems especially apt: "'Fool,' said my muse to me, "look in thy heart and write.'" More importantly, the feel of an English alexandrine depends at least as much on how the translator handles the line as on some intrinsic property of it, properties that have become associated with a given verse form change and can, to some extent, be changed, and Hugo's alexandrines seem especially in need of a more expansive English equivalent, if only to accommodate his tone and gestures. (Additional arguments specific to Hugo's verse might be gleaned from my literary-historical discussion of the French alexandrine.) Conversely, endorsements of particular properties of iambic pentameter should not exclude the alexandrine from the translator's repertoire. It is sometimes claimed, for example, that an iambic pentameter line can be delivered more rapidly and thereby avoid sounding pompous. But this claim, even if true, presumably applies more to verse plays than lyric poetry. Finally, as inspiring as successful translations in heroic couplets are (Richard Wilbur's versions of Molière come to mind), the untapped possibilities of the English alexandrine may be more enticing.

Whatever the challenges of translating verse poetry in verse, even metered verse, the idea of a verse translation is relatively uncontroversial. Rhyming, by contrast, may be the leading cause of consternation among readers of poetry in translation. Infidelity to the original is the main charge here, though readers arguably ought to be more critical of poor aesthetic results. (If the original is of high quality, a faithful translation that produces a mediocre poem is, in reality, unfaithful, and potentially performs a disservice to the poem, the poem's author, and poetry in general; a successful poetic imitation, even if it strays from the spirit of the original, will at least be worth something as a poem.) At any rate, aesthetically satisfying rhymes do not inherently produce unfaithful translations, however much they may heighten the reader's suspicions, and they ideally help keep a translation faithful. My rhymes aspire to the ease and the beauty of Hugo's precisely because I want my translations to remain faithful to those important qualities of his poetry. Yet for all of the emphasis I place on crafting English alexandrines and English rhyming couplets, I do not so much seek formal parity – twelve syllables for twelve syllables, one rhyme for one rhyme – as affective equivalence. Poetic translations should first and foremost feel like the originals. In practice this means that I occasionally drop a rhyme or alter the scheme of the couplets. For some verse forms, I skirt the rhyme-for-rhyme approach still more. When translating quatrains with either *abab* or *abba* rhyme schemes, for example, I generally concentrate on the rhyme that closes the stanza, and even then let rhythm and line integrity perform much of the poetic work:

> And today my eyes are only open half-way;
> I don't turn around even when my name is called;
> I am full of stupor and ennui, like a man
> Who wakes before dawn without having slept at all.
> ('Veni, Vidi, Vixi')

> [Maintenant, mon regard ne s'ouvre qu'à demi;
> Je ne me tourne plus même quand on me nomme;
> Je suis plein de stupeur et d'ennui, comme un homme
> Qui se lève avant l'aube et qui n'a pas dormi. («Veni, Vidi, Vixi»)]

For at least one other Hugolian stanza, the consistency of my rhymes varies substantially from poem to poem, sometimes within the same poem. The stanza in question has an *aabccb* rhyme scheme, and consists of two pairs of alexandrine couplets divided by a six-syllable 'half-alexandrine' that rhymes with another six-syllable line following the second couplet. One of the most striking features of this stanza is the interplay between the long lines and the short lines:

Forced by the steps he took to come up off the ground,
The leaves that were lying in the peopleless woods
      Went flying in a pack.
In the same way sometimes, when the soul is sad, our thoughts
Fly upwards on their wounded wings for a moment,
      Then suddenly fall back.   ('Olympio's Sadness')

[Les feuilles qui gisaient dans le bois solitaire,
S'efforçant sous ses pas de s'élever de terre,
      Couraient dans le jardin;
Ainsi, parfois, quand l'âme est triste, nos pensées
S'envolent un moment sur leurs ailes blessées,
      Puis retombent soudain.   («Tristesse d'Olympio»)]

As the verse expands following the third line, then contracts in the final line, the poetry enacts the sensation of briefly entertaining a hope. Rhyme plays only a part in this effect, and my translation efforts are geared accordingly toward keeping the line lengths, syntax, and closing phrase intact. On other occasions, however, both or one of the couplet rhymes can take on greater prominence:

The pale night lifted its face into the clouds;
Things were dissolving, diminished, colourless
      In the moon's distant eyes.
When night falls, or rises from the ashes at day's end,
All at once one senses sadness descend
      And anxiety rise.   ('Magnitudo Parvi')

[La pâle nuit levait son front dans les nuées;
Les choses s'effaçaient, blêmes, diminuées,
      Sans forme et sans couleur;
Quand il monte de l'ombre, il tombe de la cendre;
On sentait à la fois la tristesse descendre
      Et monter la douleur.   («Magnitudo Parvi»)]

The rising and falling effect in 'Olympio's Sadness' is reversed here and expressed in a different timbre as sadness descends and anxiety rises. In the first couplet, the rhythm resulting from the list of adjectives is arguably more prominent than the rhyme. In the second couplet, the pause occasioned by the line break and rhyme is crucial to the impact of the final line. The rising anxiety comes across as more devastating than the falling sadness; nightfall (or moonrise) does not bring about peace or some other opposite of sadness, but apprehension. My translation tries to reflect the importance of the pause and the various oppositions at play in Hugo's verse – so much so that, besides retaining the couplet rhyme and the closing rhyme, I have shortened the final alexandrine to emphasize the pause, and I have reworked Hugo's phrasing to keep some of the more striking images, the moon and the ashes, active and in focus. The moral of the story is that the importance of any given poetic feature – rhyme, diction, imagery, or whatever – cannot be determined in advance, and that staying faithful to the original cannot be reduced to formal or verbal fidelity.

Some general descriptions of my translations will better outline my approach to translating Hugo than a lengthy theoretical discussion. With the exception of 'The Expiation', my translations contain the same number of lines as the originals, and I strive to maintain the formal integrity of individual lines, especially with regard to sharp caesuras and enjambments. (Readers with some French will not, I think, experience a rhythmic jolt when glancing occasionally at the facing original.) My alexandrines are 'loose', mostly iambic (no 'Night Before Christmas' effect) and regular enough to suggest norms analogous to those of the French while allowing for frequent rhythmic substitution and syllabic variation – in short, verse that ideally keeps the length and content of the line intact yet is supple enough to match Hugo's twists and turns. Verbal fidelity is a priority for me, to the point where I can imagine a reader surprised to find that some of the most fluid rhyming lines are also some of the most accurate word-for-word translations. In some instances where literal meaning may be obscured in an otherwise faithful rendering, I provide an explanatory note in back of the book. Readers will have to decide for themselves whether I step over the line, so to speak, regarding matters of fidelity and licence. One of the best tests for readers who know French is to read one of my translations straight through, then read the original and compare the experiences. For readers with little or no French, I offer the closing passage from 'Clearing' ('Éclaircie') as a test case:

A gleam, a faint ray that shoots from the cradle
A woman balances on a cottage threshold
Glazes the flowers, fields, and waves, then turns to gold
When striking a grave near the church it sinks behind.
The day plunges into the sea, and tries to find
Its shadow, kisses it through the surf and is gone.
Everything is quiet, mild, appeased: God looks on.

[Une lueur, rayon vague, part du berceau
Qu'une femme balance au seuil d'une chaumière,

Dore les champs, les fleurs, l'onde, et devient lumière
En touchant un tombeau qui dort près du clocher.
Le jour plonge au plus noir du gouffre, et va chercher
L'ombre, et la baise au front sous l'eau sombre et hagarde.
Tout est doux, calme, heureux, apaisé; Dieu regarde.]

The degree of verbal fidelity in this example may be low for my translations taken as a whole, but the passage is fairly typical of poems translated in rhyming alexandrine couplets. A prose version with slashes to mark the line breaks would go something like this: 'A glimmer, a vague ray, issues from the cradle/ which a woman is balancing on the threshold of a cottage,/ gilds the fields, flowers, waves, and turns to light/ when touching a grave that sleeps near a steeple./ The day dives into the blackest [part] of the abyss, and goes looking for/ [its] shadow, and kisses it on the forehead beneath the sombre and haggard water./ Everything is mild, calm, happy, appeased; God looks on.'

Though not always a conscious strategy, the drive to render the original poem's power and beauty while remaining as faithful as possible to its particular words and effects may be the working principle behind my translations. My rhymes, like my rhythms, aim at potent flexibility: I do not hesitate to use half- and other less-than-full rhymes, for example, sometimes with the goal of producing a 'soft rhyme' closer to the feel of the French. (English rhythms and rhymes can sound more definitive than the French – perhaps another argument in favour of the English alexandrine, with its leisurely reputation, against crisp and short pentameter verse.) As with my rhythmic substitutions, though, I try not to employ near rhymes with so great a frequency as to diminish their effect, obscure important formal patterns, or disrupt the poem's musical atmosphere. And while I take care to reproduce rhymes and other formal features of Hugo's verse, I do not fetishize any single feature: I may make an extra effort to bring across Hugo's start-and-stop rhythms, for example, but I don't try to preserve every caesura. Tact and attention to local effects are often better guides to translation than abstract rules or principles, and a successful poetic translation will inevitably be a strong interpretation of the poem.

Selecting and Presenting Hugo's Poems

Hugo's work demands selection for reasons that go beyond its vast size. To be sure, at a time when editors strongly prefer to publish poets in *Complete* and *Collected* volumes, it is already significant that no publisher is tempted to venture even a selectively complete translation of Hugo – 'Victor Hugo's Poems of Exile', or some such thing. Publishing a translation of *one* of Hugo's collections is barely imaginable. *Contemplations,* for example, contains over 150 poems, of which a few are over fifteen pages long, several over ten pages, and many over five pages. Even if publication size were not an issue, though, any translator hoping that Hugo's poetry will reach readers and that readers will enjoy it (any translator who, in short, cares deeply about the poetry) would still want to present the poems in a selected form. To put the matter in an ungenerous perspective, Hugo's poems vary as much in quality as they do in size and subject matter. Stated in another way, Hugo's best qualities are scattered throughout his work. When first reading his poetry, it helps to have a guide.

Fortunately with Hugo, most poems seem to select themselves. While one does not need to search far to find wildly divergent views on what is Hugo's best poetry, many poems appear regularly enough in anthologies to be considered standards. Any selection of his poetry that failed to include, say, 'Tomorrow, at dawn …' or 'Boaz Asleep', would either be wilfully perverse or risk appearing so. The regularly included poems are, happily, among Hugo's best: when selecting work to translate I never felt I had to compromise my aesthetic judgment in order to make room for an anthology piece I did not like. At most, some poem which was not my first choice, like 'Olympio's Sadness', nevertheless contained enough strong moments to win me over. In the vast majority of cases – with poems such as 'The Djinns', 'To Albrecht Dürer', 'The Spinning Wheel of Omphale', 'At Villequier', 'Shepherds and Flocks', and 'The Infanta's Rose' – the question of leaving out was never an issue and should not be one. Some lesser known poems also seemed to me to demand inclusion, both because they appealed to me and because they translated well. In this category I would place selections like 'Rapture', 'My Two Daughters', 'Letter', 'Open Windows', 'Jeannine Asleep', and 'The Sister of Mercy', poems which, while not obscure, are perhaps less likely to find their way into short anthologies of Hugo's poetry. The usual suspects and the lesser known gems account for virtually every poem in my selected Hugo. Even the temptation to include additional poems in order to show the poet's range proved as rare as the feeling that I was including an anthology piece I did not like. Hugo's best poems amply demonstrate his variety.

My main aim in presentation is to collect the poems in such a way as to help readers enjoy and understand them. For this reason, I have supplied explanatory notes, but placed them in the back of the volume, to be consulted or ignored as the reader sees fit. The notes consist mostly of glosses on proper names and topical references, translations of phrases in languages other than French or English and clarifications of some translated words or passages. Occasionally I offer interpretative suggestions, especially if they involve basic disputes over meaning, but I try to keep these comments to a minimum. For most collections, I provide some information complementary or additional to that which can be found in this introduction, such as more detailed accounts of publication and historical context. The poems, meanwhile, are unsullied by footnote markings and marginalia, and the translations are placed on pages opposite to the originals so that the reader who wants to compare the French and the English poems can do so with convenience, or read in one language, as he or she prefers.

If it can be said with justice that Hugo of all poets gains something when his work is viewed as a whole, it can also be said, and with equal justice, that Hugo of all poets gains something through careful selection and presentation. In saying this, I do not wish to echo distantly Gide's lament; I hope to translate more of Hugo's poetry some day. For now, though, a selection creative and crafted, if by Hugolian standards Lilliputian, will do more for English readers than any volume of run-of-the-mill translations. Given time, it may also create the demand for more.

Steven Monte
March 2001

Acknowledgements

I would like to thank Leah Price, David Southward, Matthew Greenfield, and Stephen Lewis for their timely suggestions and much more than editorial work on this book. Translating and introducing a poet like Hugo is a daunting project, and I feel fortunate to have had their help and support along the way.

Selected Poetry

From *Odes et Ballades*
(1822, 1823, 1824, 1826, 1828)

À Mes Odes

Le poëte, inspiré lorsque la terre ignore,
Ressemble à ces grands monts que la nouvelle aurore
    Dore avant tous à son réveil,
    Et qui, longtemps vainqueurs de l'ombre,
    Gardent jusque dans la nuit sombre
    Le dernier rayon du soleil.

From *Odes and Ballads*

To My Odes

The poet, inspired when the world is unaware,
Is like those giant peaks on which the dawn's red flare
    Alights with its first displays,
      And which, having long since pushed the shadows back,
      Up until the moment when the heavens turn black,
    Hold onto the sun's last rays.

From *Les Orientales* (1829)

La Captive

On entendait le chant des oiseaux
aussi harmonieux que la poésie.
                    Sadi., *Guilistan*

Si je n'étais captive,
J'aimerais ce pays,
Et cette mer plaintive,
Et ces champs de maïs,
Et ces astres sans nombre,
Si le long du mur sombre
N'étincelait dans l'ombre
Le sabre des spahis.

Je ne suis point tartare
Pour qu'un eunuque noir
M'accorde ma guitare,
Me tienne mon miroir.
Bien loin de ces Sodomes,
Au pays dont nous sommes,
Avec les jeunes hommes
On peut parler le soir.

Pourtant j'aime une rive
Où jamais des hivers
Le souffle froid n'arrive
Par les vitraux ouverts,
L'été, la pluie est chaude,
L'insecte vert qui rôde
Luit, vivante émeraude,
Sous les brins d'herbe verts.

From *Orientalia*

The Captive

*One heard birdsong as harmonious
as poetry.*
Sadi., *Guilistan*

If I weren't a captive here
I would love this distant land,
And this melancholy sea,
And these ripened fields of wheat,
And these heavens' countless stars,
If along these darkened walls,
The Spahis' crescent swords,
Didn't glimmer in the dark.

I'm not a Tartar woman.
No black eunuch needs
To hand me my guitar or hold
My mirror up for me.
Far from all these Sodomites
In the lands from which we come,
One can even talk with young
Unmarried men at night.

And yet I love these mild shores
Where the coldest winter blasts
Never arrive, or hurry past
The open windows and doors –
Where the rain is warm in summer
And that green fly tinted gold
Glows like a living emerald
Under the green blades of grass.

Smyrne est une princesse
Avec son beau chapel;
L'heureux printemps sans cesse
Répond à son appel,
Et, comme un riant groupe
De fleurs dans une coupe,
Dans ses mers se découpe
Plus d'un frais archipel.

J'aime ces tours vermeilles,
Ces drapeaux triomphants,
Ces maisons d'or, pareilles
À des jouets d'enfants;
J'aime, pour mes pensées
Plus mollements bercées,
Ces tentes balancées
Au dos des éléphants.

Dans ce palais de fées,
Mon cœur, plein de concerts,
Croit, aux voix étouffées
Qui viennent des déserts,
Entendre les génies
Mêler les harmonies
Des chansons infinies
Qu'ils chantent dans les airs!

J'aime de ces contrées
Les doux parfums brûlants,
Sur les vitres dorées
Les feuillages tremblants,
L'eau que la source épanche
Sous le palmier qui penche,
Et la cigogne blanche
Sur les minarets blancs.

Smyrna is a kind of queen
With its crown that looks on all,
Where happy springtime can be seen,
Responding to its call,
And, like groups of flowers one sees
All laughing in a pot,
More than one archipelago
Spills over into its seas.

I love the red towers, the noise
Of pennants blowing in the breeze –
These triumphant pennants – and these
Gold roofs like children's toys;
And, to rock my passing thoughts back
And forth more gently, I love
These high tents balanced on top of
An elephant's back.

In these enchanted palaces,
Always hearing melodies,
I would swear that I hear djinns
In the muffled voices a breeze
Brings in from the desert, where
They generate harmonies
That blend into the countless songs
They sing into the air.

I love the sweet and burning
Scents of this land. I adore
The foliage trembling
Above a gold window or door,
Water bubbling from a spring
Beneath a bending palm tree,
And white storks on white minarets
Surrounded by the sea.

J'aime en un lit de mousses
Dire un air espagnol,
Quand mes compagnes douces,
Du pied rasant le sol,
Légion vagabonde
Où le sourire abonde,
Font tournoyer leur ronde
Sous un rond parasol.

Mais surtout, quand la brise
Me touche en voltigeant,
La nuit j'aime être assise,
Être assise en songeant,
L'œil sur la mer profonde,
Tandis que, pâle et blonde,
La lune ouvre dans l'onde
Son éventail d'argent.

Clair de lune

Per amica silentia lunae.
Virgile

La lune était sereine et jouait sur les flots.
La fenêtre enfin libre est ouverte à la brise,
La sultane regarde, et la mer qui se brise,
Là-bas, d'un flot d'argent brode les noirs îlots.

De ses doigts en vibrant s'échappe la guitare.
Elle écoute… Un bruit sourd frappe les sourds échos.
Est-ce un lourd vaisseau turc qui vient des eaux de Cos,
Battant l'archipel grec de sa rame tartare?

Sont-ce des cormorans qui plongent tour à tour,
Et coupent l'eau, qui roule en perles sur leur aile?
Est-ce un djinn qui là-haut siffle d'une voix grêle,
Et jette dans la mer les créneaux de la tour?

I like to sing a Spanish air
Lying on a bed of moss,
While my sweet companions there –
A band of women – toss
Their hair and batter the ground
With their feet, where smiles abound
And everyone can dance their round
Underneath a parasol.

But especially when a breeze
Caresses me and swirls around,
At evening I like to sit down,
Sit down alone and dream,
Staring across the sea, while the man
In the moon casts his pale spells,
Opening up his silver fan
When the water's surface swells.

Moonlight

Per amica silentia lunae.
Virgil

The moonlight was serene and playing on the waves.
The window finally comes loose and opens to the air.
The sultana looks out, and the wrinkled sea weaves
Its silver threads among the dark islets out there.

The guitar jingles, dropping from her fingers to the floor.
She listens... A muffled sound strikes the muffled echoes.
Is it some Turkish vessel packed with goods from Cos
Beating the Greek islands with its Tartar oar?

Are those things vultures there, swooping suddenly
And hitting water turning to pearls beneath their wings?
Is that a genie up there shrilly whistling
And throwing crenellations of its tower in the sea?

Qui trouble ainsi les flots près du sérail des femmes?
Ni le noir cormoran, sur la vague bercé,
Ni les pierres du mur, ni le bruit cadencé
Du lourd vaisseau, rampant sur l'onde avec des rames.

Ces sont des sacs pesants, d'où partent des sanglots.
On verrait, en sondant la mer qui les promène,
Se mouvoir dans leurs flancs comme une forme humaine…
La lune était sereine et jouait sur les flots.

Les Djinns

E come i gru van cantando lor lai
Facendo in aer di se lunga riga,
Cosi vid'io venir traendo guai
Ombre portate dalla detta briga.
                                    Dante

Et comme les grues qui font dans
l'air de longues files vont chantant
leur plainte, ainsi je vis venir traînant
des gémissements les ombres emportées
par cette tempête.

Mur, ville
Et port,
Asile
De mort,
Mer grise
Où brise
La brise,
Tout dort.

Dans la plaine
Naît un bruit.
C'est l'haleine
De la nuit.
Elle brame
Comme une âme
Qu'une flamme
Toujours suit!

What's troubling the waves near the harem and its shores?
Not black cormorants hovering above the swells,
Nor stones from a wall, and not the cadenced rhythm
Of a packed vessel crawling through the water with its oars.

Those things out there from which you can hear sobbing are sacks.
Watching how the current causing them to drift behaves
You might just make out some struggling human forms...
The moonlight was serene and playing on the waves.

The Djinns

E come i gru van cantando lor lai
Facendo in aer di se lunga riga,
Cosi vid'io venir traendo guai
Ombre portate dalla detta briga.
                                    Dante

And as cranes go singing their lays,
making a long line of themselves in
the air, so I saw coming toward us,
dragging cries, shades borne by the
aforesaid violence.

Walls, town,
And port:
Haven
For Death.
Grey seas.
Winds keep
Blowing.
Worlds sleep.

In the plains
A noise stirs.
It's the breath
Of the night.
It rings out
Like the soul
That a flame
Flies about.

La voix plus haute
Semble un grelot. –
D'un nain qui saute
C'est le galop.
Il fuit, s'élance,
Puis en cadence
Sur un pied danse
Au bout d'un flot.

La rumeur approche,
L'écho la redit.
C'est comme la cloche
D'un couvent maudit; –
Comme un bruit de foule,
Qui tonne et qui roule,
Et tantôt s'écroule,
Et tantôt grandit.

Dieu! la voix sépulcrale
Des Djinns!… Quel bruit ils font!
Fuyons sous la spirale
De l'escalier profond.
Déjà s'éteint ma lampe,
Et l'ombre de la rampe,
Qui le long du mur rampe,
Monte jusqu'au plafond.

C'est l'essaim des Djinns qui passe,
Et tourbillonne en sifflant!
Les ifs, que leur vol fracasse,
Craquent comme un pin brûlant.
Leur troupeau, lourd et rapide,
Volant dans l'espace vide,
Semble un nuage livide
Qui porte un éclair au flanc.

Ils sont tout près! – Tenons fermée
Cette salle, où nous les narguons.
Quel bruit dehors! Hideuse armée
De vampires et de dragons!
La poutre du toit descellée
Ploie ainsi qu'une herbe mouillée,
Et la vieille porte rouillée
Tremble, à déraciner ses gonds!

The higher voice
Is like a bell
Tied to a cat,
A jumping dwarf.
It leaps, lets go,
Then, keeping time,
Spins on its toe
Over a wave.

The sound comes closer.
Echoes call it back,
Like the mission bell
Of some evil cult,
Or noise in a crowd
Rumbling and flowing,
Sometimes collapsing,
And sometimes growing.

My God! the eerie air
Of the Djinns! What a noise!
Let's hide below the steps
Of the high spiral stair!
My lamp's already out,
The rails' shadows reeling,
Twisting along the wall,
And climbing the ceiling!

The swarm of Djinns is passing
With its spinning and its shrieks!
The yews it breaks in pieces
Crackle loud like burning pines.
And the speeding horde beneath
Flying into empty space
Is like an ashen stormcloud
Hiding lightning in its sheath.

They're almost here! Secure the room
So completely we can taunt them!
What a noise! An evil army
Of flying dragons and vampires!
The unsealed timbers of the roof
Are bending like a field of grass
And the rusty gate is shaking
As if each hinge were coming off!

Cris de l'enfer! voix qui hurle et qui pleure!
L'horrible essaim, poussé par l'aquilon,
Sans doute, ô ciel! s'abat sur ma demeure.
Le mur fléchit sous le noir bataillon.
La maison crie et chancelle penchée,
Et l'on dirait que, du sol arrachée,
Ainsi qu'il chasse une feuille séchée,
Le vent la roule avec leur tourbillon!

Prophète! si ta main me sauve
De ces impurs démons des soirs,
J'irai prosterner mon front chauve
Devant tes sacrés encensoirs!
Fais que sur ces portes fidèles
Meure leur souffle d'étincelles,
Et qu'en vain l'ongle de leurs ailes
Grince et crie à ces vitraux noirs!

Ils sont passés! – Leur cohorte
S'envole, et fuit, et leurs pieds
Cessent de battre ma porte
De leurs coups multipliés.
L'air est plein d'un bruit de chaînes,
Et dans les forêts prochaines
Frissonnent tous les grands chênes,
Sous leur vol de feu pliés!

De leurs ailes lontaines
Le battement décroit,
Si confus dans les plaines,
Si faible, que l'on croit
Ouïr la sauterelle
Crier d'une voix grêle,
Ou pétiller la grêle
Sur le plomb d'un vieux toit.

D'étranges syllabes
Nous viennet encor; –
Ainsi, des arabes
Quand sonne le cor,
Un chant sur la grève
Par instants s'élève,
Et l'enfant qui rêve
Fait des rêves d'or.

Hellish shrieks! Sobs and voices screaming out!
Blown here by the north wind, the awful swarm
Heavens! is surely battering my house.
The wall is buckling beneath the dark storm.
The house, tottering and swaying, cries out –
You would swear that it, unmoored from the ground,
Were being lifted up and spun around
Like a dried leaf a wind gust blows about!

    Prophet! if you deliver me
    From these demons of the darkness,
    I will prostrate my shaven head
    In front of your holy censers.
    Make sure that these trustworthy doors
    Snuff out the sparks the Djinns let pass,
    And that the sharp claws on their wings
    Scratch in vain at this blackened glass!

      They've passed by! The massive horde
      Is flying off, and their feet
      Aren't battering my windows
      With their knocking any more.
      Chains clink in the air still warm
      And, in the nearby forests,
      The oaks are shaking, bent down
      By the passing of the swarm.

        The beating of their wings
        Now far-away, grows less,
        So spread out in the plains,
        So feeble, one might guess
        That one were hearing rough
        Voices of cicadas
        Or tiny stones of hail
        Crackling on the roof.

          Jumbled syllables
          Are still reaching us,
          As when Arabs hear
          The sound of a horn:
          All along the shore
          Chanted songs unfold,
          And the dreaming child
          Dreams a dream of gold.

Les Djinns funèbres,
Fils du trépas,
Dans les ténèbres
Pressent leur pas;
Leur essaim gronde:
Ainsi, profonde,
Murmure une onde
Qu'on ne voit pas.

Ce bruit vague
Qui s'endort,
C'est la vague
Sur le bord;
C'est la plainte,
Presque éteinte,
D'une sainte
Pour un mort.

On doute
La nuit …
J'écoute: –
Tout fuit,
Tout passe;
L'espace
Efface
Le bruit.

Rêverie

Lo giorno se n'andava, et l'aer bruno
Toglieva gli animai che sono 'n terra,
Dalle fatiche loro.

Dante

Oh! laissez-moi! c'est l'heure où l'horizon qui fume
Cache un front inégal sous un cercle de brume,
L'heure où l'astre géant rougit et disparaît.
Le grand bois jaunissant dore seul la colline:
On dirait qu'en ces jours où l'automne décline,
Le soleil et la pluie ont rouillé la forêt.

Oh, what will rise up now, what will be born in its train
Over there – while I sit here dreaming at my pane
And shadows in the corridor are spreading out their nets:
Some Moorish city, dazzling and rising from the dark,
Which, like a rocket shooting upwards in an arc,
Will rip this haze open with its blazing minarets!

Let it come and give life to everything I sing,
Oh spirit! – as in an autumn sky that's darkening –
And cast its magical reflection in my eye,
And, dying out at length in muffled echoes in the mist,
With the thousand towers of its fairy palaces,
Raise its violet crenellations in the sky!

Rapture

And then I heard a loud voice.
Revelations

Alone with all the stars above and ocean under me,
Not a cloud in heaven, not a sail on the sea,
I started seeing deeper than the real world rushing by.
And the forests, the mountains, nature, everything,
Seemed to speak and question, in confused murmuring,
     The waves of the sea, the fires in the sky.

And the infinite legions of stars that one sees,
In a loud voice, a deep voice, a thousand harmonies,
Were singing, and their fiery coronas seemed to nod;
And the breakers, which can never be chained and never rest,
Were singing, curling back the foaming on their crest:
     'It is the Lord, the Lord our God!'

From *Les Feuilles d'automne* (1831)

La Pente de la rêverie

Obscuritate rerum verba sæpe obscurantur.
Gervasius Tilbertensis.

Amis, ne creusez pas vos chères rêveries;
Ne fouillez pas le sol de vos plaines fleuries;
Et quand s'offre à vos yeux un océan qui dort,
Nagez à la surface ou jouez sur le bord.
Car la pensée est sombre! Une pente insensible
Va du monde réel à la sphère invisible;
La spirale est profonde, et quand on y descend,
Sans cesse se prolonge et va s'élargissant,
Et pour avoir touché quelque énigme fatale,
De ce voyage obscur souvent on revient pâle!

L'autre jour, il venait de pleuvoir, car l'été,
Cette année, est de bise et de pluie attristé,
Et le beau mois de mai dont le rayon nous leurre,
Prend le masque d'avril qui sourit et qui pleure.
J'avais levé le store aux gothiques couleurs.
Je regardais au loin les arbres et les fleurs.
Le soleil se jouait sur la pelouse verte
Dans les gouttes de pluie, et ma fenêtre ouverte
Apportait du jardin à mon esprit heureux
Un bruit d'enfants joueurs et d'oiseaux amoureux.
Paris, les grands ormeaux, maison, dôme, chaumière,
Tout flottait à mes yeux dans la riche lumière
De cet astre de mai dont le rayon charmant
Au bout de tout brin d'herbe allume un diamant!
Je me laissais aller à ces trois harmonies,
Printemps, matin, enfance, en ma retraite unies;
La Seine, ainsi que moi, laissait son flot vermeil
Suivre nonchalamment sa pente, et le soleil
Faisait évaporer à la fois sur les grèves
L'eau du fleuve en brouillards et ma pensée en rêves!

From *Autumn Leaves*

The Slope of Reverie

Obscuritate rerum verba sæpe obscurantur.
Gervasius Tilbertensis.

My friends, don't delve into your favourite reveries,
Don't burrow through your soil growing flowers and trees,
And when your vision conjures sleeping seas with hidden floors,
Swim across their surfaces or play along their shores.
Because thought is sombre! An invisible ravine
Descends from the real world to the sphere that can't be seen.
The spiralling is deep and, when one is in its throes,
Extends without pausing and increases as one goes,
And, having sensed some great enigma one brushed past,
One often comes back from the voyage there aghast!

The other day it had just finished raining. For the spring,
This year, is overrun with storms and buffeting.
And brilliant May, enticing us the moment it appears,
Has donned the mask of April and is laughing through its tears.
I lifted up my window shades tinted like stained glass.
I was looking at the elm trees, the flowers, and the grass
Across the distant courtyard over which the sunlight played
In raindrops – everything my open pane displayed
And brought in from the garden, as if from above:
The sounds of children playing and the sounds of birds in love.
Everything was floating past my eyes in that light
Streaming from the May sun and enchanting every sight:
Paris and its lofty elms, domes, chimneys, pavement, glass,
A diamond blinking on the tip of every blade of grass.
I let myself relax into this triple harmony –
Morning, spring, and childhood – made one in my retreat.
The Seine, like me, had let its eddies and its streams
Follow their own course, while the sun's vermilion beams,
Striking the water, simultaneously made
The river turn to fog and my thoughts turn to dreams!

Alors, dans mon esprit, je vis autour de moi
Mes amis, non confus, mais tels que je les vois
Quand ils viennent le soir, troupe grave et fidèle,
Vous avec vos pinceaux dont la pointe étincelle,
Vous, laissant échapper vos vers au vol ardent,
Et nous tous écoutant en cercle, ou regardant.
Ils étaient bien là tous, je voyais leurs visages,
Tous, même les absents qui font de longs voyages,
Puis tous ceux qui sont morts vinrent après ceux-ci,
Avec l'air qu'ils avaient quand ils vivaient aussi.
Quand j'eus, quelques instants, des yeux de ma pensée,
Contemplé leur famille à mon foyer pressée,
Je vis trembler leurs traits confus, et par degrés
Pâlir en s'effaçant leurs fronts décolorés,
Et tous, comme un ruisseau qui dans un lac s'écoule,
Se perdre autour de moi dans une immense foule.

Foule sans nom! chaos! des voix, des yeux, des pas.
Ceux qu'on n'a jamais vus, ceux qu'on ne connaît pas.
Tous les vivants! – cités bourdonnant aux oreilles
Plus qu'un bois d'Amérique ou des ruches d'abeilles,
Caravanes campant sur le désert en feu,
Matelots dispersés sur l'océan de Dieu,
Et, comme un pont hardi sur l'onde qui chavire,
Jetant d'un monde à l'autre un sillon de navire,
Ainsi que l'araignée entre deux chênes verts
Jette un fil argenté qui flotte dans les airs!

Les deux pôles! le monde entier! la mer, la terre,
Alpes aux fronts de neige, Etnas au noir cratère,
Tout à la fois, automne, été, printemps, hiver,
Les vallons descendant de la terre à la mer
Et s'y changeant en golfe, et des mers aux campagnes
Les caps épanouis en chaînes de montagnes,
Et les grands continents, brumeux, verts ou dorés,
Par les grands océans sans cesse dévorés,
Tout, comme un paysage en une chambre noire
Se refléchit avec ses rivières de moire,
Ses passants, ses brouillards flottant comme un duvet,
Tout dans mon esprit sombre allait, marchait, vivait!
Alors, en attachant, toujours plus attentives,
Ma pensée et ma vue aux mille perspectives
Que le souffle du vent ou le pas des saisons

And so, in my mind, I saw my friends surrounding me,
Not confusedly, but in the way that one would see
The loyal troupe gathering just like we always met:
You, with your paintbrushes twinkling as if wet,
You, with all those fiery verses you would fling,
Everyone in a circle, watching, listening.
All of us were there; I could see every face,
Even those now living in some faraway place;
And after them, departed friends began to arrive
With all the same expressions as when they were alive.
For a time I contemplated in my mind's eye
This family huddled round my hearth, and wondered why.
Then I saw their trembling features warp and, gradually,
Their foreheads turn pale and dissolve in front of me,
And everyone, like a stream that flows into a sea,
Became completely lost in a dark immensity.

A nameless crowd! chaos! only footsteps, voices, eyes,
Those whom one has never seen, those one can't surmise.
Everyone living! – cities buzzing more than trees
In Amazon's jungles or a hive full of bees,
Caravans encamping in a desert that's on fire,
Sailors dispersed across the sea of God the Father,
And, like a raft the swell is threatening to smother,
Casting out a furrowed wake from one world to the other,
Just as a spider casts a silver thread that floats
In the breeze, suspended between two leafy oaks!

The two poles! the world itself! the earth and sea below,
Etnas with their blackened cores, Alps topped with snow,
Everything at once: spring, winter, summer, fall,
Valleys sloping down from land to sea, across it all,
And changing into gulfs, seas engulfing the plains,
Headlands expanding into cliffs and mountain chains,
And continents – misty, green, or gold – which the sea
In all of its expanses swallowed up unceasingly.
Everything, like a landscape on a photographic plate,
Was mirrored in its silky streams and ever-shifting state,
Its passers-by, its fogs and mists adrift like down –
Everything inside me walked and lived and moved around!
And then, while attaching my increasingly keen
Thought and vision onto all the outlooks on this scene
The wind's exhalations or the seasons' steady pace

M'ouvrait à tous moments dans tous les horizons,
Je vis soudain surgir, parfois du sein des ondes,
À côté des cités vivantes des deux mondes,
D'autres villes aux fronts étranges, inouïs,
Sépulcres ruinés des temps évanouis,
Pleines d'entassements, de tours, de pyramides,
Baignant leurs pieds aux mers, leur tête aux cieux humides.
Quelques-unes sortaient de dessous des cités
Où les vivants encor bruissent agités,
Et des siècles passés jusqu'à l'âge où nous sommes
Je pus compter ainsi trois étages de Romes.
Et tandis qu'élevant leurs inquiètes voix,
Les cités des vivants résonnaient à la fois
Des murmures du peuple ou du pas des armées,
Ces villes du passé, muettes et fermées,
Sans fumée à leurs toits, sans rumeurs dans leurs seins,
Se taisaient, et semblaient des ruches sans essaims.
J'attendais. Un grand bruit se fit. Les races mortes
De ces villes en deuil vinrent ouvrir les portes,
Et je les vis marcher ainsi que les vivants,
Et jeter seulement plus de poussière aux vents.
Alors, tours, aqueducs, pyramides, colonnes,
Je vis l'intérieur des vieilles Babylones,
Les Carthages, les Tyrs, les Thèbes, les Sions,
D'où sans cesse sortaient des générations.

Ainsi j'embrassais tout: et la terre, et Cybèle;
La face antique auprès de la face nouvelle;
Le passé, le présent; les vivants et les morts;
Le genre humain complet comme au jour du remords.
Tout parlait à la fois, tout se faisait comprendre,
Le pélage d'Orphée et l'étrusque d'Évandre,
Les runes d'Irmensul, le sphinx égyptien,
La voix du nouveau monde aussi vieux que l'ancien.

Or, ce que je voyais, je doute que je puisse
Vous le peindre: c'était comme un grand édifice
Formé d'entassements de siècles et de lieux;
On n'en pouvait trouver les bords ni les milieux;
À toutes les hauteurs, nations, peuples, races,
Mille ouvriers humains, laissant partout leurs traces,
Travaillaient nuit et jour, montant, croisant leurs pas,
Parlant chacun leur langue et ne s'entendant pas;

Divulged to me each moment and all over the place,
I suddenly saw – sometimes coming from the surge
And foreign in appearance – other cities emerge
Beside the living cities of the two worlds at this stage:
Sepulchres in ruins from some long since vanished age
With heaps of rubble, pyramids, and towers vast in size
Bathing their feet in oceans and their heads in humid skies.
Some cities were streaming from beneath another town
Where the living, agitated, rustled up and down,
And I could make out levels of Rome in three stages
By tracing all the centuries up to our age's.
And while they were raising anxious voices all around,
The cities of the living were beginning to resound
With marching armies and the people's murmuring.
The cities of the past, like some mute and closed-up thing,
With smokeless chimneys, emptied-out and echoless streets,
Were quiet, and each seemed like a hive without its bees.
I was waiting. Noises sounded. The dead woke in scores
And nations of them came out to open their doors;
I saw them walking like the living here and there
Except that they were stirring up more dust in the air.
Then aqueducts and pyramids, columns made of bronze –
I saw the inner workings of the ancient Babylons,
The Carthages, the Tyres, Thebes, Jerusalem,
From which generations were streaming without end.

I embraced it all: Cybele and Nature, too,
The face of the old beside the face of the new,
The living and the dead, yesteryear and today,
All the human species as if on Judgement Day.
Everyone spoke and understood each other speak:
Evander's Etruscan, Orpheus's antique Greek,
The sphinx of ancient Egypt, the runes of Irmensul,
The voices of the new world as ancient as the old.

What I saw – I doubt very much if speech like this
Can paint it for you: it was like a large edifice
Fashioned out of heaped-up centuries and places.
At every level there were different nations and races;
You couldn't find its centre or determine its extent.
Night and day, a thousand human workers came and went
Passing by each other, climbing, banding and disbanding,
Speaking their own languages and not understanding,

Et moi je parcourais, cherchant qui me réponde,
De degrés en degrés cette Babel du monde.

La nuit avec la foule, en ce rêve hideux,
Venait, s'épaississant ensemble toutes deux,
Et, dans ces régions que nul regard ne sonde,
Plus l'homme était nombreux, plus l'ombre était profonde.
Tout devenait douteux et vague, seulement
Un souffle qui passait de moment en moment,
Comme pour me montrer l'immense fourmilière,
Ouvrait dans l'ombre au loin des vallons de lumière,
Ainsi qu'un coup de vent fait sur les flots troublés
Blanchir l'écume, ou creuse une onde dans les blés.

Bientôt autour de moi les ténèbres s'accrurent,
L'horizon se perdit, les formes disparurent,
Et l'homme avec la chose et l'être avec l'esprit
Flottèrent à mon souffle, et le frisson me prit.
J'étais seul. Tout fuyait. L'étendue était sombre.
Je voyais seulement au loin, à travers l'ombre,
Comme un océan les flots noirs et pressés,
Dans l'espace et le temps les nombres entassés!

Oh! cette double mer du temps et de l'espace
Où le navire humain toujours passe et repasse,
Je voulus la sonder, je voulus en toucher
Le sable, y regarder, y fouiller, y chercher,
Pour vous en rapporter quelque richesse étrange,
Et dire si son lit est de roche ou de fange.
Mon esprit plongea donc sous ce flot inconnu,
Au profond de l'abîme il nagea seul et nu,
Toujours de l'ineffable allant à l'invisible…
Soudain, il s'en revint avec un cri terrible,
Ébloui, haletant, stupide, épouvanté,
Car il avait au fond trouvé l'éternité.

While I, in search of someone with whom I might converse,
Walked through every level of this Babel universe.

In this horrific dream, along with night came a crowd,
And both condensed and thickened together like a cloud,
And in those regions through which no gaze can descend
The shadows were increasing in proportion to the men.
Everything was vague and uncertain; a gust
Or breath of wind, shuttling back and forth in the dusk,
Was the only thing disclosing distant valleys of light
As if to show the swarm to me in all its eerie might:
In the same way breezes blanch an ocean's rolling sheet
Of waves with foam, or part a field of harvest wheat.

And soon the shadows gathered over me and revolved,
The skyline vanished, and all forms in it dissolved;
And man along with matter, being with the mind,
Floated on my breath and sent a shiver down my spine.
I was alone. The world was fleeing. Skies looked grim.
I could only see, across the dark horizon's rim,
Rushing waves, like ocean swells, all over the place,
Numerals piled up and inside time and space!

Oh! that double ocean, that sea of space and time
The human vessel crosses and recrosses all the time –
I wished to sound its depths, and I wished to touch its sands,
To look at it, to dig through it, to search through its expanse,
That I might bring something rich and strange back to you,
And tell you if its floors were rock or mud completely through.
And so my mind dove downwards, past what it had known,
Into that abyss where it swam naked and alone,
Moving from what can't be said to that which can't be seen …
Suddenly it came to its senses with a scream,
Astonished, panting, horrified, attempting to break free,
Because, in those depths, it had found eternity.

Soleils couchants (II)

Le jour s'enfuit des cieux; sous leur transparent voile
De moments en moments se hasarde une étoile;
La nuit, pas à pas, monte au trône obscur des soirs;
Un coin du ciel est brun, l'autre lutte avec l'ombre,
Et déjà, succédant au couchant rouge et sombre,
Le crépuscule gris meurt sur les coteaux noirs.

Et là-bas, allumant ses vitres étoilées,
Avec sa cathédrale aux flèches dentelées,
Les tours de son palais, les tours de sa prison,
Avec ses hauts clochers, sa bastille obscurcie,
Posée au bord du ciel comme une longue scie,
La ville aux mille toits découpe l'horizon.

Oh! qui m'emportera sur quelque tour sublime
D'où la cité sous moi s'ouvre comme un abîme!
Que j'entende, écoutant la ville où nous rampons,
Mourir sa vaste voix, qui semble un cri de veuve,
Et qui, le jour, gémit plus haut que le grand fleuve,
Le grand fleuve irrité, luttant contre les ponts!

Que je voie, à mes yeux en fuyant apparues,
Les étoiles des chars se croiser dans les rues,
Et serpenter le peuple en l'étroit carrefour,
Et tarir la fumée au bout des cheminées,
Et, glissant sur le front des maisons blasonnées,
Cent clartés naître, luire et passer tour à tour!

Que la vieille cité, devant moi, sur sa couche
S'étende, qu'un soupir s'échappe de sa bouche,
Comme si de fatigue on l'entendait gémir!
Que, veillant seul, debout sur son front que je foule,
Avec mille bruits sourds d'océan et de foule,
Je regarde à mes pieds la géante dormir!

Setting Suns (II)

The light flees from heaven. Beneath the sky's transparent veil
A star ventures out now and then, dim and pale.
The night, step by step, climbs to evening's throne and fills
Some sky with brown, while some struggles with the dark;
And already, following the sun's violet arc,
The grey dusk is dying up along the blackened hills.

And over there the city with its starry panes alit,
With its vast cathedral and the steeples under it,
The towers of its palaces and prisons, every wall
And clockface, every tall and sombre fortress too,
Laid out on the skyline like the teeth of a saw –
The city with its thousand roofs cuts the sky in two.

Take me to some high ledge of a tower, like a cliff's,
From which the town opens up beneath like an abyss!
That I may hear this city through which we make our way
Compose itself or cry out, like a widow, in its pains,
Or groan even louder than the river in the day,
The great river, struggling against the bridges' chains!

That I may see, coming into view as starry streaks,
The sudden sparks of carriages crossing in the streets,
The people winding through the narrow alleyways,
The smoke dissolve above the chimneys like black foam,
And, gliding onto the façades of blazoned homes,
A hundred lights be born, grow bright, and pass away!

And may the ageing city lie and stretch itself out
In front of me, and may a sigh escape from its mouth
As though a groan of weariness were rising from the street!
May I stand watch alone there on the city's brow
With all the oceanic noises of the crowd
And look down on the giant sleeping at my feet!

Soleils couchants *(VI)*

Le soleil s'est couché ce soir dans les nuées.
Demain viendra l'orage, et le soir, et la nuit;
Puis l'aube, et ses clartés de vapeurs obstruées;
Puis les nuits, puis les jours, pas du temps qui s'enfuit!

Tous ces jours passeront; ils passeront en foule
Sur la face des mers, sur la face des monts,
Sur les fleuves d'argent, sur les forêts où roule
Comme un hymne confus des morts que nous aimons.

Et la face des eaux, et le front des montagnes,
Ridés et non vieillis, et les bois toujours verts
S'iront rajeunissant; le fleuve des campagnes
Prendra sans cesse aux monts le flot qu'il donne aux mers.

Mais moi, sous chaque jour courbant plus bas ma tête,
Je passe, et, refroidi sous ce soleil joyeux,
Je m'en irai bientôt, au milieu de la fête,
Sans que rien manque au monde, immense et radieux!

Setting Suns (VI)

The sun this evening has set among the clouds.
Tomorrow there'll be storms, and the evening, and the night,
Then dawn, with its glimmering mists slowly clearing,
Then the nights, then the days – time's footsteps disappearing.

These days will pass away; they will pass away in crowds
From the faces of the oceans and the faces of the hills,
From the silver rivers and the forests which sway
Like a requiem blending with the souls we care for still.

And the faces of the waters, and the foreheads of the hills
Wrinkled without having grown old, and evergreens
Will keep rejuvenating. The streams will ceaselessly
Take water from the mountaintops and give it to the sea.

But I, bending lower with the weight of each day,
Am passing by, and – chilled again in this ecstatic sun –
About to leave, though celebration here won't have ended,
And none of this world's radiance will have gone away!

From *Les Chants du crépuscule* (1835)

À la Colonne

Plusieurs pétitionnaires demandent que la Chambre intervienne pour faire transporter les cendres de Napoléon sous la colonne de la place Vendôme.

Après une courte déliberation, la Chambre passe à l'ordre du jour.

(CHAMBRE DES DÉPUTÉS. – *Séance du 7 octobre 1830*.)

Oh! quand il bâtissait, de sa main colossale
Pour son trône, appuyé sur l'Europe vassale,
    Ce pilier souverain,
Ce bronze, devant qui tout n'est que poudre et sable,
Sublime monument, deux fois impérissable,
    Fait de gloire et d'airain;

Quand il le bâtissait, pour qu'un jour dans la ville
Ou la guerre étrangère ou la guerre civile
    Y brisassent leur char,
Et pour qu'il fît pâlir sur nos places publiques
Les frêles héritiers de vos nom magnifiques,
    Alexandre et César!

C'était un beau spectacle! – Il parcourait la terre
Avec ses vétérans, nation militaire
    Dont il savait les noms;
Les rois fuyaient; les rois n'étaient point de sa taille;
Et, vainqueur, il allait par les champs de bataille
    Glanant tous leurs canons.

Et puis, il revenait avec la grande armée,
Encombrant de butin sa France bien-aimée,
    Son Louvre de granit,
Et les Parisiens poussaient des cris de joie,
Comme font les aiglons, alors qu'avec sa proie
    L'aigle rentre à son nid!

From *The Songs of Daybreak*

To the Column

Several petitioners asked the Chamber to intervene in order to have
the ashes of Napoleon transported to and placed beneath the column
at the *Place Vendôme*.
    After a short deliberation, the Chamber moved on to its agenda for
that day.
(CHAMBER OF REPRESENTATIVES – session of 7 October 1830.)

When he (for his throne backed by Europe, his vassal)
Was building this huge, commanding pillar to which
    Nothing corresponds –
This monument that makes all things compared with it
Powder and sand; this twice undying feat because it is
    Made of glory and bronze;

When he was building it, so that some future day
Either a foreign or a civil war might break
    The wheels of its chariot,
And that he might make all of those feeble heirs
Of august Caesar and Alexander the Great
    Turn pale from fear of it,

It was a beautiful sight! He walked the grounds
Along with his veterans, whose names he all knew,
    Nation in arms and renown.
The kings ran away; the kings weren't of his stature.
And so he went through battlefields, gleaning canons
    So he could melt them down.

And then he came home with his illustrious army,
Burdening his dear France with plunder, and his Louvre
    With a granite display.
And all of the Parisians shouted from their chest
Like eaglets when the eagle returns to its nest
    Carrying its prey.

Et lui, poussant du pied tout ce métal sonore,
Il courait à la cuve où bouillonnait encore
    Le monument promis.
Le moule en était fait d'une de ses pensées.
Dans la fournaise ardente il jetait à brassées
    Les canons ennemies!

Puis il s'en revenait gagner quelque bataille.
Il dépouillait encore à travers la mitraille
    Maints affûts dispersés;
Et, rapportant ce bronze à la Rome française,
Il disait aux fondeurs penchés sur la fournaise:
    — En avez-vous assez?

C'était son œuvre à lui! — Les feux du polygone,
Et la bombe, et le sabre, et l'or de la dragonne
    Furent ses premiers jeux.
Général, pour hochets il prit les Pyramides;
Empereur, il voulut, dans ses vœux moins timides,
    Quelques chose de mieux.

Il fit cette colonne! — Avec sa main romaine
Il tordit et mêla dans l'œuvre surhumaine
    Tout un siècle fameux,
Les Alpes se courbant sous sa marche tonnante,
Le Nil, le Rhin, le Tibre, Austerlitz rayonnante,
    Eylau froid et brumeux.

Car c'est lui qui, pareil à l'antique Encelade,
Du trône universel essaya l'escalade,
    Qui vingt ans entassa,
Remuant terre et cieux avec une parole,
Wagram sur Marengo, Champaubert sur Arcole,
    Pélion sur Ossa!

Oh! quand par un beau jour, sur la place Vendôme,
Homme dont tout un peuple adorait le fantôme,
    Tu vins grave et serein,
Et que tu découvris ton œuvre magnifique,
Tranquille, et contenant d'un geste pacifique
    Tes quatre aigles d'airain;

And he, pushing this resounding metal as he went,
Approached the furnace where the promised monument
    Was boiling in its vat.
The mould had been fashioned out of one of his thoughts.
He dragged the cannons to the glowing forge and tossed
    Armfuls of them into that!

Then he went to war again to win some other battle.
He stripped many gun carriages that were scattered
    Among the grape-shot in the rough.
And, taking this bronze back with him to France's Rome,
He said to the melters leaning over the glow,
    'Now do you have enough?'

It was *his* work. A fortress's leaping flames,
A bomb, a sabre, golden tassels, were the games
    He first played as commander.
As general, he took the pyramids – child's play –
As emperor, less timidly, he wanted in his way
    Something even grander.

He built this column! – blending, twisting, hammering
The century into this superhuman thing
    Stamped with his Roman fist.
The Alps bowed down beneath his thundering steps,
The Nile, the Rhine, the Tiber, blazing Austerlitz,
    Eylau, frozen in mist.

For he, like ancient Enceladus, tried to scale
The universe's throne, and for twenty years
    Amassed something awesome,
Moving earth and heaven with a single word,
Wagram on Marengo, Champaubert on Arcole,
    Pelion on Ossa!

When you, whose spirit an entire nation worshipped,
Came to the *Place Vendôme* one brilliant day,
    And greeted our response,
Grave and serene, you unveiled your great work
So tranquil, and containing in a gesture of peace,
    Your four eagles of bronze;

À cette heure où les tiens t'entouraient par cent mille;
Où, comme se pressaient autour de Paul-Émile
  Tous les petits Romains,
Nous, enfants de six ans, rangés sur ton passage,
Cherchant dans ton cortège un père au fier visage,
  Nous te battions des mains;

Oh! qui t'eût dit alors, à ce faîte sublime,
Tandis que tu rêvais sur le trophée opime
  Un avenir si beau,
Qu'un jour à cet affront il te faudrait descendre
Que trois cents avocats oseraient à ta cendre
  Chicaner ce tombeau!

At that hour, when a hundred thousand supporters
Surrounded you, we six-year-old children lined up
     To watch as you passed through:
Like the Roman boys around Paullus-Aemilius,
We searched for a father's face in your procession
     And clapped our hands for you!

Who could have said to you then, at that height,
While you were dreaming of some ultimate glory
     And greater times to come,
That one day you would be reduced to this state –
That three hundred lawyers would dare to separate
     Your ashes from your tomb!

From *Les Voix intérieures* (1837)

À Albert Durer

Dans les vieilles forêts où la sève à grands flots
Court du fût noir de l'aulne au tronc blanc des bouleaux,
Bien des fois, n'est-ce pas? à travers la clairière,
Pâle, effaré, n'osant regarder en arrière,
Tu t'es hâté, tremblant et d'un pas convulsif,
O mon maître Albert Dure, ô vieux peintre pensif!

On devine, devant tes tableaux qu'on vénère,
Que dans les noirs taillis ton œil visionnaire
Voyait distinctement, par l'ombre recouverts,
Le faune aux doigts palmés, le sylvain aux yeux verts,
Pan, qui revêt de fleurs l'antre où tu te recueilles,
Et l'antique dryade aux mains pleines de feuilles.

Une forêt pour toi, c'est un monde hideux.
Le songe et le réel s'y mêlent tous les deux.
Là se penchent rêveurs les vieux pin, les grands ormes
Dont les rameaux tordus font cent coudes difformes,
Et dans ce groupe sombre agité par le vent
Rien n'est tout à fait mort ni tout à fait vivant.
Le cresson boit; l'eau court; les frênes sur les pentes,
Sous la broussaille horrible et les ronces grimpantes,
Contractent lentement leurs pieds noueux et noirs;
Les fleurs au cou de cygne ont les lacs pour miroirs;
Et, sur vous qui passez et l'avez réveillée,
Mainte chimère étrange à la gorge écaillée,
D'un arbre entre ses doigts serrant les larges nœuds,
Du fond d'un antre obscur fixe un œil lumineux.
O végétation! esprit! matière! force!
Couverte de peau rude ou de vivante écorce!

From *Inner Voices*

To Albrecht Dürer

In ancient forests where the tree sap flows in surges
From the alders' black trunks to the white boughs of birches,
Many times – am I not right? – you would hurry through a glade
Not daring to look behind you – trembling and afraid
And pale, agitated in your walk as if distraught –
My venerable master, Albrecht Dürer, deep in thought!

When looking intently at your paintings, one perceives
That your visionary eye could clearly penetrate
Into the underbrush's shadows and see
Web-fingered fauns, slender sylphs with green eyes,
Pan wreathing flowers on the caves where you would meditate,
And antique dryads with their hands full of leaves.

For you, a dark forest is a hideous affair.
Dreams and reality both blend together there.
There, dreamers lean down – pines, and elms whose branches dangle
And twist about at every conceivable angle.
In this sombre group, which, now and then, the winds revive,
Nothing's really dead, nor entirely alive.
The watercress drinks; the waters rush; the ash tree
Pulls its gnarled feet back toward the banks gradually
Beneath the creeping vines and the terrifying brakes.
The swan-necked flowers there are mirrored in the lakes;
And for the passer-by who has roused them from their sleep,
Many a strange monster with a scaly throat will squeeze
Some tree's giant knots between its fingers, and stare
At you with glowing eyes from deep inside its lair.
Vegetation! Spirit! Matter! Energy within
Covered by a rough hide or a tree's living skin!

Aux bois, ainsi que toi, je n'ai jamais erré,
Maître, sans qu'en mon cœur l'horreur ait pénétré,
San voir tressaillir l'herbe, et, par le vent bercées,
Pendre à tous les rameaux de confuses pensées.
Dieu seul, ce grand témoin des faits mystérieux,
Dieu seul le sait, souvent, en de sauvages lieux,
J'ai senti, moi qu'échauffe une secrète flamme,
Comme moi palpiter et vivre avec une âme,
Et rire, et se parler dans l'ombre à demi-voix,
Les chênes monstrueux qui remplissent les bois.

«Jeune homme, ce méchant fait …»

Jeune homme, ce méchant fait une lâche guerre.
Ton indignation ne l'épouvante guère.
Crois-moi donc, laisse en paix, jeune homme au noble cœur,
Ce Zoïle à l'œil faux, ce malheureux moqueur.
Ton mépris? mais c'est l'air qu'il respire. Ta haine?
La haine est son odeur, sa sueur, son haleine:
Il sait qu'il peut souiller sans peur les noms fameux,
Et que pour qu'on le touche il est trop venimeux.
Il ne craint rien; pareil au champignon difforme
Poussé dans une nuit au pied d'un chêne énorme,
Qui laisse les chevreaux autour de lui paissant
Essayer leur dent folle à l'arbuste innocent;
Sachant qu'il porte en lui des vengences trop sûres,
Tout gonflé de poison il attend les morsures.

Master, like you, I've never wandered through the trees
Without a sense of awe in my heart, and unease,
Without seeing grasses shake, and, hanging from the boughs,
Clusters of confused thoughts rocking in the breeze.
God alone – that witness of mysterious things –
God knows how often I have felt the glimmerings
Of something which I, warmed by secret fires, feel
Lives and throbs as I do, and whose soul is as real,
And laughs, and whispers to itself as I advance:
The monstrous oak trees that fill the woods' expanse.

'The war that scoundrel wages ...'

The war that scoundrel wages is cowardly and low.
Young man with a noble heart, believe me, let him go –
That false-eyed Zoïlus, that mocker full of gall,
Your indignation hardly touches him at all.
Your disdain? The air he breathes in. Your antipathy?
Hatred is his odour, his sweat, his atmosphere.
He knows he can tarnish famous names impudently
And is so venomous that no one dares come near.
He fears nothing. Like a twisted mushroom that has grown
At the foot of an enormous oak overnight
Allowing all the nearby sheep that graze and roam
To chew into the innocent shrub with all their might ...
Knowing that sure revenge is always in his sights,
Swelling with poison, he waits for the bites.

La Vache

Devant la blanche ferme où parfois vers midi
Un vieillard vient s'asseoir sur le seuil attiédi,
Où cent poules gaîment mêlent leurs crêtes rouges,
Où, gardiens du sommeil, les dogues dans leurs bouges
Écoutent les chansons du gardien du réveil,
Du beau coq vernissé qui reluit au soleil,
Une vache était là tout à l'heure arrêtée.
Superbe, énorme, rousse et de blanc tachetée,
Douce comme une biche avec ses jeunes faons,
Elle avait sous le ventre un beau groupe d'enfants,
D'enfants aux dents de marbre, aux cheveux en brousailles
Frais, et plus charbonnés que de vieilles murailles,
Qui, bruyants, tous ensemble, à grands cris appelant
D'autres qui, tout petits, se hâtaient en tremblant,
Dérobant sans pitié quelque laitière absente,
Sous leur bouche joyeuse et peut-être blessante
Et sous leurs doigts pressant le lait par mille trous,
Tiraient le pis fécond de la mère au poil roux.
Elle, bonne et puissante et de son trésor pleine,
Sous leurs mains par moments faisant frémir à peine
Son beau flanc plus ombré qu'un flanc de léopard,
Distraite, regardait vaguement quelque part.

The Cow

In front of the white farm, where, sometimes, around noon,
An old man comes to sit on the stoop warmed by the sun,
Where a hundred hens mix their red crests together,
Where the bulldogs, those guardians of sleep, are forever
Listening to the songs of the guardian of waking
(The rooster whose glaze shines brilliantly in the light),
A cow had stopped grazing and was standing on the lawn.
She was superb, enormous, spotted red and white,
As mild as a doe taking care of a fawn.
She had a group of small children underneath her –
Children with marble teeth and thick, dishevelled hair
More charcoal-coloured than an old blackened wall,
Who, squealing loudly and at once, would shout and call
To other small friends who hurried there in nervous bands
And pitilessly stole from some absent milkwoman
With their gleeful, perhaps wounding, mouths – and their hands,
Tugging on the many fruitful teats of the udder,
Squeezed all the milk from this ruddy-coloured mother,
While she, generous, strong, and filled with riches within,
Was making her belly shaded like a leopard's skin
Quiver underneath – though showing no signs of resistance –
And vaguely gazing somewhere off into the distance.

From *Les Rayons et les ombres* (1840)

«Comme dans les étangs …»

Comme dans les étangs assoupis sous les bois,
Dans plus d'une âme on voit deux choses à la fois,
Le ciel, qui teint les eaux à peine remuées
Avec tous ses rayons et toutes ses nuées,
Et la vase, – fond morne, affreux, sombre et dormant,
Où des reptiles noirs fourmillent vaguement.

Écrit sur le vitre d'une fenêtre flammande

J'aime le carillon dans tes cités antiques,
O vieux pays gardien de tes mœurs domestiques,
Noble Flandre, où le Nord se réchauffe engourdi
Au soleil de Castille et s'accouple au Midi!
Le carillon, c'est l'heure inattendue et folle,
Que l'œil croit voir, vêtue en danseuse espagnole,
Apparaître soudain par le trou vif et clair
Que ferait en s'ouvrant une porte de l'air.
Elle vient, secouant sur les toits léthargiques
Son tablier d'argent plein de notes magiques,
Réveillant sans pitié les dormeurs ennuyeux,
Sautant à petits pas comme un oiseau joyeux,
Vibrant, ainsi qu'un dard qui tremble dans la cible;
Par un frêle escalier de cristal invisible,
Effarée et dansante, elle descend des cieux;
Et l'esprit, ce veilleur fait d'oreilles et d'yeux,
Tandis qu'elle va, vient, monte et descend encore,
Entend de marche en marche errer son pied sonore!

From *Sunbeams and Shadows*

'Just as in a forest's drowsy pools ...'

Just as in a forest's drowsy pools and rain-filled holes,
One can see two things at once in many souls:
Heaven – setting barely stirring waters ablaze
With all of its white clouds and all of its rays,
And the mud – with its murky depths one doesn't sound,
Where shadowy reptiles vaguely swarm around.

Written on the pane of a Flemish window

I love the carillons pealing in your ancient towns,
Oh agèd country, guardian of the customs of the home,
Noble Flanders, where the North heats up drowsily
In Castille's sun, then couples itself with the Midi!
Carillons are the wild and unexpected hour
Clothed as a Spanish dancer one believes one sees
Suddenly stepping through a lighted, living hole
A portal of air would make, opening in a breeze.
She appears, overflowing with her magic notes, and moves
Shaking her silver apron out over the roofs,
Piteously waking up the sleeping and the bored,
Flitting about with tiny steps like a bird,
And quivering like a dart sticking in a bull's eye.
Trembling and dancing, she descends from the sky
On a delicate stairway of invisible crystal.
And while she roams, comes back, falls, and reascends the air,
The mind, that watchman made of ears and of eyes,
Listens to her ringing foot glide from stair to stair!

Tristesse d'Olympio

Les champs n'étaient point noirs, les cieux n'étaient pas mornes;
Non, le jour rayonnait dans un azur sans bornes
    Sur la terre étendu,
L'air était plein d'encens et les prés de verdures
Quand il revit ces lieux où par tant de blessures
    Son cœur s'est répandu!

L'automne souriait; les coteaux vers la plaine
Penchaient leurs bois charmants qui jaunissaient à peine;
    Le ciel était doré;
Et les oiseaux, tournés vers celui que tout nomme,
Disant peut-être à Dieu quelque chose de l'homme,
    Chantaient leur chant sacré!

Il voulut tout revoir, l'étang près de la source,
La masure où l'aumône avait vidé leur bourse,
    Le vieux frêne plié,
Les retraites d'amour au fond des bois perdues,
L'arbre où dans les baisers leurs âmes confondues
    Avaient tout oublié!

Il chercha le jardin, la maison isolée,
La grille d'où l'œil plonge en une oblique allée,
    Les vergers en talus.
Pâle, il marchait. – Au bruit de son pas grave et sombre,
Il voyait à chaque arbre, hélas! se dresser l'ombre
    Des jours qui ne sont plus!

Il entendait frémir dans la forêt qu'il aime
Ce doux vent qui, faisant tout vibrer en nous-même,
    Y réveille l'amour,
Et, remuant le chêne ou balançant la rose,
Semble l'âme de tout qui va sur chaque chose
    Se poser tour à tour!

Les feuilles qui gisaient dans le bois solitaire,
S'efforçant sous ses pas de s'élever de terre,
    Couraient dans le jardin;
Ainsi, parfois, quand l'âme est triste, nos pensées
S'envolent un moment sur leurs ailes blessées,
    Puis retombent soudain.

Olympio's Sadness

The fields were not black; the heavens were not sad.
No, the day was blazing with a limitless blue
    On the earth spread out below,
The air was filled with incense and the meadows with green
When he saw again those places where – after so much pain –
    His heart had let go!

Autumn was smiling; the hills beyond the plain
Were leaning down their barely yellowing leaves;
    The day was gold and long;
And the birds, having turned toward the One who names all,
Telling God perhaps something human that they saw,
    Were singing their sacred song!

He wished to see it all again; the pool near the source,
The hut where alms-giving had emptied their purse,
    The ash tree, bent and curled;
The love retreats lost in the depths of the woods,
The tree where – souls entwined with kisses – they had stood
    And forgotten the world!

He looked for the garden, the orchard on the hill,
The side path through the iron gate that caught the eye,
    The house out of the way.
He walked on, pale. And with the tread of every step,
He would see shadows from the trees he passed start up
    And days that had passed away!

In those woods that he loved he heard the mild pulse
Of winds which make everything inside us convulse
    And stir the love that's there,
And which, lifting boughs or setting roses trembling,
Seem the soul of nature passing over every thing
    Alighting here and there!

Forced by the steps he took to come up off the ground,
The leaves that were lying in the peopleless woods
    Went flying in a pack.
In the same way sometimes, when the soul is sad, our thoughts
Fly upwards on their wounded wings for a moment,
    Then suddenly fall back.

Il contempla longtemps les formes magnifiques
Que la nature prend dans les champs pacifiques;
    Il rêva jusqu'au soir;
Tout le jour il erra le long de la ravine,
Admirant tour à tour le ciel, face divine,
    Le lac, divin miroir!

Hélas! se rappelant ses douces aventures,
Regardant, sans entrer, par-dessus les clôtures,
    Ainsi qu'un paria,
Il erra tout le jour. Vers l'heure où la nuit tombe,
Il se sentit le cœur triste comme une tombe,
    Alors il s'écria:

– «O douleur! j'ai voulu, moi dont l'âme est troublée,
Savoir si l'urne encor conservait la liqueur,
Et voir ce qu'avait fait cette heureuse vallée
De tout ce que j'avais laissé là de mon cœur!

«Que peu de temps suffit pour changer toutes choses!
Nature au front serein, comme vous oubliez!
Et comme vous brisez dans vos métamorphoses
Les fils mystérieux où nos cœurs sont liés!

«Nos chambres de feuillage en halliers sont changées!
L'arbre où fut notre chiffre est mort ou renversé;
Nos roses dans l'enclos ont été ravagées
Par les petits enfants qui sautent le fossé.

«Un mur clôt la fontaine où, par l'heure échauffée,
Folâtre, elle buvait en descendant des bois;
Elle prenait de l'eau dans sa main, douce fée,
Et laissait retomber des perles de ses doigts!

«On a pavé la route âpre et mal aplanie,
Où, dans le sable pur se dessinant si bien,
Et de sa petitesse étalant l'ironie,
Son pied charmant semblait rire à côté du mien!

«La borne du chemin, qui vit des jours sans nombre,
Où jadis pour m'attendre elle aimait à s'asseoir,
S'est usée en heurtant, lorsque la route est sombre,
Les grands chars gémissants qui reviennent le soir.

For a long time he meditated on the brilliant forms
Nature takes on in peaceful fields from dawn to dusk
  And dreams make clearer.
He wandered the entire day along the ravine
Admiring in turn the sky, heaven's face,
  And the lake, heaven's mirror!

Alas! thinking back over his sweet encounters,
Looking, without entering, over fence-enclosed fields
  As if he'd been cast out,
He wandered the length of the day. And when night fell
He felt his heart constrict as though he heard a funeral bell
  And then cried out aloud:

'O misery! How I, with my troubled soul, wanted
To know if the urn still preserved some sweet wine
And find out what this smiling valley had done
With that part of myself I had left behind!

'So little time is needed for everything to change!
Serene-faced Nature, how quickly you forget!
And, in your transformations, how quickly you cut
The ties our hearts are bound by and on which they're set!

'Our leafy bowers have been torn into tatters.
The tree we carved our names on is knocked on its edge.
Our roses in the cloistered garden have been ravaged
By all the small children jumping over the hedge.

'A wall shuts in the fountain which, on hot summer days,
Would drink deep and chuckle in its basin. And when
It would take the water in its hands, sweet fairy,
Pearls slipped through its fingers as they fell down again.

'They've even paved that rough and poorly levelled road
Where her foot, playing in the sand, would draw a line
Displaying the irony of her petite-ness –
Her charming foot seemed to be laughing next to mine!

'The milestone near the road, which had seen countless days
And which she loved to sit on while waiting for me,
Is worn from being knocked against by heavy, groaning carts
Returning in the evening when the road is hard to see.

«La forêt ici manque et là s'est agrandie.
De tout ce qui fut nous presque rien n'est vivant;
Et, comme un tas de cendre éteinte et refroidie,
L'amas des souvenirs se disperse à tout vent!

«N'existons-nous donc plus? Avons-nous eu notre heure?
Rien ne la rendra-t-il à nos cris superflus?
L'air joue avec la branche au moment où je pleure;
Ma maison me regarde et ne me connaît plus.

«D'autres vont maintenant passer où nous passâmes.
Nous y sommes venus, d'autres vont y venir;
Et le songe qu'avaient ébauché nos deux âmes,
Ils le continueront sans pouvoir le finir!

«Car personne ici-bas ne termine et n'achève;
Les pires des humains sont comme les meilleurs;
Nous nous réveillons tous au même endroit du rêve.
Tout commence en ce monde et tout finit ailleurs.

«Oui, d'autres à leur tour viendront, couples sans tache,
Puiser dans cet asile heureux, calme, enchanté,
Tout ce que la nature à l'amour qui se cache
Mêle de rêverie et de solemnité!

«D'autres auront nos champs, nos sentiers, nos retraites;
Ton bois, ma bien-aimée, est à des inconnus.
D'autres femmes viendront, baigneuses indiscrètes,
Troubler le flot sacré qu'ont touché tes pieds nus!

«Quoi donc! c'est vainement qu'ici nous nous aimâmes!
Rien ne nous restera de ces coteaux fleuris
Où nous fondions notre être en y mêlant nos flammes!
L'impassible nature a déjà tout repris.

«Oh! dites-moi, ravins, frais ruisseaux, treilles mûres,
Rameaux chargés de nids, grottes, forêts, buissons,
Est-ce que vous ferez pour d'autres vos murmures?
Est-ce que vous direz à d'autres vos chansons?

«Nous vous comprenions tant! doux, attentifs, austères,
Tous nos échos s'ouvraient si bien à votre voix!
Et nous prêtions si bien, sans troubler vos mystères,
L'oreille aux mots profonds que vous dites parfois!

'Here, some trees are missing; over there, it's overgrown.
Almost nothing from then is living now. What one sees
Is like a heap of ash, once glowing, that has cooled,
A pile of memories scattered on the breeze!

'Do *we* still exist? Have we had our hour then?
Will nothing give it back? no matter what we cry out for?
The air plays with branches at the same time I'm crying.
The house looks at me and doesn't know me anymore.

'Now others are going to come and walk where we walked.
We came here; they'll come here. Time we spent they will spend.
And the dream which our two souls began to sketch in –
It will go on without the power to end!

'For no one down here brings himself to completion.
The worst man, like the best, has the same tale he tells.
We all seem to wake up in the same place of the dream.
Everything begins here and will finish somewhere else.

'Yes, others, blameless couples, will come in their turn
To this serene retreat, this joyous scenery,
To breathe in what nature, for the love that is hiding,
Infuses with dreaming and solemnity!

'And others will possess our fields, our pathways, and our bowers,
Your woods will belong to those unknown to us, my love.
And other women – indiscreet bathers – will come here
To stir the lake your feet touched and dangled above!

'Is it in vain then that we loved each other here?
Nothing will be left of those hills in the back
Where we melted our being while mixing our flames!
Nature has already taken everything back.

'So tell me, ravines and fresh streams, trellised vines,
Nest-burdened branches, hills to which the wood belongs,
Will you continue to murmur to others?
Will you keep singing to others your songs?

'How well we understood you! Attentive to your voice,
Our echoes would answer you time and time again!
How gladly we lent (without disturbing your rites)
An ear to those deep words you utter now and then!

«Répondez, vallon pur, répondez, solitude,
O nature abritée en ce désert si beau,
Lorsque nous dormirons tous deux dans l'attitude
Que donne aux morts pensifs la forme du tombeau,

«Est-ce que vous serez à ce point insensible
De nous savoir couchés, morts avec nos amours,
Et de continuer votre fête paisible,
Et de toujours sourire et de chanter toujours?

«Est-ce que, nous sentant errer dans vos retraites,
Fantômes reconnus par vos monts et vos bois,
Vous ne nous direz pas de ces choses secrètes
Qu'on dit en revoyant des amis d'autrefois?

«Est-ce que vous pourrez, sans tristesse et sans plainte,
Voir nos ombres flotter où marchèrent nos pas,
Et la voir m'entraîner, dans une morne étreinte,
Vers quelque source en pleurs qui sanglote tout bas?

«Et s'il est quelque part, dans l'ombre où rien ne veille,
Deux amants sous vos fleurs abritant leurs transports,
Ne leur irez-vous pas murmurer à l'oreille:
— Vous qui vivez, donnez une pensée aux morts!

«Dieu nous prête un moment les prés et les fontaines,
Les grands bois frissonnants, les rocs profonds et sourds,
Et les cieux azurés et les lacs et les plaines,
Pour y mettre nos cœurs, nos rêves, nos amours;

«Puis il nous les retire. Il souffle notre flamme;
Il plonge dans la nuit l'antre où nous rayonnons;
Et dit à la vallée, où s'imprima notre âme,
D'effacer notre trace et d'oublier nos noms.

«Eh bien! oubliez-nous, maisons, jardin, ombrages!
Herbe, use notre seuil! ronce, cache nos pas!
Chantez, oiseaux! ruisseaux, coulez! croissez, feuillages!
Ceux que vous oubliez ne vous oublieront pas.

«Car vous êtes pour nous l'ombre de l'amour même!
Vous êtes l'oasis qu'on rencontre en chemin!
Vous êtes, ô vallon, la retraite suprême
Où nous avons pleuré nous tenant par la main!

'Answer me, valley, answer me, o Solitude!
O Nature sheltered in this desert that's in bloom,
When both of us are sleeping in that grave position
The thoughtful dead take on in the confines of the tomb,

'Will you be so unmoved by us, even then,
Knowing that we're dead with all we've loved? And will you
Continue with your quiet festivities then
And still go on smiling and go on singing too?

'And when you sense our spirits wandering through you –
Familiars recognized by forest, hill, and glen –
Won't you confide in us and tell us those secrets
One shares with old friends when one sees them again?

'Will you be able, without sadness or lamenting,
To watch our spirits drifting where our footsteps used to fall,
And see her pull me in a sad embrace toward water
Sobbing softly so you hardly hear it at all?

'And if, in the shade where nothing watches, there are lovers
Sheltering their ecstasies beneath some flower-bed,
Won't you go up to them and whisper in their ears:
"You who are living, give a thought to the dead!"?

'God lends us meadows and fountains for a moment,
The vast, trembling forests, the blue skies above,
The deep and deaf rocks, and the lakes, and the plains
To place in them our hearts, our dreams, and our love –

And then he takes them back. He extinguishes our flame.
He plunges into darkness the cave we blazed about,
And tells the valley where our souls have been imprinted
To forget our names and rub all traces of us out.

'Go ahead then, houses, garden, shadows, forget us!
Hide our footsteps, brambles! Overrun our thresholds too!
Sing, birds! Flow onward, rivers! And grow, grass and leaves!
Those whom you've forgotten won't forget about you.

' – For you are the shadow of love itself for us;
You are the oasis we discover in life's sand;
And you, o valley, are the ultimate refuge
Where we've cried, holding each other by the hand!

«Toutes les passions s'éloignent avec l'âge,
L'une emportant son masque et l'autre son couteau,
Comme un essaim chantant d'histrions en voyage
Dont le groupe décroît derrière le coteau.

«Mais toi, rien t'efface, amour! toi qui nous charmes,
Toi qui, torche ou flambeau, luis dans notre brouillard.
Tu nous tiens par la joie, et surtout par les larmes.
Jeune homme on te maudit, on t'adore viellard.

«Dans ces jours où la tête au poids des ans s'incline,
Où l'homme, sans projets, sans but, sans visions,
Sent qu'il n'est déjà plus qu'une tombe en ruine
Où gisent ses vertues et ses illusions;

«Quand notre âme en rêvant descend dans nos entrailles,
Comptant dans notre cœur, qu'enfin la glace atteint,
Comme on compte les morts sur un champ de batailles,
Chaque douleur tombée et chaque songe éteint,

«Comme quelqu'un qui cherche en tenant une lampe,
Loin des objets réels, loin du monde rieur,
Elle arrive à pas lents par une obscure rampe
Jusqu'au fond désolé du gouffre intérieur;

«Et là, dans cette nuit qu'aucun rayon n'étoile,
L'âme, en un repli sombre où tout semble finir,
Sent quelque chose encor palpiter sous un voile… –
C'est toi qui dors dans l'ombre, ô sacré souvenir!»

Oceano Nox

Saint-Valery-sur-Somme.

Oh! combien de marins, combiens de capitaines
Qui sont partis joyeux pour des courses lointaines,
Dans ce morne horizon se sont évanouis!
Combien ont disparu, dure et triste fortune!
Dans une mer sans fond, par une nuit sans lune,
Sous l'aveugle océan à jamais enfouis!

54

'All of the passions drift away as we grow older,
Carrying off their masks, their knives, and what they will,
Like a caravan of travelling actors whose singing
Disperses when the troupe passes over a hill.

'But you, enchanting Love, nothing quenches your flame.
You light us in our fog and warm us in our cold.
You keep us with joy and especially with tears.
When young, we curse you; we revere you when we're old.

'And on those days when we are weighed down by the years,
When the man without a vision, goal, or urging to create
Senses he is nothing but a tomb in ruins
Into which his virtues and illusions have been laid,

'When our reflecting soul descends into our self
To count in our heart ice at last has forced to yield
Each fallen sorrow and each dream that's been snuffed out
The way one counts the bodies on a battlefield,

'Like a man who is searching, holding up a lamp,
The soul arrives with slow steps and by some dark stair –
Far from real objects and far from the mocking world –
At the innermost abyss of ourselves – and it's there,

'Within that night where no ray sparkles, that the soul,
In a nook where everything appears to cease to be,
Senses something palpitating still beneath a veil:
Sleeping in the shadows, you, sacred memory!'

Oceano Nox

Saint-Valery-sur-Somme.

How many sailors, and how many captains
Who set out in joy for some faraway land
Have gone beneath the skyline and disappeared from sight!
How many have vanished – hard and sad destiny –
In a soundless ocean, on a moonless night,
And are buried forever inside the blind sea!

Combien de patrons morts avec leurs équipages!
L'ouragan de leur vie a pris toutes les pages,
Et d'un souffle il a tout dispersé sur les flots!
Nul ne saura leur fin dans l'abîme plongée.
Chaque vague en passant d'un butin s'est chargée;
L'une a saisi l'esquif, l'autre les matelots!

Nul ne sait votre sort, pauvres têtes perdues!
Vous roulez à travers les sombres étendues,
Heurtant de vos fronts morts des écueils inconnus.
Oh! que de vieux parents, qui n'avaient plus qu'un rêve,
Sont morts en attendant tous les jours sur la grève
       Ceux qui ne sont pas revenus!

On s'entretient de vous parfois dans les veillées.
Maint joyeux cercle, assis sur des ancres rouillées,
Mêle encor quelque temps vos noms d'ombre courverts
Aux rires, aux refrains, aux récits d'aventures,
Aux baisers qu'on dérobe à vos belles futures,
Tandis que vous dormez dans les goëmons verts!

On demande: — Où sont-ils? sont-ils rois dans quelque île?
Nous ont-ils délaissés pour un bord plus fertile? —
Puis votre souvenir même est enseveli.
Le corps se perd dans l'eau, le nom dans la mémoire.
Le temps, qui sur toute ombre en verse une plus noire,
Sur le sombre océan jette le sombre oubli.

Bientôt des yeux de tous votre ombre est disparue.
L'un n'a-t-il pas sa barque et l'autre sa charrue?
Seules, durant ces nuits où l'orage est vainqueur,
Vos veuves aux fronts blancs, lasses de vous attendre,
Parlent encor de vous en remuant la cendre
       De leur foyer et de leur cœur!

Et quand la tombe enfin a fermé leur paupière,
Rien ne sait plus vos noms, pas même une humble pierre
Dans l'étroit cimetière où l'écho nous répond,
Pas même un saule vert qui s'effeuille à l'automne,
Pas même la chanson naïve et monotone
Que chant un mendiant à l'angle d'un vieux pont!

How many dead captains along with their crews!
Hurricanes have carried off the pages of their lives
And strewn them with gusts of wind across the ocean!
Buried in the deep, no one will ever know their end.
Every wave that passes by possesses a treasure:
One clutches at the ship, another at the men!

No one knows how you met your end, poor lost souls.
You are rolling across the sombre expanses,
Knocking up against reefs and drifting with the foam.
How many parents, with a dream and nothing more,
Have died waiting all those days along the shore
      For those who never came home!

You're talked about now and then at evening gatherings.
Sitting on rusted anchors, circles of old friends
Sometimes blend your shadowy names with the air,
With laughter and song and stories of adventures,
With kisses taken from your once glowing futures
While you are sleeping in the seaweed's green hair!

Someone asks, 'Where are they? Are they kings of some island?
Have they abandoned us for some happier shore?'
Even reminders of you soon become enshrouded,
Your body lost in water, your name in memory:
Time, pouring ever blacker shadows on each shadow,
Casts a dark forgetfulness over a dark sea.

And soon your shadow passes from the eyes of the world.
Doesn't this man have his vessel, that his plough to tend?
Alone, on those nights when stormclouds flash in fits and starts,
Your widows, worn out from always waiting up for you,
Speak your names staring at the ashes they sift through
      In their hearths and their hearts!

And when at last the grave has closed their eyelids too,
Nothing knows your names anymore, not one stone
Inside the narrow graveyard where echoes answer us –
Not even the autumn willow, green and flowering,
Not even the song, naive and monotonous,
A beggar in the corner of a bridge will sometimes sing!

Où sont-ils, les marins sombrés dans les nuits noires?
O flots, que vous savez de lugubres histoires!
Flots profonds, redoutés des mères à genoux!
Vous vous les racontez en montant les marées,
Et c'est ce qui vous fait ces voix désespérées
Que vous avez le soir quand vous venez vers nous!

Nuits de juin

L'été, lorsque le jour a fui, de fleurs couverte
La plaine verse au loin un parfum enivrant;
Les yeux fermés, l'oreille aux rumeurs entr'ouverte,
On ne dort qu'à demi d'un sommeil transparent.

Les astres sont plus purs, l'ombre paraît meillure;
Un vague demi-jour teint le dôme éternel;
Et l'aube douce et pâle, en attendant son heure,
Semble toute la nuit errer au bas du ciel.

Where are they, the sailors sunken in the black night?
O waves, what melancholy histories you hide!
Waves kneeling mothers dread, deep and dangerous:
You exchange these stories while scaling the tide,
And that is what makes those voices desperate –
Those voices you release at dusk when you come toward us!

June Nights

In summer when the day has gone, the flowering fields
Pour out their scents, intoxicating and deep.
With eyes closed, ears open to the sounds the earth yields,
The world only half-sleeps a transparent sleep.

The stars are purer then; the darkness seems to shake.
A half day vaguely tints the heavens with its light.
And the sweet and pale dawn, as if waiting to break,
Wanders at the bottom of the sky the whole night.

From *Les Châtiments* (1853)

Souvenir de la nuit du 4

L'enfant avait reçu deux balles dans la tête.
Le logis était propre, humble, paisible, honnête;
On voyait un rameau bénit sur un portrait.
Une vieille grand'mère était là qui pleurait.
Nous la déshabillions en silence. Sa bouche,
Pâle, s'ouvrait; la mort noyait son œil farouche;
Ses bras pendants semblaient demander des appuis.
Il avait dans sa poche une toupie en buis.
On pouvait mettre un doigt dans les trous de des plaies.
Avez-vous vu saigner la mûre dans les haies?
Sone crâne était ouvert comme un bois qui se fend.
L'aïeule regarda déshabiller l'enfant,
Disant: — Comme il est blanc! approchez donc la lampe.
Dieu! ses pauvres cheveux sont collés sur sa tempe! —
Et quand se fut fini, le prit sur ses genoux.
La nuit était lugubre; on entendait des coups
De fusil dans la rue où l'on en tuait d'autres.
— Il faut ensevelir l'enfant, dirent les nôtres.
Et l'on prit un drap blanc dans l'armoire en noyer.
L'aïeule cependent l'approchait du foyer
Comme pour réchauffer ses membres déjà roides.
Hélas! ce que la mort touche de ses mains froides
Ne se réchauffe plus aux foyers d'ici-bas!
Elle pencha la tête et lui tira ses bas,
Et dans ses vieilles mains prit les pieds du cadavre.
— Est-ce que ce n'est pas une chose qui navre!
Cria-t-elle! monsieur, il n'avait pas huit ans!
Ses maîtres, il allait en classe, étaient contents.
Monsieur, quant il fallait que je fisse une lettre,
C'est lui qui l'écrivait. Est-ce qu'on va se mettre
À tuer les enfants maintenant? Ah! mon Dieu!
On est donc des brigands! Je vous demande un peu,
Il jouait ce matin, là, devant la fenêtre!
Dire qu'ils m'ont tué ce pauvre petit être!
Il passait dans la rue, ils ont tiré dessus.
Monsieur, il était bon et doux comme un Jésus.

From *Punishments*

Memory of the Night of the Fourth

The child had received two bullets in the head.
The lodging was tidy, modest, peaceful, unassuming.
A blessed branch hung above the portrait near the bed.
The grandmother was there. All you heard were her cries.
We undressed him in silence. The boy's pallid lips
Opened. Death drowned out and glazed his wild eyes.
His drooping arms almost seemed to ask for support.
We found a wooden top in his pocket and some cord.
His skull was cracked open like a log that had split.
His wound was so large you could put your thumb through it.
Have you ever seen mulberries bleeding in a field?
The grandmother watched us undressing him and said,
'Look how pale he is! Come closer to the light!
His poor curls are sticking to the top of his head.'
And when we had finished, she took him on her knees.
The night was ruthless. Rifles crackled in the streets
Where the soldiers were shooting others in the head.
'You will have to cover up the child,' someone said.
Someone else took a sheet out of the walnut armoire.
The grandmother, however, brought him closer to the fire
As if to warm his already stiffening limbs.
Whatever death touches with his cold hands down here,
Alas! can't be warmed by our fires again.
She leaned his head backwards and pulled off his socks,
Then rubbed the corpse's toes in her quivering hands.
'Isn't this a sight that we aren't meant to withstand?'
She shouted. 'Sir, he wasn't even eight years old!
His teachers – he studied – said he did as he was told
And stayed alert. Whenever I had to write a note
Or a long letter, sir, it was always he who wrote.
Are they going to kill children as well now? They must
Be truly evil then. Does it not fill you with disgust?
This morning he was playing near the window outside.
To say that they have taken this little child's life!
He was passing by and they shot him in cold blood.
He was a baby Jesus, so sweet and so good.

Moi je suis vieille, il est tout simple que je parte;
Cela n'aurait rien fait à monsieur Bonaparte
De me tuer au lieu de tuer mon enfant! –
Elle s'interrompit, les sanglots l'étouffant,
Puis elle dit, et tous pleuraient près de l'aïeule:
– Que vais-je devenir à présent toute seule?
Expliquer-moi cela, vous autres, aujourd'hui.
Hélas! je n'avais plus de sa mère que lui.
Pourquoi l'a-t-on tué? je veux qu'on me l'explique.
L'enfant n'a pas crié vive la République. –
Nous nous taisions, debout et graves, chapeau bas,
Tremblant devant ce deuil qu'on ne console pas.

Vous ne compreniez point, mère, la politique.
Monsieur Napoléon, c'est son nom authentique,
Est pauvre et même prince; il aime les palais;
Il lui convient d'avoir des chevaux, des valets,
De l'argent pour son jeu, sa table, son alcôve,
Ses chasses; par la même occasion, il sauve
La famille, l'église et la société;
Il veut avoir Saint-Cloud, plein de rose l'été,
Où viendront l'adorer les préfets et les maires;
C'est pour cela qu'il faut que les vieilles grand'mères,
De leur pauvres doigts gris que fait trembler le temps,
Cousent dans le linceul des enfants de sept ans.

Ce que le poëte se disait en 1848

Tu ne dois pas chercher le pouvoir, tu dois faire
Ton œuvre ailleurs; tu dois, esprit d'une autre sphère,
Devant l'occasion reculer chastement.
De la pensée en deuil doux et sévère amant,
Compris ou dédaigné des hommes, tu dois être
Pâtre pour les garder et pour les bénir prêtre.
Lorsque les citoyens, par la misère aigris,
Fils de la même France et du même Paris,
S'égorgent; quand, sinistre, et soudain apparue,
La morne barricade au coin de chaque rue
Monte et vomit la mort de partout à la fois,

I am old, sir: if I died, it might make some sense.
It wouldn't have cost Monsieur Bonaparte a cent
To have killed me instead of killing my child!'
She broke off, choking on her sobs for awhile.
We cried with her. Then suddenly she changed her tone:
'What am I going to do now that I am alone?
Explain that to me, each and every one of you.
There's nothing of his mother now that I have lost him too.
Tell me why they kill the defenceless and the weak.
The child never shouted, *Long live the Republic!*'
We were silent, hats in hand, and could offer no relief,
Trembling in the face of inconsolable grief.

Mother, you don't understand: politics is a game.
Monsieur Napoleon – that's his authentic name –
Is poor and yet a prince. He loves his palaces.
It's fitting he has horses and valets, and always is
Providing for his bedroom, gambling, and his table.
For only by maintaining all of this is he able
To save 'the family, the church, society'.
He wants to own Saint-Cloud so officials from the city
Can smell the summer roses when they come to pay respect.
This is the reason ageing mothers should expect
To use their fingers prone to tremble in the cold
To sew the shrouds of children who are seven years old.

What the poet said to himself in 1848

You shouldn't seek power, but do what work you would
Somewhere else. Otherworldly as you are, you should
Retreat modestly in front of opportunity.
Severe and mild lover of grief-burdened thought,
Whether scorned or understood by men, you should be
A shepherd who will guard them and a priest who will bless.
And when your countrymen, embittered by poverty,
Offspring of the same France and Paris, nonetheless
Butcher each other, piling metal, stone, and wood
Into barricades at every corner, as the air
Disperses the smoke and vomits death everywhere –

Tu dois y courir seul et désarmé; tu dois
Dans cette guerre impie, abominable, infâme,
Présenter ta poitrine et répandre ton âme,
Parler, prier, sauver les faibles et les forts,
Sourire à la mitraille et pleurer sur les morts;
Puis remonter tranquille à ta place isolée,
Et là, défendre, au sein de l'ardente assemblée,
Et ceux qu'on veut proscrire et ceux qu'on croit juger,
Renverser l'échafud, servir et protéger
L'ordre et la paix, qu'ébranle un parti téméraire,
Nos soldats trop aisés à tromper, et ton frère,
Le pauvre homme du peuple aux cabanons jeté,
Et les lois, et la triste et fière liberté;
Consoler, dans ces jours d'anxiété funeste,
L'art divin qui frissonne et pleure, et pour le reste
Attendre le moment suprême et décisif.

Ton rôle est d'avertir et de rester pensif.

L'Expiation

I

Il neigeait. On était vaincu par sa conquête.
Pour la première fois l'aigle baissait la tête.
Sombres jours! l'empereur revenait lentement,
Laissant derrière lui brûler Moscou fumant.
Il neigeait. L'âpre hiver fondait en avalanche.
Après la plaine blanche une autre plane blanche.
On ne connaissait plus les chefs ni le drapeau.
Hier la grande armée, et maintenant troupeau.
On ne distinguait plus les ailes ni le centre:
Il neigeait. Les blessés s'abritaient dans le ventre
Des chevaux morts; au seuil des bivouacs désolés
On voyait des clairons à leur poste gelés
Restés debout, en selle et muets, blancs de givre,
Collant leur bouche en pierre aux trompettes de cuivre.
Boulets, mitraille, obus, mêlés aux flocons blancs,
Pleuvaient; les grenadiers, surpris d'être tremblants,

You should run out, alone and unarmed, and you should
Expose your chest and open your soul to the throng
Who fight this unholy, abominable war;
And speak, pray, save both the weak and the strong;
Smile at the grape-shot, but mourn the dead most;
Then climb back, tranquil, to your isolated post,
And there, in the heat of the assembly, defend
Those they would exile and those they would condemn;
Overturn the death penalty; serve and protect
Peace and order, overrun by a reckless sect,
And our soldiers, all too easily duped; and you should free
Your brother, the people's man denied liberty,
The laws, and Freedom, proud and sad, that used to thrive –
And in these days, fearful to everyone alive,
Comfort art when it sobs, administer the balm,
And wait for the decisive moment to arrive.

Your role is to warn and stay thoughtful and calm.

The Expiation

I

It was snowing. Every falling flake spelled defeat.
The eagle was forced to bow its head the first time.
Dismal days! The emperor led the slow retreat,
Leaving smoke- and flame-gutted Moscow behind.
It was snowing. Winter collapsed the terrain.
A plain of white followed by another white plain.
Was that an officer? A flag? You couldn't say.
The *grande armée* the day before, a herd today.
You couldn't make out flanks or the centre's divides.
It was snowing. Wounded men found shelter in the sides
Of dead horses. You saw buglers, standing upright
In their saddles at their posts, and staring blankly – mute and white
And frozen, as some weary regiment would pass –
Their stony lips welded to the instrument's brass.
Bullets, grape-shot, shrapnel, and the white flakes of snow
Fell together. The grenadiers held to a slow

Marchaient pensifs, la glace à leur moustache grise.
Il neigeait, il neigeait toujours! la froide bise
Sifflait; sur le verglas, dans des lieux inconnus,
On n'avait pas de pain et l'on allait pieds nus.
Ce n'étaient plus des cœurs vivants, des gens de guerre;
C'était un rêve errant dans la brume, un mystère,
Une procession d'ombres sous le ciel noir.
La solitude vaste, épouvantable à voir,
Partout apparaissait, muette vengeresse.
Le ciel faisait sans bruit avec la neige épaisse
Pour cette immense armée un immense linceul.
Et, chacun se sentant mourir, on était seul.
– Sortira-t-on jamais de ce funeste empire?
Deux ennemis! le Czar, le Nord. Le Nord est pire.
On jetait les canons pour brûler les affûts.
Qui se couchait, mourait. Groupe morne et confus,
Ils fuyaient; le désert dévorait le cortège.
On pouvait, à des plis qui soulevaient la neige,
Voir que des régiments s'étaient endormis là.
O chutes d'Annibal! Lendemains d'Attila!
Fuyards, blessés, mourants, caissons, brancards, civières,
On s'écrasait aux ponts pour passer les rivières.
On s'endormait dix mille, on se réveillait cent.
Ney, que suivait naguère une armée, à présent
S'évadait, disputant sa montre à trois cosaques.
Toutes les nuits, qui vive! alerte, assauts! attaques!
Ces fantômes prenaient leur fusil, et sur eux
Il voyaient se ruer, effrayants, ténébreux,
Avec des cris pareils aux voix des vautours chauves,
D'horribles escadrons, tourbillons d'hommes fauves.
Toute une armée ainsi dans la nuit se perdait.
L'empereur était là, debout, qui regardait.
Il était comme un arbre en proie à la cognée.
Sur ce géant, grandeur jusqu'alors épargnée,
Le malheur, bûcheron sinistre, était monté;
Et lui, chêne vivant, par la hache insulté,
Tresaillant sous le spectre aux lugubres revanches,
Il regardait tomber autour de lui ses branches.
Chefs, soldats, tous mouraient. Chacun avait son tour.
Tandis qu'environnant sa tente avec amour,
Voyant son ombre aller et venir sur la toile,
Ceux qui restaient, croyant toujours à son étoile,
Accusaient le destin de lèse-majesté,

And trembling pace. Ice bit into every moustache.
It was snowing. It was always snowing! Winds would lash
Exposed flesh and whistle. Men would march with naked feet
Over ice, in unknown regions, without any bread to eat.
They weren't living hearts anymore, or men of war,
But a dream wandering into the fog, a mystery,
A shadowy procession on the sky's darkened floor.
Solitude, enormous and frightening to see,
Appeared everywhere, like an avenging ghost.
The sky was weaving a shroud with its snows
Over the army, thick and silent as a sigh.
Each soldier was alone feeling he was going to die.
'Will we ever leave this country God himself would curse?'
Two enemies: the Czar, the North. The North is worse.
They scavenged the canons to burn the frames' wood.
Whoever slept died. They no longer withstood
Assaults. They fled. Drifts covered troops everywhere.
And you could see, beneath the folds of snow and through the haze,
Entire regiments who had gone to sleep there.
Downfalls like Hannibal's! Attila-like next days!
Caissons, stretchers, carriage wheels; deserters, wounded men
Crushed themselves at bridges to cross a swollen stream.
Ten thousand went to sleep; one hundred woke again.
Ney, whom an army had been following, could be seen
Escaping, selling off his watch to three Cossacks.
And every night: 'Who goes there?... Alert!' Assaults. Attacks.
These phantoms grabbed their guns, and saw whirlwinds of men
Rushing down on them, in the shadows, at their backs,
With screams like those of vultures ripping carrion.

An entire army perished that way in the night.
The emperor was there, watching, standing upright.
He stood like a tree being pounded by an axe.
Sinister Misfortune levelled its attacks
On this giant whose grandeur had been spared until then.
And he, the oak at which the hatchet aimed its blow,
Quivering under spectres of revenge and punishment,
Was watching his branches fall into the snow.
Enlisted men and officers alike. They all went.
Surrounding the emperor with their loyalty,
And watching his shadow come and go on the tent,
Those who remained, trusting in his destiny,
Accused Fate of desertion and *lèse-majesté*.

Lui se sentit soudain dans l'âme épouvanté.
Stupéfait du désastre et ne sachant que croire,
L'empereur se tourna vers Dieu; l'homme de gloire
Trembla; Napoléon comprit qu'il expiait
Quelque chose peut-être, et, livide, inquiet,
Devant ses légions sur la neige semées:
– Est-ce le châtiment, dit-il, Dieu des armées? –
Alors il s'entendit appeler par son nom
Et quelqu'un qui parlait dans l'ombre lui dit: non.

II

Waterloo! Waterloo! Waterloo! morne plaine!
Comme une onde qui bout dans une urne trop pleine,
Dans ton cirque de bois, de coteaux, de vallons,
La pâle mort mêlait les sombres bataillons.
D'un côté c'est l'Europe et de l'autre la France.
Choc sanglant! des héros Dieu trompait l'espérance;
Tu désertais, victoire, et le sort était las.
O Waterloo! je pleure et je m'arrête, hélas!
Car ces derniers soldats de la dernière guerre
Furent grands; ils avaient vaincu toute la terre,
Chassé vingt rois, passé les Alpes et le Rhin,
Et leur âme chantait dans les clairons d'airain!

Le soir tombait; la lutte était ardente et noire.
Il avait l'offensive et presque la victoire;
Il tenait Wellington acculé sur un bois.
Sa lunette à la main, il observait parfois
Le centre du combat, point obscur où tressaille
La mêlée, effroyable et vivante broussaille,
Et parfois l'horizon, sombre comme la mer.
Soudain, joyeux, il dit: Grouchy! – C'était Blücher.
L'espoir changea de camp, le combat changea d'âme,
La mêlée en hurlant grandit comme une flamme.
La batterie anglaise écrasa nos carrés.
La plaine où frissonnaient les drapeaux déchirés,
Ne fut plus, dans les cris des mourants qu'on égorge,
Qu'un gouffre flamboyant, rouge comme une forge;
Gouffre où les régiments, comme des pans de murs,
Tombaient, où se couchaient comme des épis mûrs
Les haut tambours-majors aux panaches énormes,

His soul sensed horror creeping in and courage leave.
Stunned at the event, not knowing what to believe,
The emperor turned his eyes toward God; the once great
Man trembled; for Napoleon knew he must expiate
Some sin of his. Enraged and anxious, he swore
In front of his legions scattered in the snow.
'Is this my punishment,' he shouted, 'God of war?'
And someone speaking in the shadows answered, 'No.'

II

Waterloo! Your field stands, desolate and grim.
Like water boiling in a pot filled to the rim –
In your circle of forests, valleys, and glens,
Pale death mingled with the sombre regiments.
On one side, Europe; on the other side, France.
Brutal shock! God thwarted heroes' hopes and plans.
Victory and Fate deserted them at last.
Oh Waterloo! I sob, then stop my tears, alas!
For these last soldiers who waged the last war
Were truly great. They had conquered the world,
Deposed twenty kings, crossed the Alps and the Rhine:
Their souls sang like bronze trumpets blowing in one line!

Night fell. The fight went on, though you could barely see.
He had the offensive and almost victory.
He was holding Wellington prone against a wood.
Eyeglass in hand, he looked whenever he could
Toward the conflict's centre, a living patch of trees
Shuddering with struggle – a vague point ahead –
Or else at the horizon's depths, as dark as the sea's.
In joy he shouted, 'Groushee!' It was Blücher instead.
Hope switched sides. The combat had a change of heart.
With a sudden howl, the battle caught like fire and spread.
The English artillery ripped our troops apart.
The plain where tattered flags were once all you saw
Was no more than a furnace-like gulf, glowing red
Amidst the cries of dying men the battle consumed.
– An abyss where regiments, like sections of a wall,
Cracked and fell; where drum-majors, helmeted and plumed,
Lay like ears of corn among the wounded and the dead.

Où l'on entrevoyait des blessures difformes!
Carnage affreux! moment fatal! l'homme inquiet
Sentit que la bataille entre ses mains pliait.
Derrière un mamelon la garde était massée.
La garde, espoir suprême et suprême pensée!
– Allons! faites donner la garde, cria-t-il! –
Et Lanciers, Grenadiers aux guêtres de coutil,
Dragons que Rome eût pris pour des légionnaires,
Cuirassiers, Cannoniers qui traînaient des tonnerres,
Portant le noir colback ou le casque poli,
Tous, ceux de Friedland et ceux de Rivoli,
Comprenant qu'ils allaient mourir dans cette fête,
Saluèrent leur dieu, debout dans la tempête.
Leur bouche, d'un seul cri, dit: vive l'empereur!
Puis, à pas lents, musique en tête, sans fureur,
Tranquille, souriant à la mitraille anglaise,
La garde impériale entra dans la fournaise.
Hélas! Napoléon, sur sa garde penché,
Regardait, et, sitôt qu'ils avaient débouché
Sous les sombres canons crachant des jet de soufre,
Voyait, l'un après l'autre, en cet horrible gouffre,
Fondre ces régiments de granit et d'acier
Comme fond une cire au souffle d'un baiser.
Ils allaient, l'arme au bras, front haut, grave, stoïques,
Pas un ne recula. Dormez, morts héroïques!
Le reste de l'arméee hésitait sur leurs corps
Et regardait mourir la garde. – C'est alors
Qu'élevant tout à coup sa voix désespérée,
La Déroute, géante à la face effarée,
Qui, pâle, épouvantant les plus fiers bataillons,
Changeant subitement les drapeaux en haillons,
À de certains moments, spectre fait de fumées,
Se lève grandissante au milieu des armées,
La Déroute apparut au soldat qui s'émeut,
Et se tordant les bras, cria: Sauve qui peut!
Sauve qui peut! affront! horreur! toutes les bouches
Criaient; à travers champs, fous, éperdus, farouches,
Comme si quelque souffle avait passé sur eux,
Parmi les lourds caissons et les fourgons poudreux,
Roulant dans les fossés, se cachant dans les seigles,
Jetant schakos, manteaux, fusils, jetant les aigles,
Sous les sabres prussiens, ces vétérans, ô deuil!
Tremblaient, hurlaient, pleuraient, couraient! – En un clin d'œil,

A slaughter! Fatal moment! Looking up from his plans,
The troubled man sensed the fight was slipping through his hands.
The *garde* was still massed behind a nearby hill.
The imperial guard, last hope and last resort!
'Let's do it then!' he shouts. 'Call the guard to report!'
And Lancers, gaitered Grenadiers with boots tucked under,
Dragoons which Rome itself would draft as legionnaires,
Cuirassiers, Gunners dragging lightning and thunder
And wearing shining helmets and colbacks – like a sea,
All of them – those of Friedland and those of Rivoli –
Knowing they were going to die in this game,
Saluted their god, standing upright in the storm,
And cried in unison, 'Long live the emperor!'
And then, at an even pace, to music, without fear,
Smiling at the grape-shot, with no thought of retreat,
They all marched straight into the furnace's heat.
Alas! And Napoleon, expectant, looked about
The battlefield as soon as they had issued out
Where canons spat streams of sulfur with a hiss.
He saw those regiments of granite and steel
Melt, one by one, in that fiery abyss
Like candles near a brazier or wax on a seal.
They went, rifles up, foreheads high, grave and stoic.
None turned back. Rest now, for your deaths were heroic!
The others felt their limbs shake then stand straight again,
Watching the guard slowly die. It was then
That Rout itself, a giant with a horrifying face,
Raising its desperate voice to a scream,
Pale, striking fear into the sturdiest of men,
Tearing flags to shreds, ripping hearts at the seam,
Appearing as a spectre of smoke now and then –
Drifted though the ranks and grew larger. It began
To shout to anxious soldiers, 'Save yourself if you can!'

Save yourself if you can! Disgrace! Everyone
Was shouting, crazed and flustered, confused in the fray.
As if a breath passed over them, these veterans –
Among the heavy caissons and the ammunition vans,
Tossing shakos, rifles, coats, and eagles away,
Rolling in the ditches, hiding in the beds of rye –
Trembled, wept, and ran!
                    In the blink of an eye,

Comme s'envole au vent une paille enflammée,
S'évanouit ce bruit qui fut la grande armée,
Et cette plaine, hélas! où l'on rêve aujourd'hui,
Vit fuir ceux devant qui l'univers avait fui!
Quarante ans sont passés, et ce coin de la terre,
Waterloo, ce plateau funèbre et solitaire,
Ce champ sinistre où Dieu mêla tant de néants,
Tremble encor d'avoir vu la fuite des géants!

Napoléon les vit s'écouler comme un fleuve;
Hommes, chevaux, tambours, drapeaux; — et dans l'épreuve
Sentant confusément revenir son remords,
Levant les mains au ciel, il dit: mes soldats morts,
Moi vaincu! mon empire est brisé comme verre.
Est-ce le châtiment cette fois, Dieu sévère? —
Alors parmi les cris, les rumeurs, le canon,
Il entendit la voix qui lui répondait: Non!

III

Il croula. Dieu changea la chaîne de l'Europe.

Il est, au fond des mers que la brume enveloppe,
Un roc hideux, débris des antiques volcans.
Le Destin prit des clous, un marteau, des carcans,
Saisit, pâle et vivant, ce coleur du tonnerre,
Et, joyeux, s'en alla sur le pic centenaire
Le clouer, excitant par son rire moqueur
Le vautour Angleterre à lui ronger le cœur.

Évanouissement d'une splendeur immense!
Du soleil qui se lève à la nuit qui commence,
Toujours l'isolement, l'abandon, la prison;
Un soldat rouge au seuil, la mer à l'horizon.
Des rochers nus, des bois affreux, l'ennui, l'espace,
Des voiles s'enfuyant somme l'espoir qui passe,
Toujours le bruit des flots, toujours le bruits des vents!
Adieu, tente de pourpre aux panaches mouvants,
Adieu, le cheval blanc que César éperonne!
Plus de tambours battant aux champs, plus de couronne,
Plus de rois prosternés dans l'ombre avec terreur,
Plus de manteau traînant sur eux, plus d'empereur!

The sound which was once the *grande armée* died away
Like a piece of burning straw consumed by a breeze,
And this ring of fields, alas! where we dream today,
Saw those before whom the universe fled flee!
Forty years have passed, but the plain nonetheless,
Waterloo, battlefield of France against alliance,
This valley in which God scattered so much nothingness,
Still trembles from having seen the flight of those giants!

Napoleon watched them, like a river, course ahead:
Men, drums, horses, flags – while he, behind the pack,
Vaguely sensing his remorse ebbing back,
Lifted up his hands and shouted, 'So many dead!
The battle lost! My empire broken like glass!
Is *this* my punishment, God? The final blow?'
Among the shouts, the noises, canon shot shrieking past,
He heard a voice he heard before. It answered, 'No.'

III

He crumbled. God himself changed Europe's boundaries.

There lies, in the depths of fog-covered seas,
A rock formed from volcanoes long since sunk under.
Fate picked up a hammer, nails and pillories,
Then seized this pale but living thief of thunder,
And gleefully flew to a peak that stands apart
To nail him there, and prod, with a mocking laugh,
The English vulture to devour his heart.

Vanishing of a vast magnificence!
From sunrise to the moment night fell on the shore,
There was always his cell, solitude, abandonments;
The sea on the horizon, a redcoat at the door.
Naked boulders, savage forests, space and ennui,
Passing sails vanishing like hope on the sea,
The breakers' constant roar, the breezes' constant sigh!
Adieu, purple tent and bobbing plumes passing by!
Adieu, white horse which Caesar would spur!
No more battlefield drums, no more crowns, and no more
Terrified kings bowing down to the floor,
No more mantle hanging over them – no more emperor!

Napoléon était retombé Bonaparte.
Comme un romain blessé par la flèche du Parthe,
Saignant, morne, il songeait à Moscou qui brûla.
Un caporal anglais lui disait: halte-là!
Son fils aux mains des rois! sa femme aux bras d'un autre!
Plus vils que le pourceau qui dans l'égout se vautre,
Son sénat qui l'avait adoré l'insultait.
Au bord des mers, à l'heure où la bise se tait,
Sur les escarpements croulant en noirs décombres,
Il marchait, seul, rêveur, captif des vagues sombres,
Sur les monts, sur les flots, sur les cieux, triste et fier.
L'œil encore ébloui des batailles d'hier,
Il laissait sa pensée errer à l'aventure.
Grandeur, gloire, ô néant! calme de la nature!
Des aigles qui passaient ne le connaissaient pas.
Les rois, ses guichetiers, avaient pris un compas
Et l'avaient enfermé dans un cercle inflexible.
Il expirait. La mort de plus en plus visible
Se levait dans sa nuit et croissait à ses yeux
Comme le froid matin d'un jour mystérieux.
Son âme palpitait, déjà presque échappée.
Un jour enfin il mit sur son lit son épée,
Et se coucha près d'elle, et dit: c'est aujourd'hui!
On jeta le manteau de Marengo sur lui.
Ses batailles du Nil, du Danube, du Tibre,
Se penchaient sur son front, il dit: me voici libre!
Je suis vainqueur! je vois mes aigles accourir!
Et, comme il retournait sa tête pour mourir,
Il aperçut, un pied dans la maison déserte,
Hudson-Lowe guettant par la porte entrouverte.
Alors, géant broyé sous le talon des rois,
Il cria: — la mesure est comble cette fois!
Seigneur! c'est maintenant fini! Dieu que j'implore,
Vous m'avex châtié! — la voix dit: — pas encore!

IV

O noirs événements, vous fuyez dans la nuit!
L'empereur mort tomba sur l'empire détruit.
Napoléon alla s'endormir sous le saule.
Et les peuples alors, de l'un à l'autre pôle,
Oubliant le tyran, s'éprirent du héros.
Les poëtes, marquant au front les rois bourreaux,

Napoleon went back to being Bonaparte.
Like a Roman wounded by a Parthian dart,
Bleeding and brooding, he saw Moscow's fires flare.
An English corporal would bark out 'Halt right there!'
His son in hands of kings, his wife in someone else's arms!
Viler than swine in sewer mud, the senators
Who had worshipped him before insulted him now.
He'd walk along the shore when the blasts settled down
Alone, on escarpments crumbling into debris,
And dream there, captivated by the wrinkling of the sea,
Sad and proud, moving over mountains, waves, and skies.
Yesterday's battles still dazzling his eyes,
He let his thoughts wander at random on the roughs.
The eagles passing by didn't know who he was.
Grandeur, glory, nothingness! The calmness of the place!
His jailers, the kings, took out a compass and traced
An inflexible circle around him like a vice.
He was dying. A more and more visible death
Was rising in his night and growing clear in his eyes
Like the frozen dawn of some mysterious day.
His shivering soul seemed already on its way.
Finally one day he put his sword on his bed
And lay down next to it, declaring, 'It's today.'
They threw the mantle of Marengo over him.
His battles on the Danube, the Tiber, and the Nile
Leaned over his forehead. He said, 'Now I can smile.
I'm free, victorious! I see my eagles coming near!'
But the moment he turned to meet death without fear,
He saw someone's foot move in the house's empty wing:
Hudson-Lowe was waiting by the half-open door.
And then the giant, pinned beneath the talons of kings,
Cried out, 'My cup is overflowing with regret.
Oh Lord! It's finished now! Oh God whom I implore,
You've punished me this time!' The voice said, 'No, not yet.'

IV

Black events! You flee into night's darkest skies!
The emperor fell dead on the empire's demise.
Napoleon went to sleep beneath a willow tree.
And everyone, from one pole to the other, suddenly
Forgot the autocrat and fell in love with the man.
The poets, branding murderous tyrants, were solemn

Consolèrent, pensifs, cette gloire abattue.
À la colonne veuve on rendit la statue.
Quant on levait les yeux, on le voyait debout
Au-dessus de Paris, serein, dominant tout,
Seul, le jour dans l'azur et la nuit dans les astres.
Panthéons, on grava son nom sur vos pilastres!
On ne regarda plus qu'un seul côté des temps;
On ne se souvint plus que des jours éclatants;
Cet homme étrange avait comme enivré l'histoire;
La justice à l'œil froid disparut sous sa gloire;
On ne vit plus qu'Eylau, Ulm, Arcole, Austerlitz;
Comme dans les tombeaux des romains abolis,
On se mit à fouiller dans ces grandes années;
Et vous applaudissiez, nations inclinées,
Chaque fois qu'on tirait de ce sol souverain
Ou le consul de marbre, ou l'empereur d'airain!

V

Le nom grandit quand l'homme tombe;
Jamais rien de tel n'avait lui.
Calme, il écoutait dans sa tombe
La terre qui parlait de lui.

La terre disait: «la victoire
»A suivi cet homme en tous lieux.
»Jamais tu n'as vu, sombre histoire,
»Un passant plus prodigieux!

»Gloire au maître qui dort sous l'herbe!
»Gloire à ce grand audacieux!
»Nous l'avons vu gravir, superbe,
»Les premiers échelons des cieux!

»Il envoyait, âme acharnée,
»Prenant Moscou, prenant Madrid,
»Lutter contre la destinée
»Tous les rêves de son esprit.

»À chaque instant, rentrant en lice,
»Cet homme aux gigantesques pas
»Proposait quelque grand caprice
»À Dieu qui n'y consentait pas.

And conciliatory toward this fallen eminence.
His statue was placed again atop the widowed column.
Whenever you looked up, you would see him standing there
Serene, above Paris, dominating the air,
By day framed in azure, at night by stars – alone.
Pantheons, they chiselled his name in your stone!
One could only see one side of time through the haze.
One only remembered the illustrious days.
He had, it seemed, intoxicated history.
Cold-eyed justice disappeared before his glory.
People saw only Ulm, Eylau, and Austerlitz.
As if they were digging in Rome's burial pits,
They began to rummage through the years that came before,
And every time someone pulled a bronze emperor
Or a marble consul from this sovereign soil
You submissive nations clapped and cried out for more!

V

A man's name grows the moment he falls.
Nothing before had shone so brilliantly.
He listened to the earth talk of him
From the grave, and felt tranquillity.

The earth would shout aloud, 'Victory
Followed this man everywhere.
History, you never saw anyone pass
As grand or imposing as he.

'Glory to him who sleeps underground!
Glory to the bold!' it would cry.
'We have seen him, magnificent,
Climb the first steps of the sky!

'His restless mind would send abroad
The dreams of his soul, so that he
Might take Moscow, might take Madrid,
Might wrestle with destiny.

'At every instance, entering the lists,
This man whose strides caused lands to split,
Proposed some grand caprice to God
Who would never consent to it.

»Il n'était presque plus un homme.
»Il disait, grave et rayonnant,
»En regardant fixement Rome:
»C'est moi qui règne maintenant!

»Il voulait, héros et symbole,
»Pontif et roi, phare et volcan,
»Faire du Louvre un Capitole
»Et de Saint-Cloud un Vatican.

»César, il eût dit à Pompée:
»Sois fier d'être mon lieutenant!
»On voyait luire son épée
»Au fond d'un nuage tonnant.

»Il voulait, dans les frénésies
»De ses vastes ambitions,
»Faire devant ses fantaisies
»Agenouiller les nations,

»Ainsi qu'en une urne profonde,
»Mêler races, langues, esprits,
»Répandre Paris sur le monde,
»Enfermer le monde en Paris!

»Comme Cyrus dans Babylone,
»Il voulait sous sa large main
»Ne faire du monde qu'un trône
»Et qu'un peuple du genre humain,

»Et bâtir, malgré les huées,
»Un tel empire sous son nom,
»Que Jéhovah dans les nuées
»Fût jaloux de Napoléon!»

VI

Enfin, mort triomphait, il vit sa délivrance,
Et l'océan rendit son cercueil à la France.

L'homme, depuis douze ans, sous le dôme doré
Reposait, par l'exil et par la mort sacré;

'He was almost no longer a man.
Brooding, with a gleam on his brow,
He would say, staring straight at Rome:
I am the one who rules now!

'He wished to be a symbol, a hero too,
Pope, king, volcano, guiding light,
To make a Capitol out of the Louvre,
A Vatican out of Saint-Cloud.

'As Caesar, he'd have said to Pompey:
"Be proud you are my lieutenant!"
You could see his sword shimmering
In clouds where thunder came and went.

'He wanted, in the frenzies of
His boundless ambition to reign,
To make the nations kneel before
The fantasies of his brain,

'Mix races, languages, and souls
As if in one enormous urn,
Scatter Paris into the world,
Enclose the world in it in turn!

'Like Cyrus, he desired to place
The world under one command,
And make, beneath his massive hand,
One people of the human race,

'And build, in spite of all the taunts,
Such an empire in his name,
That God himself, in the clouds above,
Was jealous of Napoleon's fame!'

VI

Finally Death triumphed. He saw his deliverance.
And the ocean carried his casket back to France.

Beneath a gold dome, twelve years after his decease,
Hallowed by exile and death, he slept in peace.

En paix! – quand on passait près du monument sombre,
On se le figurait, couronne au front, dans l'ombre,
Dans son manteau semé d'abeilles d'or, muet,
Couché sous cette voûte où rien ne remuait,
Lui, l'homme qui trouvait la terre trop étroite,
Le sceptre en sa main gauche, et l'épée en sa droite,
À ses pieds son grand aigle ouvrant l'œil à demi,
Et l'on disait: c'est là qu'est César endormi!

Laissant dans la clarté marcher l'immense ville,
Il dormait; il dormait confiant et tranquille.

VII

Une nuit, – c'est toujours la nuit dans le tombeau, –
Il s'éveilla. Luisant comme un hideux flambeau,
D'étranges visions emplissaient sa paupière;
Des rires éclataient sous son plafond de pierre;
Livide, il se dressa, la vision grandit;
O terreur! une voix qu'il reconnut, lui dit:

– Réveille-toi. Moscou, Waterloo, Sainte-Hélène,
L'exil, les rois geôliers, l'Angleterre hautaine
Sur ton lit accoudée à ton dernier moment,
Sire, cela n'est rien. Voici le châtiment:

La voix alors devint âpre, amère, stridente,
Comme le noir sarcasme et l'ironie ardente;
C'était le rire amer mordant un demi-dieu.

– Sire! on t'a retiré de ton Panthéon bleu!
Sire! on t'a descendu de ta haute colonne!
Regarde: des brigands, dont l'essaim tourbillonne,
D'affreux bohémiens, des vainqueurs de charnier
Te tiennent dans leurs mains et t'ont fait prisonnier.
À ton orteil d'airain leur patte infâme touche.
Ils t'ont pris. Tu mourus, comme un astre se couche,
Napoléon-le-Grand, empereur; tu renais
Bonaparte, écuyer du cirque Beauharnais.
Te voilà dans leurs rangs, on t'a, l'on te harnache.
Ils t'appellent tout haut grand homme, entr'eux, ganache.
Ils traînent, sur Paris, qui les voit s'étaler,

In peace! When people passed the sombre monument
They imagined him there in the dark, confident
With his crown and his imperial coat sown with bees,
Asleep beneath that vault where nothing stirs, at ease –
The man who found the world too narrow for his sight,
Sceptre in his left hand, sabre in his right,
His eagle at his feet half opening its eye –
And they would say: 'Caesar sleeps there to rise no more.'

Allowing the enormous city to pass by,
He slept there; he slept there, untroubled, tranquil, sure.

VII

Then one night – it is always night in the grave –
He awoke. Flickering like torches in a cave,
Strange apparitions filled his eyes. He heard a groan.
Laughter burst from under his ceiling of stone.
Angered, he sat up. The vision was immense.
The horror! A voice he recognized from past events

Said, 'Awake. Moscow, Saint Helena, Waterloo,
Exile, jailer-kings, and England watching over you
In your last hour, all the guards that came and went –
That's nothing, your majesty. Behold your punishment ...'

The voice turned bitter then, as caustic and as free
As a dark sarcasm, or a scathing irony:
A laugh to mock a demi-god a crown once sat upon.

'Sire, they've removed from your blue Pantheon!
Sire, they've pulled you from the column where you rested!
Look, all the thieves, with which the nation is infested,
Charnel-house victors, and the low-life that appals,
Have taken you prisoner and hold you in their claws.
Their talons touch the bronze toe they once cringed before.
They've taken you. You die as the great emperor,
Napoleon; like a star, you're reborn the next day
As Bonaparte, horseman of the *Cirque Beauharnais*.
There you are in their ranks! They dress you for the part.
In public, you're the great one, in private, the old fart.
They drag across Paris all those shows the crowds follow:

Des sabres qu'au besoin ils sauraient avaler.
Aux passants attroupés devant leur habitacle,
Ils disent, entends-les: — Empire à grand spectacle!
Le pape est engagé dans la troupe; c'est bien,
Nous avons mieux; le czar en est; mais ce n'est rien,
Le czar n'est qu'un sergent, le pape n'est qu'un bonze.
Nous avons avec nous le bonhomme de bronze!
Nous sommes les neveux du grand Napoléon! —
Et Fould, Magnan, Rouher, Parieu caméléon,
Font rage. Ils vont montrant un sénat d'automates.
Ils ont pris de la paille au fond des casemates
Pour empailler ton aigle, ô vainqueur d'Iéna!
Il est là, mort, gisant, lui qui si haut plana,
Et du champ de bataille il tombe au champ de foire.
Sire, de ton vieux trône ils recousent la moire.
Ayant dévalisé la France au coin d'un bois,
Ils ont à leurs haillons du sang, comme tu vois,
Et dans son bénitier Sibour lave leur linge.
Toi, lion, tu les suis; leur maître, c'est le singe.
Ton nom leur sert de lit, Napoléon premier.
On voit sur Austerlitz un peu de leur fumier.
Ta gloire est un gros vin dont leur honte se grise;
Cartouche essaie et met ta redingote grise;
On quête des liards dans le petit chapeau;
Pour tapis sur la table ils ont mis ton drapeau;
À cette table immonde où le grec devient riche,
Avec le paysan on boit, on joue, on triche.
Tu te mêles, compère, à ce tripot hardi,
Et ta main qui tenait l'étendard de Lodi,
Cette main qui portait la foudre, ô Bonaparte,
Aide à piper les dés et fait sauter la carte.
Ils te forcent à boire avec eux, et Carlier
Pousse amicalement d'un coude familier
Votre majesté, sire, et Piétri dans son antre
Vous tutoie, et Maupas vous tape sur le ventre.
Faussaires, meurtriers, escrocs, forbans, voleurs,
Ils savent qu'ils auront, comme toi, des malheurs;
Leur soif en attendant vide la coupe pleine,
À ta santé; Poissy trinque avec Sainte-Hélène.

Regarde! bals, sabbats, fêtes matin et soir.
La foule au bruit qu'ils font se culbute pour voir;
Debout sur le tréteau qu'assiège une cohue

Swords which, when they need to, they know how to swallow.
To passers-by who crowd their homes, they like to say
(Just listen to them shouting), 'Empire on display!
The pope's joined our troupe: he has a certain appeal.
We've better: the czar. But even he's no big deal.
The czar is just a sergeant; the pope is just a flea.
The bronze gentleman is, so to speak, family.
For we are the nephews of the great Napoleon!'
And Fould, Magnan, Rouher, and Parieu the Protean
Are the rage. People hold their bogus senate in awe.
Oh victor of Jena, they have scraped all the straw
From casemates so they could stuff your eagle with it!
– He's dead now, he who flew the heavens' length and width.
He has tumbled from a battleground to a fair. –
They're restitching the silk on your throne here and there.
Having raped France behind some out-of-the-way tree,
They've rags of blood all over them, as you can see,
And Sibour does their wash in a baptismal font.
A monkey leads them, lion. You aren't what they want.
Your name, Napoleon the First, is an excuse.
Their dung hangs down from Austerlitz, and they abuse
Your glory like a wine they're intoxicated on.
Cartouche eyes your grey frock coat, then puts it on.
They beg crowds for pennies with the hats they take off.
They've spread out your flag like a giant tablecloth.
And on this massive table where the Greek strikes it rich,
They drink with the peasants, and cheat them when they wish.
You mingle with this gambling crowd and play your part,
And your hand which once held the flag in Lodi's skies,
That hand which used to carry thunder, Bonaparte,
Helps pull cards from under the deck and load the dice.
They force you to drink with them, and Carlier
Likes to elbow you in an intimate way.
When Pietri converses with you in his nest,
You're his dear friend. Maupas taps you on the chest.
Con-artists, murderers, forgers, swindlers, thieves –
They know they will have troubles like yours in life's arena.
In the meantime, they drink their full cups to the lees.
To your health! Poissy clinks a glass with Saint Helena.

Look! Balls and sabbath dances, parties day and night.
Allured by their own noise, crowds press to get a view.
And standing on the stage, above the pit where people fight,

Qui rit, bâille, applaudit, tempête, siffle, hue,
Entouré de pasquins agitant leur grelot,
– Commencer par Homère et finir par Callot!
Épopée! épopée! oh! quel dernier chapitre! –
Près de Troplong paillasse et de Baroche pitre,
Devant cette baraque, abject et vil bazar
Où Mandrin mal lavé se déguise en César,
Riant, l'affreux bandit, dans sa moustache épaisse,
Toi, spectre impérial, tu bats la grosse caisse. –

L'horrible vision s'éteignit. – L'empereur,
Désespéré, poussa dans l'ombre un cri d'horreur,
Baissant les yeux, dressant ses mains épouvantées;
Les Victoires de marbre à la porte sculptées,
Fantômes blancs debout hors du sépulcre obscur,
Se faisaient du doigt signe et, s'appuyant au mur,
Écoutaient le titan pleurer dans les ténèbres.
Et Lui, cria: démon aux visions funèbres,
Toi qui me suis partout, que jamais je ne vois,
Qui donc es-tu? – Je suis ton crime, dit la voix. –
La tombe alors s'emplit d'une lumière étrange
Semblable à la clarté de Dieu quand il se venge;
Pareils aux mots que vit resplendir Balthazar,
Deux mots dans l'ombre écrits flamboyaient sur César;
Bonaparte, tremblant comme un enfant sans mère,
Leva sa face pâle et lut: – DIX-HUIT-BRUMAIRE!

Au Peuple

Il te ressemble; il est terrible et pacifique.
Il est sous l'infini le niveau magnifique;
Il a le mouvement, il a l'immensité.
Apaisé d'un rayon et d'un souffle agité,
Tantôt c'est l'harmonie et tantôt le cri rauque.
Les monstres sont à l'aise en sa profondeur glauque;
La trombe y germe; il a des gouffres inconnus
D'où ceux qui l'ont bravé ne sont pas revenus;
Sur son énormité le colosse chavire;
Comme toi le despote, il brise le navire;

Laugh and yawn, applaud and struggle, whistle, boo;
Surrounded by jesters shaking bells as they go
(Beginning with Homer and ending with Callot!
An epic! An epic! And the last scene's coming soon!);
Near Troplong the joker and Baroche the buffoon;
In front of this fair-booth, this repulsive bazaar,
Where Mandrin, dressed as Caesar, sits unwashed and laughing hard
Through the bandito mustache he twists to wring the scum –
Imperial spectre, you beat the party drum!'

The terrifying vision disappeared. The emperor,
With lowered eyes, and hands raised in front of his face,
Cried out in horror, desperation, and disgrace;
While all the marble victories sculpted on the door –
White apparitions standing outside in the gloom –
Were pointing, and, leaning on the wall of the tomb,
Listening to the titan sobbing in obscurity.
He shouted out, 'Demon whose visions are all black,
Who follow me everywhere, whom I never see,
Who are you then?' – 'I am your crime,' it answered back.
Then the tomb filled with light, as bizarre and as wild
As the glow of God when he allows vengeance to fall.
And just as with the writing Balthazar read on the wall,
Two words were flickering on shadows gathered there.
Bonaparte, trembling like a motherless child,
Lifted his face and read aloud *Eighteen Brumaire!*

To the People

It resembles you. It is awe-inspiring and at peace.
Its wrinkled plain dazzles and reflects infinities.
It possesses movement and depth; it is immense.
Softened by a sunbeam, ruffled by a breeze,
It is harmony sometimes, and sometimes dissonance.
Monsters are at home in its fathomless black.
Waterspouts brew there; it's an unknown abyss
From which those who've braved it have never come back.
Colossi are capsized in its infiniteness.
Just as you with despots, it pulls ships from on high.

Le fanal est sur lui comme l'esprit sur toi;
Il foudroie, il caresse, et Dieu seul sait pourquoi;
Sa vague, où l'on entend comme des chocs d'armures,
Emplit la sombre nuit de monstrueux murmures,
Et l'on sent que ce flot, comme toi, gouffre humain,
Ayant rugi ce soir, dévorera demain.
Son onde est une lame aussi bien que le glaive;
Il chante un hymne immense à Vénus qui se lève;
Sa rondeur formidable, azur universel,
Accepte en son miroir tous les astres du ciel;
Il a la force rude et la grâce superbe;
Il déracine un roc, il épargne un brin d'herbe;
Il jette comme toi l'écume aux fiers sommets,
O Peuple; seulement, lui, ne trompe jamais
Quand, l'œil fixe, et debout sur sa grève sacrée,
Et pensif, on attend l'heure de sa marée.

Stella

Je m'étais endormi la nuit près de la grève.
Un vent frais m'éveilla, je sortis de mon rêve,
J'ouvris les yeux, je vis l'étoile du matin.
Elle resplendissait au fond du ciel lointain
Dans une blancheur molle, infinie et charmante.
Aquilon s'enfuyait emportant la tourmente.
L'astre éclatant changeait la nuée en duvet.
C'était une clarté qui pensait, qui vivait;
Elle apaisait l'écueil où la vague déferle;
On croyait voir une âme à travers une perle.
Il faisait nuit encor, l'ombre régnait en vain,
Le ciel s'illuminait d'un sourire divin.
La lueur argentait le haut du mât qui penche;
Le navire était noir, mais la voile était blanche;
Des goélands debout sur un escarpement,
Attentifs, contemplaient l'étoile gravement
Comme un oiseau céleste et fait d'une étincelle;
L'océan, qui ressemble au peuple, allait vers elle,
Et, rugissant tout bas, la regardait briller,
Et semblait avoir peur de la faire envoler.

Like the Spirit over you, lanterns pass over it.
It thunders, it caresses, and God alone knows why.
Its waves, like colliding suits of armour, pound and ring,
And fill the dark night with their monstrous murmuring.
And one senses that it, like you, gulf of sorrow,
Having roared this evening, will devour tomorrow.
Its wave crests are blade-like and sharp as sabres are.
It sings a giant hymn when it sees the evening star.
Its circle captures azure and the clouds as they pass.
It accepts all the stars of heaven in its glass.
It possesses brute force and an elegant grace.
It uproots a boulder; it spares a blade of grass.
Like you, it throws foam at the proud heights of space,
Oh People; only it won't deceive or turn aside,
When, pensive, staring outward from the rim of its shore,
One stands there, waiting for the rising of its tide.

Stella

I went to sleep that night somewhere close to the sea.
A cold wind woke me up; I broke out of my dream.
I opened my eyes and I saw the morning star.
It was shining in a mild whiteness. From afar
Its flickering, enchanting light seemed infinite.
The wind fled, carrying off agony with it.
The star emerged and transformed the clouds into down.
It seemed a living, thinking brightness looking down
On reefs it softened where the rollers broke in curls.
You thought you were looking at a soul through a pearl.
Then it was night again. Shadows reigned and passed by.
A divine smile lit up the entire sky.
A mast, leaning forward, turned to silver in the light.
The ship itself was black, but its sail shimmered white;
The gulls, perched above on a rock, looked out to sea
And up at the star they watched attentively
As though it were some celestial bird made from a spark.
The sea, the people's image, motioned toward it in the dark,
And, blushing all over, watched it blaze down like day
And seemed to be afraid of frightening it away.

Un ineffable amour emplissait l'étendue.
L'herbe verte à mes pieds frisonnait éperdue,
Les oiseaux se parlaient dans les nids; une fleur
Qui s'éveillait me dit: C'est l'étoile ma sœur.
Et pendant qu'à longs plis l'ombre levait son voile,
J'entendis une voix qui venait de l'étoile
Et qui disait: — Je suis l'astre qui vient d'abord.
Je suis celle qu'on croit dans la tombe et qui sort.
J'ai lui sur le Sina, j'ai lui sur le Taygète;
Je suis le caillou d'or et de feu que Dieu jette,
Comme avec une fronde, au front noir de la nuit.
Je suis ce qui renaît quand un monde est détruit.
O nations! je suis la Poésie ardente.
J'air brillé sur Moïse et j'ai brillé sur Dante.
Le lion Océan est amoureux de moi.
J'arrive. Levez-vous, vertu, courage, foi!
Penseurs, esprits! montez sur la tour, sentinelles!
Paupières, ouvrez-vous! allumez-vous, prunelles!
Terre, émeus le sillon; vie éveille le bruit;
Debout vous qui dromez; — car celui qui me suit,
Car celui qui m'envoie en avant la première,
C'est l'ange Liberté, c'est le géant Lumière!

«Sonnez, sonnez toujours …»

Sonnez, sonnez toujours, clairons de la pensée.

Quand Josué rêveur, la tête aux cieux dressée,
Suivi des siens, marchait, et, prophète irrité,
Sonnait de la trompette autour de la cité,
Au premier tour qu'il fit, le roi se mit à rire;
Au second tour, riant toujours, il lui fit dire:
— Crois-tu donc renverser ma ville avec du vent?
À la troisième fois l'arche allait en avant,
Puis les trompettes, puis toute l'armée en marche,
Et les petis enfants venaient cracher sur l'arche,
Et, soufflant dans leur trompe, imitaient le clairon;
Au quatrième tour, bravant les fils d'Aaron,
Entre les vieux créneaux tout brunis par la rouille,

An ineffable love poured into the expanse.
The grass was trembling, as if shaking in a trance.
The birds were chattering in the trees. Suddenly
A flower woke up and said: 'The star that you see
Is my sister.' And while the dawn was lifting the night's
Long, pleated veil – I heard a voice come from the light
Which said: 'I'm the star that is sent forward first,
She who people think is in the grave I have burst.
I have shone on Sinai, I have shone on Taygetos.
I am the gold and fiery pebble God throws
As if with a slingshot, into the void.
I am what's reborn when a world is destroyed.
Nations of the world, I am impassioned Poetry.
I have blazed on Moses and on Dante Alighieri.
Now the lion Ocean itself is my lover.
I am coming. Awake, faith and courage! It's the hour,
Thinkers and souls! Sentinels, climb your towers!
Eyelids, open up! And all you pupils, ignite!
Earth, move your furrows; all you sleepers, stand upright!
And life, wake up your noises – for the one who follows me,
The one who is sending me forward in the night,
Is heaven's giant light, the angel Liberty.'

'Blow forever, trumpets of thought …'

Blow forever, trumpets of thought, blow forever!

When Joshua, that irritable prophet and dreamer,
Marched his men around the city, looking up at the sky
And blowing his trumpet at the walls he walked by,
The first time, the king laughed when they passed, and long after.
The second time, unable to control his laughter,
He yelled: 'You're going to topple my city with a breeze?'
The third time, when they placed the ark in front, and companies
Of men in ranks advanced behind the trumpeters,
The little children came out to spit on the ark
And mimic the trumpets with an upturned nose.
The fourth time, braving Israel's columns and rows,
And watching through the crenellations red with rust,

Les femmes s'asseyaient en filant leur quenouille,
Et se moquaient, jetant des pierres aux Hébreux;
À la cinquième fois, sur ces murs ténébreux,
Aveugles et boiteux vinrent, et leurs huées
Raillaient le noir clairon sonnant sous les nuées;
À la sixième fois, sur sa tour de granit
Si haute qu'au sommet l'aigle faisait son nid,
Si dure que l'éclair l'eût en vain foudroyée,
Le roi revint, riant à gorge déployée,
Et cria: – ces Hébreux sont bons musiciens! –
Autour du roi joyeux, riaient tous les anciens
Qui le soir sont assis au temple, et délibèrent.

À la septième fois, les murailles tombèrent.

«*Cette nuit, il pleuvait …*»

Cette nuit, il pleuvait, la marée était haute,
Un brouillard lourd et gris couvrait toute la côte,
Les brisants aboyaient comme des chiens, le flot
Aux pleurs du ciel profond joignait son noir sanglot,
L'infini secouait et mêlait dans son urne
Les sombres tournoîments de l'abîme nocturne;
Les bouches de la nuit semblaient rugir dans l'air.

J'entendais le canon d'alarme sur la mer.
Des marins en détresse appelaient à leur aide.
Dans l'ombre où la rafale aux rafales succède,
Sans pilote, sans mât, sans ancre, sans abri,
Quelque vaisseau perdu jetait son dernier cri.
Je sortis. Une vieille, en passant effarée,
Me dit: – il a péri. C'est une chasse-marée.
Je courus à la grève et ne vis qu'un linceul
De brouillard et de nuit, et l'horreur, et moi seul;
Et la vague, dressant sa tête sur l'abîme,
Comme pour éloigner un témoin de son crime,
Furieuse, se mit à hurler après moi.

Women sat on the walls, spinning wool as they discussed
Affairs, and mocked the Hebrews by throwing stones below.
The fifth time, the blind and the lame came out to throw
Mockeries and insults from the shadowy walls
As trumpets came and went underneath blaring calls.
The sixth time, standing on a tower so high
That eagles nested there, so firm its stone defied
The lightning bolts striking it from out of a cloud,
The king returned, and, laughing heartily and loud,
Shouted, 'These Hebrews are excellent musicians!'
And all the old men who debate propositions
At temple in the evening were laughing hard as well.

The seventh time, the walls of the city cracked and fell.

'It was raining that night ...'

It was raining that night. The ocean tide was high.
The fog along the coast, thick and grey, hid the sky.
The breakers were howling like dogs, and the swell
Was mixing its sobs with the raindrops that fell.
Infinity was shaking and stirring each turn
And twist of the evening's abyss in its urn.
The mouths of the night were glowing red in the air.

Warning canons fired on the ocean somewhere.
Sailors in distress were calling for help.
Without a pilot, shelter, or an anchor, or a mast,
Some lost ship was throwing out its final cry
In darkness where each blast was followed by a blast.
I went out. An old, frightened woman passing by
Said to me, 'It's over. The bark was overthrown.'
I hurried to the shore and saw only a shroud
Of night and fog, and horror, and myself there alone.
And the surf, lifting up its head from time to time,
As if to chase away a witness from its crime,
Began to hurl a furious invective at me.

Qu'es-tu donc, Dieu jaloux, Dieu d'épreuve et d'effroi,
Dieu des écroulements, des gouffres, des orages,
Que tu n'es pas content de tant de grands naufrages,
Qu'après tant de puissants et de forts engloutis,
Il te reste du temps encor pour les petits,
Que sur les moindres fronts ton bras laisse sa marque,
Et qu'après cette France, il te faut cette barque!

What are you then, jealous God, God of misery,
God of fear, God of ruin, God of storms and the abyss,
That you aren't content with the havoc you wreak,
That after the powerful and the strong, nonetheless
You still find time to crush the vessels of the weak,
That on the humblest foreheads your arm leaves its mark,
That after France itself, you had to sink that bark!

From *Les Contemplations* (1856)

Autrefois (1830–1843)

'Le poëte s'en va dans les champs ...'

Le poëte s'en va dans les champs; il admire,
Il adore, il écoute en lui-même une lyre;
Et le voyant venir, les fleurs, toutes les fleurs,
Celles qui des rubis font pâlir les couleurs,
Celles qui des paons même éclipseraient les queues,
Les petites fleurs d'or, les petites fleurs bleues,
Prennent, pour l'accueillier agitant leurs bouquets,
De petits airs penchés ou de grands airs coquets,
Et, familièrement, car cela sied aux belles:
«Tiens! c'est notre amoureux qui passe!» disent-elles.
Et, pleins de jour et d'ombre et de confuses voix,
Les grands arbres profonds qui vivent dans les bois,
Tous ces vieillards, les ifs, les tilleuls, les érables,
Les saules tout ridés, les chênes vénérables,
L'orme au branchage noir, de mousse appesanti,
Comme les ulémas quand paraît le muphti,
Lui font de grands saluts et courbent jusqu'à terre
Leurs têtes de feuillée et leurs barbes de lierre,
Contemplent de son front la sereine lueur,
Et murmurent tout bas: C'est lui! c'est le rêveur!

Mes Deux Filles

Dans le frais clair-obscur du soir charmant qui tombe,
L'une pareille au cygne et l'autre à la colombe,
Belles, et toutes joyeuses, ô douceur!
Voyez, la grande sœur et la petite sœur
Sont assises au seuil du jardin, et sur elles
Un bouquet d'œillets blancs aux longues tiges frêles,
Dans une urne de marbre agité par le vent,
Se penche, et les regarde, immobile et vivant,
Et frissonne dans l'ombre, et semble, au bord du vase,
Un vol de papillons arrêté dans l'extase.

From *Contemplations*

Former Times

'*The poet goes away into the fields ...*'

The poet goes away into the fields. He admires,
He adores, he listens to his inner lyres,
And seeing him arrive, the flowers, all of them,
Those whose colours would make the brightest rubies dim,
Those whose petals outshine even a peacock's tail,
The little gold flowers and the blue ones, the pale
(As each of them greets him by shaking its bouquet)
Take on submissive or coquettish airs, and say
Familiarly, for that manner suits beauties well:
'Oh look! our little lover is passing this way!'
And then the shadow-filled and glowing trees that dwell
In the woods, resounding with the voices they let loose,
All of those ancient men, the maples and the yews,
The lindens, wrinkled willows, oaks hallowed by the years,
The black-branched elms overburdened with moss –
Like ulemas when the mufti appears
Greet him with grand gestures, and slowly bow down
Their large leafy heads and ivy beards to the ground,
Then contemplate his forehead shining in the sun,
And murmur quietly: 'It's him, the dreamy one!'

My Two Daughters

In the flickering twilight that falls from above
One looks like a swan and the other a dove:
Beautiful, alive, they catch the light of the sun.
You can see the big sister and the little one
Sitting at the gateway to a garden. Over them
A bouquet of carnations with long, fragile stems
Shaken by the wind in a marble urn
Leans forward, looks at them – fixed and living in turn –
And shivers in the shadows where it appears to be
A flight of butterflies frozen in ecstasy.

Le firmament est plein de la vaste clarté;
Tout est joie, innocence, espoir, bonheur, bonté.
Le beau lac brille au fond du vallon qui le mure;
Le champ sera fécond, la vigne sera mûre;
Tout regorge de sève et de vie et de bruit,
De rameaux verts, d'azur frissonnent, d'eau qui luit,
Et de petits oiseaux qui se cherchent querelle.
Qu'a donc le papillon? qu'a donc la sauterelle?
La sauterelle a l'herbe, et le papillon l'air
Et tous deux ont avril, qui rit dans le ciel clair.
Un refrain joyeux sort de la nature entière;
Chanson qui doucement monte et devient prière.
Le poussin court, l'enfant joue et danse, l'agneau
Saute, et laissant tomber goutte à goutte son eau,
Le vieux antre, attendri, pleure comme un visage;
Le vent lit à quelqu'un d'invisible un passage
Du poëme inouï de la création;
L'oiseau parle au parfum; la fleur parle au rayon;
Les pins sur les étangs dressent leur verte ombelle;
Les nids ont chaud. L'azur trouve la terre belle;
Onde et sphère; à la fois tous les climats flottants;
Ici l'automne, ici l'été, là le printemps.
O coteaux! ô sillons! souffles, soupirs, haleines!
L'hosanna des forêts, des fleuves et des plaines,
S'élève gravement vers Dieu, père du jour;
Et toutes les blancheurs sont des strophes d'amour;
Le cygne dit: Lumière! et le lys dit: Clémence!
Le ciel s'ouvre à ce chant comme une oreille immense.
Le soir vient; et le globe à son tour s'éblouit,
Devient un œil énorme et regarde la nuit;
Il savoure, éperdu, l'immensité sacré,
La contemplation du splendide empyrée,
Les nuages de crêpe et d'argent, le zénith,
Qui, formidable, brille et flamboie et bénit,
Les constellations, ces hydres étoilées,
Les effluves du sombre et du profond, mêlées
À vos effusions, astres de diamant,
Et toute l'ombre avec tout le rayonnement!
L'infini tout entier d'extase se soulève.
Et, pendant ce temps-là, Satan, l'envieux, rêve.

The clarity that fills up the heavens is immense.
Everything is joy, happiness, hope, innocence.
Lakes sparkle from the valley's depths that wall them in.
Fields will be fertile, grapes will cluster on the vines.
The world overflows with the vigour and the din
Of life, with branches, azure, water that shines,
And birds that are quarrelling with others their own size.
What do the grasshoppers have? And butterflies?
Grasshoppers have the lawn, and butterflies the air,
And both have this April that is laughing everywhere.
All of nature exhales a joyous refrain,
A hymn that builds softly and soon becomes a prayer.
A small chick runs, a child plays and dances, a lamb
Jumps, and, letting water drip gently like rain,
An old cavern, saddened, seems to cry like a face.
The wind reads to someone invisible a page
Of the unheard poem of the whole creation;
The birds speak to air-scents; the flowers to the sun.
The pines next to ponds spread their green parasol;
The nests are hot; the sky finds the earth beautiful,
The waves, the airy sphere, the lands adrift and shimmering:
Here is the autumn, here the summer; there the spring.
Oh hills! furrows! breaths! winds! sighs! gentle rains!
The hosanna of the forests, rivers, and plains,
Is solemnly rising toward where God is above
And every hint of white is a strophe of love.
The swan shouts out 'Light!' and the lily 'Clemency!'
Like a huge ear, the sky takes in this harmony.
Night falls; the globe itself turns dazzlingly bright,
Becomes a giant eye, and looks out on the night;
It savours, flushed and stunned, the sky's immensity
And contemplates the firmament's depths and clarity,
The clouds, crêpe-like and silvery, the zenith
Which shines, blesses, blazes through the sky's length and width,
The constellations – star-studded hydras – the streams
Of light from the darkness and the depths, blending with
Your emanations, stars of diamond and sapphire,
And all of the shadows and the flickering beams!
Infinity rises as if it were on fire.
And as it climbs, Satan, the envious one, dreams.

À André Chénier

Oui, mon vers croit pouvoir, sans se mésallier,
Prendre à la prose un peu de son air familier.
André, c'est vrai, je ris quelquefois sur la lyre.
Voici pourquoi. Tout jeune encor, tâchant de lire
Dans le livre effrayant des forêts et des eaux,
J'habitais un parc sombre où jasaient des oiseaux,
Où des pleurs souriaient dans l'œil bleu des pervenches;
Un jour que je songeais seul au milieu des branches,
Un bouvreuil qui faisait le feuilleton du bois
M'a dit: «Il faut marcher à terre quelquefois.
»La nature est un peu moqueuse autour des hommes;
»O poëte, tes chants, ou ce qu'ainsi tu nommes,
»Lui ressemblerait mieux si tu les dégonflais.
»Les bois ont des soupirs, mais ils ont des sifflets.
»L'azur luit, quand parfois la gaîté le déchire;
»L'Olympe reste grand en éclatant de rire;
»Ne crois pas que l'esprit du poëte descend
»Lorsque entre deux grands vers un mot passe en dansant.
»Ce n'est pas un pleureur que le vent en démence;
»Le flot profond n'est pas un chanteur de romance;
»Et la nature, au fond des siècles et des nuits,
»Accouplant Rabelais à Dante plein d'ennuis,
»Et l'Ugolin sinistre au Grandgousier difforme,
»Près de l'immense deuil montre le rire énorme.»

La Vie aux champs

Le soir, à la campagne, on sort, on se promène,
Le pauvre dans son champ, le riche en son domaine;
Moi, je vais devant moi; le poëte en tout lieu
Se sent chez lui, sentant qu'il est partout chez Dieu.
Je vais volontiers seul. Je médite ou j'écoute.
Pourtant, si quelqu'un veut m'accompagner en route,
J'accepte. Chacun a quelque chose en l'esprit,
Et tout homme est un livre où Dieu lui-même écrit.
Chaque fois qu'en mes mains un de ces livres tombe,
Volume où vit une âme et que scelle la tombe,
        J'y lis.

To André Chénier

Yes, my verses can, without marrying below,
Take on some familiar accents of prose.
It's true, I sometimes laugh on the lyre and reed.
Here's why. When I was young and learning how to read
From the terrifying book of the ponds and the firs
I lived near a park in which the birds would converse
And where the tears smiled in each periwinkle's eye.
One day I was alone among the branches and the sky.
A bullfinch, delivering the forest's bulletin,
Said to me: 'You should walk on the earth now and then.
Nature is somewhat of a mocker around men.
Poet, your songs, or what you make pass for them,
Would resemble her more if you let out their air.
There are sighs in the woods and there's whistling there.
The sky shines when joy rips through it, and long after.
Olympus stays great when it bursts into laughter.
Don't think that the poetic spirit declines
When a dancing word passes between two noble lines.
It's not to cry that winds blow wildly and free.
The rocks don't sing romances, nor does the sea.
And nature, through the night's and the ages' winding paths,
Coupling Dante's sorrows with the joys of Rabelais,
And sinister Ugolino with the fat Grandgousier,
Near incredible pain lets out enormous laughs.'

Life in the Fields

At evening, in the country, one goes out walking late.
The poor man in his field; the rich in his estate.
As for me, I go before myself: the poet's at home there
No matter where he goes; God's abode is everywhere.
I meditate or listen, happy to walk alone.
But if someone wants to come along or invites,
I accept. Everyone has a soul of his own
And everyone's a book in which God himself writes.
If one of these volumes tumbles into my hands
I read it.

Chaque soir donc, je m'en vais, j'ai congé,
Je sors. J'entre en passant chez des amis que j'ai.
On prend le frais, au fond du jardin, en famille.
Le serein mouille un peu les bancs sous la charmille;
N'importe! je m'assieds, et je ne sais pourquoi
Tous les petits enfants viennent autour de moi.
Dès que je suis assis, les voilà tous qui viennent.
C'est qu'ils savent que j'ai leurs goûts; ils se souviennent
Que j'aime comme eux l'air, les fleurs, les papillons,
Et les bêtes qu'on voit courir dans les sillons.
Ils savent que je suis un homme qui les aime,
Un être auprès duquel on peut jouer, et même
Crier, faire du bruit, parler à haute voix;
Que je riais comme eux et plus qu'eux autrefois,
Et qu'aujourd'hui, sitôt qu'à leurs ébats j'assiste,
Je leur souris encor, bien que je sois plus triste;
Ils disent, doux amis, que je ne sais jamais
Me fâcher; qu'on s'amuse avec moi; que je fais
Des choses en carton, des dessins à la plume;
Que je raconte, à l'heure où la lampe s'allume,
Oh! des contes charmants qui vous font peur la nuit,
Et qu'enfin je suis doux, pas fier et fort instruit.

Aussi, dès qu'on m'a vu: «Le voilà!» tous accourent.
Ils quittent jeux, cerceaux et balles; ils m'entourent
Avec leurs beaux grands yeux d'enfants, sans peur, sans fiel,
Qui semblent toujours bleus, tant on y voit le ciel!

Les petits – quand on est petit, on est très brave –
Grimpent sur mes genoux; les grands ont un air grave;
Ils m'apportent des nids de merles qu'ils ont pris,
Des albums, des crayons qui viennent de Paris;
On me consulte, on a cent choses à me dire,
On parle, on cause, on rit surtout – j'aime le rire,
Non le rire ironique aux sarcasmes moqueurs,
Mais le doux rire honnête ouvrant bouches et cœurs,
Qui montre en même temps des âmes et des perles. –

J'admire les crayons, l'album, les nids de merles;
Et quelquefois on dit, quand j'ai bien admiré:
«Il est du même avis que monsieur le curé.»
Puis, losqu'ils ont jasé tous ensemble à leur aise,
Ils font soudain, les grands s'appuyant à ma chaise,
Et les petits toujours groupés sur mes genoux,
Un silence, et cela veut dire: «Parle-nous.»

At evening then, when I have no demands,
I go out. Passing by a home I know, I make a call.
My friend and I enjoy the garden air with family.
The dew wets the benches underneath the arbour wall.
No matter: I sit down, and then, I don't know why,
All of the children start to gather round me.
As soon as I am seated, here they come, one and all,
Because they know I share their tastes; and they can recall
That I love the flowers, the butterflies, the air
And creatures one sees scurry in the furrows near there.
They know I am a man who loves and will believe them,
Someone in whose presence they can play, and maybe even
Shout, makes lots of noise, carry on in a loud voice –
That I laughed like they do at every chance I had,
And that today, when I see them at the games they enjoy,
I smile again at them, even if I am sad.
My little friends tell me that I never know how
To get angry; that they laugh with me; that somehow
I make things from scrap paper, scribbling on it,
That I tell scary stories when the lamp is being lit
Oh! so real they make your hands shake and your heart,
That I'm a kind person, not proud, and very smart.

And so, when they see me ('It's him!') they run around.
They stop playing games, hoops, and balls; they gather round
Not with fear or malice, but their big children's eyes
That always seem blue and make one think of the skies!

The little ones – when one is little, one is brave –
Climb up onto my knees; their parents' looks are grave.
They bring me the birds' nests they've found so I can see,
Their albums, their pencils come from Paris recently.
They consult with me on everything and we chat.
We talk, we joke, we laugh above all. I like that –
Not the ironic laugh that pulls us apart,
But an honest, mild laugh that opens up the heart
And the mouth, shows the teeth and the soul at its best.

I admire their pencils, their albums, each bird's nest;
And sometimes, when I like a thing a lot, I hear them say,
'*He* says the same things the priest said yesterday.'
And after they have talked for as long as they please,
And the grown-ups begin to come closer, curious,
Suddenly the little ones, still grouped around my knees,
Fall into a silence, and that means 'Talk to us.'

Je leur parle du tout. Mes discours en eux sèment
Ou l'idée ou le fait. Comme ils m'aiment, ils aiment
Tout ce que je leur dis. Je leur montre du doigt
Le ciel, Dieu qui s'y cache, et l'astre qu'on y voit.
Tout, jusqu'à leur regard, m'écoute. Je dis comme
Il faut penser, rêver, chercher. Dieu bénit l'homme,
Non pour avoir trouvé, mais pour avoir cherché.
Je dis: Donnez l'aumône au pauvre humble et penché;
Recevez doucement la leçon ou le blâme.
Donner et recevoir, c'est faire vivre l'âme!
Je leur conte la vie, et que, dans nos douleurs,
Il faut que la bonté soit au fond de nos pleurs,
Et que, dans nos bonheurs, et que, dans nos délires,
Il faut que la bonté soit au fond de nos rires;
Qu'être bon, c'est bien vivre; et que l'adversité
Peut tout chasser d'une âme, excepté la bonté;
Et qu'ainsi les méchants, dans leur haine profonde,
Ont tort d'accuser à Dieu. Grand Dieu! nul homme au monde
N'a droit, en choisissant sa route, en y marchant,
De dire que c'est toi qui l'as rendu méchant;
Car le méchant, Seigneur, ne t'est pas nécessaire.

Je leur raconte aussi l'histoire; la misère
Du peuple juif, maudit qu'il faut enfin bénir;
La Grèce, rayonnant jusque dans l'avenir;
Rome; l'antique Égypte et ses plaines sans ombre,
Et tout ce qu'on y voit sinistre et de sombre.
Lieux effrayants! tout meurt; le bruit humain finit.
Tous ces démons taillés dans des blocs de granit,
Olympe monstrueux des époques obscures,
Les Sphinx, les Anubis, les Ammons, Les Mercures,
Sont assis au désert depuis quatre mille ans.
Autour d'eux le vent souffle, et les sables brûlants
Montent comme une mer d'où sort leur tête énorme;
La pierre mutilée a gardé quelque forme
De statue ou de spectre, et rappelle d'abord
Les plis que fait un drap sur la face s'un mort;
On y distingue encor le front, le nez, la bouche,
Les yeux, je ne sais quoi d'horrible et de farouche
Qui regarde et qui vit, masque vague et hideux.
Le voyageur de nuit, qui passe à côté d'eux,
S'épouvante, et croit voir, aux lueurs des étoiles,
Des géants enchaînés et muets sous de voiles.

I tell them everything that I am able to think of,
Sow facts and ideas. Since they love me, they love
Everything I say. I point up in the air
At heaven, God hiding, and the stars one sees there.
Everything down to their eyes is intent.
I tell them one must think, dream, look. God blesses men,
Not for finding things, but for having looked for them.
I tell them: 'Give something to the poor whom you see.
Always take your lessons and the blame patiently.
Give and receive, for that's what makes a soul live!'
I tell them about life, how when hardship appears,
Kindness should be at the bottom of our tears,
And how, when hardships pass and joys follow after,
Kindness should be at the bottom of our laughter.
I also tell them that being good is living well;
Adversity can drive away all but good will,
And that the evil men who out of hatred curse their birth
Are wrong to accuse God. Great God! no one on earth
Has the right, having chosen his path and gone his way,
To say that it was you who made him that way:
For evil, Lord, isn't a necessity for you!

I talk about history: everything the Jews
Had to endure, a cursed people one should bless;
Greece, shining light into the future everywhere;
Rome; ancient Egypt, infinite and shadowless,
And everything sinister and dark one finds there.
Terrifying places! No life, no human sound.
Sculpted from granite blocks, the demons underground,
Enormous and more ancient than Olympus is,
The Sphinxes, Ammon Ras, Mercuries, Anubises
Have lain four thousand years in an empty expanse.
The wind blows around them, and the burning desert sands
Rise like a wave from which each head surfaces.
The stone has preserved the vague form the sand warps
Of a statue or a ghost, and brings to mind right away
The wrinkles a shroud makes on the face of a corpse.
You can still see the forehead, the nose, and the mouth,
The eyes, and something wild and frightening looking out,
A hideous and vague mask that's living and that stares.
The traveller passing close to them at night abruptly pales,
Thinking that he sees, by the light of the stars,
Giants, mute and shackled, stretched below the cloud veils.

Réponse à un acte d'accusation

Donc, c'est moi qui suis l'ogre et le bouc émissaire.
Dans ce chaos du siècle où votre cœur se serre,
J'ai foulé le bon goût et l'ancien vers françois
Sous mes pieds, et, hideux, j'ai dit à l'ombre: «Sois!»
Et l'ombre fut. – Voilà votre réquisitoire.
Langue, tragédie, art, dogmes, conservatoire,
Toute cette clarté c'est éteinte, et je suis
Le responsable, et j'ai vidé l'urne des nuits.
De la chute de tout je suis la pioche inepte;
C'est votre point de vue. Eh bien, soit, je l'accepte;
C'est moi que votre prose en colère a choisi;
Vous me criez: Racca; moi, je vous dis: Merci!
Cette marche du temps, qui ne sort d'une église
Que pour entrer dans l'autre, et qui se civilise,
Ces grandes questions d'art et de liberté,
Voyons-les, j'y consens, par le moindre côté
Et par le petit bout de la lorgnette. En somme,
J'en conviens, oui, je suis cet abominable homme;
Et, quoique, en vérité, je pense avoir commis
D'autres crimes encor que vous avez omis,
Avoir un peu touché les question obscures,
Avoir sondé les maux, avoir cherché les cures,
De la vieille ânerie insulté les vieux bâts,
Secoué le passé du haut jusques en bas,
Et saccagé le fond tout autant que la forme,
Je me borne à ceci: je suis ce monstre énorme,
Je suis le démagogue horrible et débordé,
Et le devastateur du vieil A B C D;
Causons.

  Quand je sortis du collège, du thème,
Des vers latins, farouche, espèce d'enfant blême
Et grave, au front penchant, aux membres appauvris;
Quand, tâchant de comprendre et de juger, j'ouvris
Les yeux sur la nature et sur l'art, l'idiome,
Peuple et noblesse, était l'image du royaume;
La poésie était la monarchie; un mot
Était un duc et pair, ou n'était qu'un grimaud;
Les syllabes pas plus que Paris et que Londre
Ne se mêlaient; ainsi marchent sans se confondre

Reply to an Act of Accusation

So I'm the scapegoat, the ogre tearing things apart.
In this age's chaos that is eating at your heart
I have trampled good taste and the verse of poetry
Under my feet, and said to darkness, 'Let there be!'
And then there was darkness. You point at what I've done.
Academies and dogmas, art, language, tragedy –
That clarity is dead now, and I am the one
Responsible: I emptied out the urn of nights.
I'm a stupid pickaxe that attacks things bit by bit.
That's your point-of-view. Well then, I welcome it.
All your angry prose is aimed directly at me.
You are yelling 'Racca'; I am answering 'Merci'.
The march of time, which only goes out of one church
To enter another, and build society,
The questions of liberty and art, now and past,
Let's look at them from every angle, I agree,
And by the little end of an opera glass.
In short, I admit it: I'm your monstrosity,
And though, to tell the truth, I have also committed
A couple other crimes that you have omitted –
Having touched on matters both profound and obscure,
Having sounded evils, having searched for their cure,
Insulted the asses on which foolishness goes,
Shaken the tradition from its head to its toes,
And ransacked the substance as often as the form,
I limit myself to this: I am that gigantic swarm,
The horrible demagogue you want me to be,
The saboteur of all the old A B C D –
Let's talk.

     When I left college, papers on a theme,
Latin verse – like a child with a head full of steam,
A pale face, a bent brow, a body falling apart;
When, trying to judge and understand, I saw art
And nature again with my eyes, the idiom
Gave one a vantage point to judge the nation from.
Poetry was monarchy then, and if a word
Wasn't aristocracy, it had to be dirt.
Syllables didn't mix any more than the shores
Of England and France; gentlemen and commoners

Piétons et cavaliers traversant le pont Neuf;
La langue était l'état avant quatrevingt-neuf;
Les mots, bien ou mal nés, vivaient parqués en castes;
Les uns, nobles, hantant les Phèdres, les Jocastes,
Les Méropes, ayant le décorum pour loi,
Et montant à Versaille aux carrosses du roi;
Les autres, tas de gueux, drôles patibulaires,
Habitant les patois; quelques-uns aux galères
Dans l'argot; dévoués à tous les genres bas;
Déchirés en haillons dans les halles; sans bas,
Sans perruque; créés pour la prose et la farce;
Populace du style au fond de l'ombre éparse;
Vilains, rustres, croquants, que Vaugelas leur chef
Dans le bagne Lexique avait marqués d'une F;
N'exprimant que la vie abjecte et familière,
Vils, dégradés, flétris, bourgeois, bons pour Molière.
Racine regardait ces marauds de travers;
Si Corneille en trouvait un blotti dans son vers,
Il le gardait, trop grand pour dire: Qu'il s'en aille;
Et Voltaire criait: Corneille s'encanaille!
Le bonhomme Corneille, humble, se tenait coi.
Alors, brigand, je vins; je m'écriai: Pourquoi
Ceux-ci toujours devant, ceux-là toujours derrière?
Et sur l'Académie, aïeule et douairière,
Cachant sous ses jupons les tropes effarés,
Et sur les bataillons d'alexandrins carrés,
Je fis souffler un vent révolutionnaire.
Je mis un bonnet rouge au vieux dictionnaire.
Plus de mot sénateur! plus de mot roturier!
Je fis une tempête au fond de l'encrier,
Et je mêlai, parmi les ombres débordés,
Au peuple noir des mots l'essaim blanc des idées;
Et je dis: Pas de mot où l'idée au vol pur
Ne puisse se poser, tout humide d'azur!
Discours affreux! – Syllepse, hypallage, litote,
Frémirent; je montai sur la borne Aristote,
Et déclarai les mot égaux, libres, majeurs.
Tous les envahisseurs et tous les ravageurs,
Tous ces tigres, les huns, les scythes et les daces,
N'étaient que des toutous auprès de mes audaces;
Je bondis hors du cercle et brisai le compas.
Je nommai le cochon par son nom; pourquoi pas?
Guichardin a nommé le Borgia! Tacite
Le Vitellius! Fauve, implacable, explicite,

Would cross the Pont Neuf without stepping out of line.
The language was the kingdom before eighty-nine.
The words, well or ill-born, were rutted into tracks.
The noble ones haunted the *Cid*s, the *Andromaque*s,
The *Mérope*s, with decorum for law, and travelling
To the court of Versailles in the carriage of the king.
The other words, in tatters, always pushed below,
Were living in *patois,* or the galleys of *argot,*
And banished to the lower genres, torn to bits
By critics in the great halls, and never wore wigs
Or hose, created for the farce and plays in prose,
Style's mob dispersed into the depths of the shadows;
Rednecks, rustics, convicts whom Vaugelas their lord
Marked with a C in the lexical prison ward –
Expressing only *common,* everyday life down there,
Degraded, vile, branded, bourgeois – fit for Molière.
Racine would look askance and call these rogues perverse.
If Corneille found one of them nestling in a verse,
He'd keep it, too generous to yell: 'Go away!'
But Voltaire would shout: '*He* gets as dirty as they!'
That Corneille was a good fellow, humble, and sly.
Then, like a bandit, I arrived; I shouted: 'Why
Are these words always on top, and those below?'
I caused a revolutionary wind to blow
Over the Academy, that dowager, and on
Her tropes hiding under her skirt; I scattered winds
Over the battalions of square alexandrines.
I put a red bonnet on the old lexicon.
No more senator words! no more plebeian words!
I revelled in the tempest of ink I had stirred
And blended, among all the shadows spilling out,
Swarms of white ideas with the black words of the crowd.
I yelled: 'There'll be no words where the idea's flight
Can't land, moistened by the azure and the light!'
Syllepsis, hypallage, litotes, stood alone
And trembled; I stood on Aristotle's milestone,
And declared the words equal, free, and of age.
All of the invasions, the ravages and rage
Of tigers, the Dacian, the Scythian, the Hun,
Were puppy love compared to what I had overrun.
I leapt out of bounds, broke the compass, cut the knot.
I called a spade a spade, a pig a pig, and why not?
Guichardin mentioned Borgia's name! And Tacitus
Vitellius! Intense, upset, ingenuous,

J'ôtai du cou de chien stupéfait son collier
D'épithètes; dans l'herbe, à l'ombre du hallier,
Je fis fraterniser la vache et la génisse,
L'une étant Margoton et l'autre Bérénice.
Alors, l'ode, embrassant Rabelais, s'enivra;
Sur le sommet du Pinde on dansait Ça ira;
Les neuf muses, seins nus, chantaient la Carmagnole;
L'emphase frissona dans sa fraise espagnole;
Jean, l'ânier, épousa la bergère Myrtil.
On entendait un roi dire: «Quelle heure est-il?»
Je massacrai l'albâtre, et la neige, et l'ivroire;
Je retirai le jais de la prunelle noire,
Et j'osai dire au bras: Sois blanc, tout simplement.
Je violai du vers le cadavre fumant;
J'y fis entrer le chiffre; ô terreur! Mithridate
Du siège de Cyzique eût pu citer la date.
Jours d'effroi! les Laïs devinrent des catins.
Force mots, par Restaut peignés tous les matins,
Et de Louis-Quatorze ayant gardé l'allure,
Portaient encor perruque; à cette chevelure
La Révolution, du haut de son beffroi,
Cria: «Transforme-toi! c'est l'heure. Remplis-toi
»De l'âme de ces mots que tu tiens prisonnière!»
Et la perruque alors rugit, et fut crinière.
Liberté! c'est ainsi qu'en nos rébellions,
Avec des épagneuls nous fîmes des lions,
Et que, sous l'ouragon maudit que nous soufflâmes,
Toutes sortes de mots se couvrirent de flammes.
J'affichai sur Lhomond des proclamations.
On y lisait: « – Il faut que nous en finissons!
»Au panier les Bouhours, les Batteux, les Brossettes!
»À la pensée humaine ils ont mis les poucettes.
»Aux armes, prose et vers! formez vos bataillons!
»Voyez où l'on est: la strophe a des bâillons,
»L'ode a les fers aux pieds, le drame est en cellule.
»Sur le Racine mort le Campistron pullule!»
Boileau grinça des dents; je lui dis: Ci-devant,
Silence! et je criai dans la foudre et le vent:
Guerre à la rhétorique et paix à la syntaxe!
Et tout quatre-vingt-treize éclata. Sur leur axe,
On vit trembler l'athos, l'ithos et le pathos.
Les matassins, lâchant Pourceaugnac et Cathos,
Poursuivant Dumarsais dans leur hideux bastringue,
Des ondes du Permesse emplirent leur seringue.

I took the dazzled dog by its neck and tore off
Its collar of fixed names: in the grass and the rough,
The cow and the heifer would converse now at peace,
The former Margoton and the latter Bérénice.
Then the ode became drunk, embracing Rabelais;
People danced *Ça ira* on Pindos night and day;
The muses bared their breasts and sang *La Carmagnole,*
Gongorism shivered in its Spanish frills and stole;
And John, the donkey driver, married Myrtilette,
The shepherdess. You heard kings ask: 'What time is it?'
I massacred ivory, alabaster, and snow;
I said to arms: 'You're white, plain white, as children know.'
I removed all the jade from the pupils of eyes.
I exhumed all the reeking carcasses from lines.
I used numbers. Terror! Mithridates referred
To the date on which the siege of Cyzique occurred.
Such fallen times! The courtesans became whores.
Combed through every morning by Restaut, many words
Still had that Louis the Fourteenth look, powdered, dyed,
And wigged throughout the day. Then the Revolution cried
From the height of its belfry at all the white hair,
'Change now! Transform yourselves! The time has come. Prepare
To fill your souls with words that you threw into chains!'
And all the wigs turned red and changed to lions' manes.
Liberty! That is how, when we rebel against the law,
We make out of cocker-spaniels lions that claw,
And why, within the hurricanes that we cause to blow,
So many words are coated with a fiery glow.
I nailed my demands on Lhomond's grammar treatise.
I wrote there: 'It's about time we put an end to this!
Throw out all the Bouhours, the Brossettes, the Batteuxs!
They twisted human thought into chains and thumbscrews.
To arms, prose and verse! Come to each other's side.
Look at what is happening: the strophe's hands are tied;
The ode's feet shackled; plays imprisoned for a scene.
Campistron battens on the corpus of Racine!'
Boileau ground his teeth; so I told him: 'Bag of winds,
Be silent!' Then I yelled into the lightning and the winds:
'Make peace with syntax! Wage war on rhetoric!'
And all of eighty-nine broke out. The world looked sick.
You could see the Athos, the ethos, and the pathos
Were shaking loose. The comic dancers left Cathos
And Pourceaugnac to seek Dumarsais with their screams,
Filling up their squirt guns in Helicon's streams.

La syllable, enjambant la loi qui la tria,
Le substantif manant, le verbe paria,
Accoururent. On but l'horreur jusqu'à la lie.
On les vit déterrer le songe d'Athalie;
Ils jetèrent au vent les cendres du récit
De Théramène; et l'astre Institut s'obscurcit.
Oui, de l'ancien régime ils ont fait tables rases,
Et j'ai battu des mains, buveur du sang des phrases,
Quand j'ai vu, par la strophe écumante et disant
Les choses dans un style énorme et rugissant,
L'Art poétique pris au collet dans la rue,
Et quand j'ai vu, parmi la foule qui se rue,
Pendre, par tous les mots que le bon goût proscrit,
La lettre aristocrate à la lanterne esprit.
Oui, je suis ce Danton! je suis ce Robespierre!
J'ai, contre le mot noble à la longue rapière,
Insurgé le vocable ignoble, son valet,
Et j'ai, sur Dangeau mort, égorgé Richelet.
Oui, c'est vrai, ce sont là quelques-uns de mes crimes.
J'ai pris et démoli la bastille des rimes.
J'ai fait plus: j'ai brisé tous les carcans de fer
Qui liaient le mot peuple, et tiré de l'enfer
Tous les vieux mots damnés, légions sépulcrales;
J'ai de la périphrase écrasé les spirales,
Et mêlé, confondu, nivelé sous le ciel
L'alphabet, sombre tour qui naquit de Babel;
Et j'ignorais pas que la main courroucée
Qui délivre le mot, délivre la pensée.

L'unité, des efforts de l'homme est l'attribut.
Tout est la même flèche et frappe au même but.

Donc, j'en conviens, voilà, déduits en style honnête,
Plusieurs de mes forfaits, et j'apporte ma tête.
Vous devez être vieux, par conséquent, papa,
Pour la dixième fois j'en fais meâ culpâ.
Oui, si Beauzée est dieu, c'est vrai, je suis athée.
La langue était en ordre, auguste, époussetée,
Fleurs-de-lis d'or, Tristan et Boileau, plafond bleu,
Les quarante fauteuils et le trône au milieu;
Je l'ai troublée, et j'ai, dans ce salon illustre,
Même un peu cassé tout; le mot propre, ce rustre,
N'était que caporal: je l'ai fait colonel;
J'ai fait un jacobin du pronom personnel,

Syllables straddling caesuras they'd disturb,
The bumpkin substantive, and the exiled verb,
Ran up. Everyone drank horror to the lees.
You saw them digging up the dream of Athalie;
They scattered the ashes of Théramène's *récit*
To the winds, and the star of the Institute went black.
They made blank slates out of the *ancien régime*.
Calling for the blood of words, I clapped and screamed
When I saw *l'Art Poétique* collared in the street,
Foaming by the strophe, only able to repeat
A few things in an enormous style, turning red –
And when I saw, among the crowd that fury led,
The words good taste did not allow come from behind
And hang the noble letter from the lantern of the mind.
Yes, I am that Danton! I am that Robespierre!
I have, fighting against the noble word's rapier,
Convinced the servant word, his valet, to strike a blow,
And slaughtered Richelet on the corpse of Dangeau.
Yes, it's all true; these are some of my crimes.
I sacked and demolished the Bastille of rhymes.
I did more: I severed all the chains that compel
The word 'people' into shackles, and dragged up from hell
The damned words of old, those ranks of the abyss,
And flattened the helixes of periphrasis.
I levelled, mixed, confused the entire alphabet,
That tower born from Babel, and did not forget
That the hand that is angered, shaking and distraught,
Delivering the word, delivers human thought.

All of human effort is directed toward the whole.
We're all the same arrow and strike the same goal.

So there you have a few of my crimes. As I said,
I plead guilty to them, and I give you my head.
You must be very old, and consequently I repeat
A loud *mea culpa* for the tenth time at least.
If Beauzée is God, then it's true, I'm atheist.
The language was in order, dusted off, and august,
Gold lilies, Boileau, Tristan, ceilings of blue stone,
And those forty armchairs that surrounded the throne.
I disturbed everything in this room, and even, well,
Broke some of the things in there; the literal
Was tobacco chew then; I promoted it to captain.
I made the personal pronoun a Jacobin,

Du participe, esclave à la tête blanchie,
Une hyène, et du verbe une hydre d'anarchie.
Vous tenez le *reum confitentem*. Tonnez!
J'ai dit à la narine: Eh mais! tu n'es qu'un nez!
J'ai dit au long fruit d'or: Mais tu n'es qu'une poire!
J'ai dit à Vaugelas: Tu n'es qu'une mâchoire!
J'ai dit aux mots: Soyez république! soyez
La fourmilière immense, et travaillez! croyez,
Aimez, vivez! – J'ai mis tout en branle, et, morose,
J'ai jeté le vers noble aux chiens noirs de la prose.

Et, ce que je faisais, d'autres l'ont fait aussi;
Mieux que moi. Calliope, Euterpe au ton transi,
Polymnie, ont perdu leur gravité postiche.
Nous faisons basculer la balance hémistiche.
C'est vrai, maudissez-nous. Le vers, qui sur son front
Jadis portait toujours douze plumes en rond,
Et sans cesse sautait sur la double raquette
Qu'on nomme prosodie et qu'on nomme étiquette,
Rompt désormais la règle et trompe le ciseau,
Et s'échappe, volant qui se change en oiseau,
De la cage césure, et fuit vers la ravine,
Et vole dans les cieux, alouette divine.

Tous les mots à présent planent dans la clarté.
Les écrivains ont mis la langue en liberté.
Et, grâce à ces bandits, grâce à ces terroristes,
Le vrai, chassant l'essaim des pédagogues tristes,
L'imagination, tapageuse aux cent voix,
Qui casse des carreaux dans l'esprit des bourgeois,
La poésie au front triple, qui rit, soupire
Et chante, raille et croit; que Plaute et que Shakespeare
Semaient, l'un sur les plebs, et l'autre sur le mob;
Qui verse aux nations la sagesse de Job
Et la raison d'Horace à travers sa démence;
Qu'enivre de l'azur la frénésie immense,
Et qui, folle sacrée aux regards éclatants,
Monte à l'éternité par les degrés du temps,
La muse reparaît, nous reprend, nous ramène,
Se remet à pleurer sur la misère humaine,
Frappe et console, va du zénith au nadir,
Et fait sur tous les fronts reluire et resplendir
Son vol, tourbillon, lyre, ouragan d'étincelles,
Et ses millions d'yeux sur ses millions d'ailes.

And the participles, slaves to the subject, were for me
Hyenas, and the verbs the beasts of anarchy.
You've the *reum confitentem*. Let loose your blows!
I said to the nostril: 'But you're only a nose!'
And I said to the long gold fruit: 'But you're a pear!'
I said to Vaugelas: 'You're a bag of hot air!'
I said to all the words: 'Be democratic, give
And work with others like an anthill. Trust and live
And love!' – I started things, then mixed others with those:
I threw the noble line to the black dogs of prose.

And what I did, others have done in their own way
Better than I. Polyhymnia, Euterpe,
And Calliope have lost their serious design.
We threw off the balance of the even-weighted line.
It's all true. Curse us. The measured line that wore
A band of twelve feathers on its forehead before
And jumped between rackets every time it was hit
By what they call prosody and good etiquette,
Breaks rules now, deceives the caesura by a word,
And escapes, shuttlecock changing into a bird,
From the cage of mid-line, and hurtles through the dark
And bright realms of azure, a heavenly skylark.

These words are now soaring in the air's clarity.
The writers have set the entire language free.
And thanks to these bandits and to these terrorists –
The Truth, chasing out swarms of pedants that resist;
Imagination, voice that resounds triumphantly
And breaks the tiles of bourgeois minds; Poetry
With its high, triple forehead, that can sigh and can cheer
And sing, believe, and scoff; and which Plautus and Shakespeare
Used to sow among plebes and mobs, which always is
Pouring out its wisdom of Job, and Horace's
Reason by means of all the madness it creates,
And which the vast frenzy of the sky intoxicates
So that crazed, star-eyed, dazzled and astonished, it will climb
To eternity itself on the staircase of time –
The muse, reappearing, leads us back and takes us in,
Begins to cry at human suffering again,
Strikes us down and consoles, goes from nadir to zenith,
And makes every forehead reflect and glisten with
Her flight, whirlwinds, lyre, hurricanes of sparklings,
And her millions of eyes on her millions of wings.

Vere Novo

Comme le matin rit sur les roses en pleurs!
Oh! les charmants petits amoureux qu'ont les fleurs!
Ce n'est dans les jasmins, ce n'est dans les pervenches
Qu'un éblouissement de folles ailes blanches
Qui vont, viennent, s'en vont, reviennent, se fermant,
Se rouvrant, dans un vaste et doux frémissement.
O printemps! quand on songe à toute les missives
Qui des amants rêveurs vont aux belles pensives,
À ces cœurs confiés au papier, à ce tas
De lettres que le feutre écrit au taffetas,
Aux messages d'amour, d'ivresse et de délire
Qu'on reçoit en avril et qu'en mai l'on déchire,
On croit voir s'envoler, au gré du vent joyeux,
Dans les prés, dans les bois, sur les eaux, dans les cieux,
Et rôder en tous lieux, cherchant partout une âme,
Et courir à la fleur en sortant de la femme,
Les petits morceaux blancs, chassés en tourbillons,
De tous les billets doux, devenus papillons.

La Fête Chez Thérèse

La chose fuit exquise et fort bien ordonnée.
C'était au mois d'avril, et dans une journée
Si douce, qu'on eût dit qu'amour l'eût faite exprès.
Thérèse la duchesse à qui je donnerais,
Si j'étais roi, Paris, si j'étais Dieu, le monde,
Quand elle ne serait que Thérèse la blonde;
Cette belle Thérèse, aux yeux de diamant,
Nous avait conviés dans son jardin charmant.

On était peu nombreux. Le chois faisait la fête.
Nous étions tous ensemble et chacun tête à tête.
Des couples pas à pas erraient de tous côtés.
C'étaient les fiers seigneurs et les rares beautés,
Les Amyntas rêvant auprès des Léonores,
Les marquises riant avec les monsignores;

Vere Novo

How the morning laughs and the tearful rose twinkles!
Look at all the little ones the flowers have made love!
It isn't the jasmines; nor is it the periwinkles
That a dazzling swarm of white wings hovers above
And goes, comes, flies away, returns, collapses there,
Then opens up again, sending shivers through the air.
Oh spring! when one thinks of all the notes that are sent
From dreamy lovers to loved ones, of all the time spent
Entrusting the heart to paper, of the ink and the pile
Of silken pages traced in some elaborate style,
Of the messages of love, intoxication, and dismay
That one receives in April and one rips to shreds in May,
Waking up to a day like this, one thinks one sees –
Prowling, flitting about on the whim of a breeze,
And searching everywhere for a soul as they whirl
Through the meadows, the woods, the water, and the skies –
The little white pieces, blown around in a swirl,
Of all the love letters now become butterflies.

The Party at Thérèse's

The thing was exquisite and superbly arranged.
It happened in April, and took place on a day
So mild you'd say love purposely made it that way.
Thérèse was the duchess about whom one says,
'Were I king, I'd give Paris, if God, the whole world,
If only she would always remain the blonde Thérèse.'
This beautiful Thérèse with diamond eyes
Had asked all of us to her garden surprise.

There weren't many of us. Selection made our set.
We were all together as well as *tête-à-tête*.
Couples were wandering in step everywhere.
There were proud lords along with rare beauties there:
Amintas were dreaming next to their Leonores,
Marquises were sharing jokes with monsignors;

Et l'on voyait rôder dans les grands escaliers
Un nain qui dérobait leur bourse aux cavaliers.

À midi, le spectacle avec la mélodie.
Pourquoi jouer Plautus la nuit? La comédie
Est une belle fille et rit mieux au grand jour.
Or, on avait bâti, comme un temple d'amour,
Près d'un bassin dans l'ombre habité par un cygne,
Un théâtre en treillage où grimpait une vigne.
Un cintre à claire-voie en anse de panier,
Cage verte où sifflait un bouvreuil prisonnier,
Couvrait toute la scène, et, sur leurs gorges blanches,
Les actrices sentaient errer l'ombre des branches.
On entendait au loin de magiques accords;
Et, tout en haut, sortant de la frise à mi-corps,
Pour atttirer la foule aux lazzis qu'il répète,
Le blanc Pulcinella sonnait de la trompette.
Deux faunes soutenaient le manteau d'Arlequin;
Trivelin leur riait au nez comme un fquin.
Parmi les ornements sculptés dans le treillage,
Colombine dormait dans un gros coquillage,
Et, quand, elle montrait son sein et ses bras nus,
On eût cru voir la conque, et l'on eût dit Vénus.
Le seigneur Pantalon, dans une niche, à droite,
Vendait des limons doux sur une table étroite,
Et criait par instants: «Seigneurs, l'homme est divin.
Dieu n'avait fait que l'eau, mais l'homme a fait le vin!»
Scaramouche en un coin harcelait de sa batte
Le tragique Alcantor, suivi du triste Arbate;
Crispin, vêtu de noir, jouait de l'éventail;
Perché, jambe pendante, au sommet du portail,
Carlino se penchait, écoutant les aubades,
Et son pied ébauchait de rêveuses gambades.

Le soleil tenait lieu de lustre; la saison
Avait brodé de fleurs un immense gazon,
Vert tapis déroulé sous maint groupe folâtre.
Rangés des deux côtés de l'agreste théâtre,
Les vrais arbers du parc, les sorbiers, les lilas,
Les ébéniers qu'avril charge de falbalas,
De leur sève embaumée exhalant les délices,
Semblaient se divertir à faire les coulisses,
Et, pour nous voir, ouvrant leurs fleurs comme des yeux,

And you could see a dwarf, on the stairs or under them,
Stealing from the purses of the knights and gentlemen.

At noon, musicians came and added melody.
Why must one play Plautus at night? Comedy
Is a beautiful girl who laughs better in the light.
And they had built a theatre for their delight
Like a temple of love, overgrown with vines and fronds,
Near a shadowy pool inhabited by swans.
An arch, like a basket handle with an opening,
And a cage from which a captured bullfinch would sing
Hung above the actresses who felt the effects
Of the shadowy bars passing over their necks.
In the distance you could hear magical harmonies,
And, poking his head out of the high curtain-frieze,
Pulcinello would blow his trumpet time after time
To attract a larger crowd to his wild pantomime.
Two fauns were holding up the curtains. Trivelin
Scoffed and then laughed in their faces, like a villain.
Columbine was sleeping in a large rippled shell
Near lattice-work that was baroque and classical.
Whenever she would bare her white arms or her breast,
You thought you saw a conch there and Venus at rest.
The lord Pantalon, in a corner on the right,
Was selling sweetened limes along with other delights
And shouting now and then: 'My lords, man is divine.
God created water, but man created wine!'
On the left Scaramouche was letting his stick land
On Alcantor, followed by the sad Aberand;
Crispin, dressed in black, waved his fan in the shade;
Carlino, legs dangling from the top of the stair,
Was leaning forward, listening to each serenade
As his feet sketched new, dreamy dance steps in the air.

The sun itself was our chandelier; while the Spring
Embroidered the lawn – a vast, flower-covered thing,
And brightened the tapestry spread out under her.
Lining the edges of the rustic theatre
The true trees of the park – lilacs and ebonies
Burdened with April's furbelows and ruff, the sorb-trees –
Amused themselves by forming the backdrop and the wings.
Exhaling their sap's mild scents and murmurings
And opening their flowers, like eyes, to see us,

Joignaient aux violons leur murmure joyeux;
Si bien qu'à ce concert gracieux et classique,
La nature mêlait un peu de sa musique.

Tout nous charmait, les bois, le jour serein, l'air pur,
Les femmes tout amour et let ciel tout azur.

Pour la pièce, elle était fort bonne, quoique ancienne.
C'était, nonchalammment assis sur l'avant-scène,
Pierrot, qui haranguait dans un grave entretien,
Un singe timbalier à cheval sur un chien.

Rien de plus. C'était simple et beau. – Par intervalles,
Le singe faisait rage et cognait ses timbales;
Puis Pierrot répliquait. – Écoutait qui voulait.
L'un faisait apporter des glaces au valet;
L'autre, galant drapé d'une cape fantasque,
Parlait bas à sa dame en lui nouant son masque;
Trois marquis attablés chantaient une chanson.
Thérèse était assise à l'ombre d'un buisson;
Les roses pâlissaient à côté de sa joue,
Et, la voyant si belle, un paon faisait la roue.

Moi, j'écoutais, pensif, un profane couplet
Que fredonnait dans l'ombre un abbé violet.

La nuit vint; tout se tut; les flambeaux s'éteignirent;
Dans les bois assombris les sources se plaignirent;
Le rossignol, caché dans son nid ténébreux,
Chanta comme un poëte et comme un amoureux.
Chacun se dispersa sous les profonds feuillages;
Les folles en riant entraînèrent les sages;
L'amante s'en alla dans l'ombre avec l'amant;
Et, troublés comme on l'est en songe, vaguement,
Ils sentaient par degrés se mêler à leur âme,
À leurs discours secrets, à leurs regards de flamme,
À leur cœur, à leurs sens, à leur molle raison,
Le clair de lune bleu qui baignait l'horizon.

They blended their whispers with every violin
So well that, for this concert – classical, continuous –
Nature mixed a little of her own music in.

Everything was charming: the woods, the day, the air.
The women were love and the sky azure there.

The play itself was good, though a bit out of date:
Pierrot was sitting near the theatre gate
Haranguing relentlessly with strong and stern words
A kettle-drumming monkey on a dog like a horse.

Nothing more. It was simple, beautiful. Now and then
The monkey screeched and banged his little kettle-drum again.
Then Pierrot. You listened only if you wished.
At one point someone brought the valet ices in a dish.
Another man dressed in a dazzling costume spoke
In hushed tones to his lady as he tied her mask and cloak.
The three dukes at table sang an old melody.
Thérèse was sitting down in the shadow of a tree;
The roses that were next to her cheeks seemed to pale,
And, seeing her beauty, a peacock spread its tail.

Pensive, I was listening to a violet abbé
Humming a couplet at the close of the day.

The night came. It was calm. All the torches went out.
The streams exchanged laments with themselves or a cloud.
The nightingale, hidden in his dark nest above,
Sang softly, like a poet or someone in love.
Everyone walked beneath the leaves' tent, or the sky's:
The foolish ones laughed as they dragged along the wise.
The lovers went away together in the shade.
And troubled, as if in a dream, by something vague,
They sensed, blending into their souls by degrees,
In their hearts, in their minds, in their hushed colloquies,
In the meaningful looks they exchanged in the night,
The distances awash with the bluish moonlight.

«Heureux l'homme …»

Heureux l'homme, occupé de l'éternel destin,
Qui, tel qu'un voyageur qui part de grand matin,
Se réveille, l'esprit rempli de rêverie,
Et dès l'aube du jour se met à lire et prie!
À mesure qu'il lit, le jour vient lentement
Et se fait dans son âme ainsi qu'au firmament.
Il voit distinctement, à cette clarté blême,
Des choses dans sa chambre et d'autres en lui-même;
Tout dort dans la maison; il est seul, il le croit,
Et cependant, fermant leur bouche de leur doigt,
Derrière lui, tandis que l'extase l'enivre,
Les anges souriants se penchent sur son livre.

Halte en marchant

Une brume couvrait l'horizon; maintenant
Voici le clair midi qui surgit rayonnant;
Le brouillard se dissout en perles sur les branches,
Et brille, diamant, au collier des pervenches.
Le vent souffle à travers les arbres, sur les toits
Du hameau noir cachant ses chaumes dans les bois;
Et l'on voit tressaillir, épars dans les ramées,
Le vague arrachement des tremblantes fumées;
Un ruisseau court dans l'herbe, entre deux hauts talus,
Sous l'agitation des saules chevelus;
Un orme, un hêtre, anciens du vallon, arbres frères
Qui se donnent la main des deux rives contraires,
Semblent, sous le ciel bleu, dire: À la bonne foi!
L'oiseau chante son chant plein d'amour et d'effroi
Et du frémissement des feuilles et des ailes;
L'étang luit sous le vol des vertes demoiselles.
Un bouge est là, montrant, dans la sauge et le thym,
Un vieux saint souriant parmi des brocs d'étain,
Avec tant de rayons et de fleurs sur la berge,
Que c'est peut-être un temple ou peut-être une auberge.
Que notre bouche ait soif, ou que ce soit le cœur,

'Happy the man ...'

Happy the man, preoccupied by destiny,
Who, like a traveller leaving at the break of day,
Awakes with a mind overwhelmed with reverie,
And, at the crack of dawn, begins to read and pray!
As he reads along, the daylight slowly filters in
And illuminates his soul like the firmament.
He sees more distinctly, as rays cover his shelf,
The things in his bedroom – and others in himself.
The house is sleeping now; he's alone, or thinks he is.
But behind him, while he is busy drinking ecstasies,
Hushing each other with a finger or a look,
Two angels, smiling, lean down over his book.

A Stop in the Middle of a Walk

A mist was covering the horizon; but now
You can see the noon's rays breaking through a cloud.
The fog dissolves in pearls on the branches and twinkles
Diamond-like, in the necklace of periwinkles.
The wind is blowing through the trees and on the roofs
Of cottages hiding their thatch in the woods.
And you can see, scattered through the limbs, the quiverings
Of the air's vague tugging on the trembling smoke strings.
A stream flows through the grass and between two banks there,
Shaking, as it passes by, the willows' leaves and hair.
An elm and a beech tree, the valley's ancient friends,
Stretch out their hands across the stream where it bends
And seem to say, 'To faith!' under skies that are clear.
The birds are singing songs full of love and full of fear,
Shiverings of leaves, and the rustling of wings.
The flight of dragonflies sets the pond shimmering.
And there's a hut that shows, in the thyme and the sage,
A smiling saint among pewter jugs stained with age.
So many rays of light and flowers shine within
It could be a temple or it could be an inn.
Whether it's our throats or our hearts that have dried up,

Gloire au Dieu bon qui tend la coupe au voyageur!
Nous entrons. «Qu'avez-vous? – Des œufs frais, de l'eau fraîche.»
On croit voir l'humble toit effondré d'un crèche.
À la source du pré, au'arbite un vert rideau,
Une enfant blonde alla remplir sa jarre d'eau,
Joyeuse et soulevant son jupon de futaine.
Pendant qu'elle plongeait sa cruche à la fontaine,
L'eau semblait admirer, gazouillant doucement,
Cette belle petite aux yeux de firmament.
Et moi, près du grand lit drapé de vieilles serges,
Pensif, je regardais un Christ battu de verges.
Eh! qu'importe l'outrage aux martyrs éclatants,
Affront de tous les lieux, crachat de tous les temps,
Vaine clameur d'aveugle, éternelle huée
Où la foule toujours s'est follement ruée!

Plus tard, le vagabond flagellé devient Dieu;
Ce front noir et saignant semble fait de ciel bleu,
Et, dans l'ombre, éclairant palais, temple, masure,
Le crucifix blanchit et Jésus-Christ s'azure.
La foule un jour suivra vos pas; allez, saignez,
Souffrez, penseurs, des pleurs de vos bourreaux baignés!
Le deuil sacre les saints, les sages, les génies;
La tremblante auréole éclôt aux gémonies,
Et, sur, ce vil marais, flotte, lueur du ciel,
Du cloaque de sang feu follet éternel.
Toujours au même but le même sort ramène:
Il est, au plus profond de notre histoire humaine,
Une sorte de gouffre, où viennent, tour à tour,
Tomber tous ceux qui sont de la vie et du jour,
Les bons, les purs, les grands, les divins, les célèbres,
Flambeaux échevelés au souffle des ténèbres;
Là se sont engloutis les Dantes disparus,
Socrate, Scipion, Milton, Tomas Morus,
Eschyle, ayant aux mains des palmes frissonnantes.
Nuit d'où l'on voit sortir leurs mémoires planantes!
Car ils ne sont complets qu'après qu'ils sont déchus.
De l'exil d'Arisitide au bûcher de Jean Huss,
Le genre humain pensif – c'est ainsi que nous sommes –
Rêve ébloui devant l'abîme des grands hommes.
Ils sont, telle est la loi des hauts destins penchant,
Tes semblables, soleil! leur gloire est leur couchant;
Et, fier Niagra dont le flot gronde et lutte,
Tes pareils: ce qu'ils ont de plus beau, c'est leur chute.

Thanks to the God who gives the traveller a cup!
We go in. 'What do you have?' – 'Eggs and water. Both fresh.'
You'd swear the sunken ceiling was the roof of a *crèche*.
At the source, covered over by a curtain on a bar,
A blonde child bent down to fill her water jar,
Holding up a skirt that was coarse and cotton-spun,
And, as she plunged her pitcher into the fountain,
The babbling water seemed entirely intent
On this pretty girl with eyes like the firmament.
And I, pensive, sitting near the source the curtain hid,
Was looking at a Christ someone built out of wood.
What do the dazzling martyrs care about outrage,
Affronts from all sides, or the spit in every age,
The vain and blind clamour, and the jeers and the shouts
Forever being raised by the maddening crowds!

Later on this wanderer becomes a God on high.
His bleeding brow appears to be made out of sky,
And shining in a palace, or a temple, or a hut,
The crucifix illuminates and Jesus reigns above.
One day the crowd will follow you – so bleed and endure,
And suffer, thinkers, washed by the tears of torturers.
Sorrow always blesses saints, the wise, the geniuses;
Trembling haloes bloom wherever misery is,
And a light from heaven floats above this awful mire:
A cesspool of blood lit by everlasting fire.
The same fate returns one to the same place again:
In the farthest reaches of the history of men
There is an abyss in which there falls, one by one,
Each of those souls who represent life, light, the sun:
The good, the pure, the famous; the great, the divine,
The torch-flames dancing in the shadowed winds of time,
Dantes who have vanished there, sunken and obscure,
Socrates and Scipio, Milton, Thomas More,
Aeschylus whose palms quake – a night from which one sees
The soar and the glow of their escaping memories!
For, until they've fallen, they don't seem complete to us.
From Aristides' exile to the stake of Jean Huss,
The race of *thinkers* has – for thus we are and have been –
Dreamed in disbelief at the abyss of great men.
Such is the law hanging on their history,
That like you, sun, it's their setting that's their glory,
And like Niagra's waves, wrestling, seething, raw,
The thing most beautiful about them is their fall.

Un de ceux qui liaient Jésus-Christ au poteau,
Et qui, sur son dos nu, jetaient un vil manteau,
Arracha de ce front tranquille une poignée
De cheveux qu'inondait la sueur résignée,
Et dit: «Je vais montrer à Caïphe cela!»
Et, crispant son poing noir, cet homme s'en alla;
La nuit était venue et la rue était sombre;
L'homme marchait; soudain, il s'arrêta dans l'ombre,
Stupéfait, pâle, et comme en proie aux visions,
Frémissant! – Il avait dans la main des rayons.

Le Rouet d'Omphale

Il est dans l'atrium, le beau rouet d'ivoire.
La roue agile est blanche, et la quenouille est noire;
La quenouille est d'ébène incrusté de lapis.
Il est dans l'atrium sur un riche tapis.

Un ouvrier d'Égine a sculpté sur la plinthe
Europe, dont un dieu n'écoute pas la plainte.
Le taureau blanc l'emporte. Europe, sans espoir,
Crie, et, baissant les yeux, s'épouvante de voir
L'Océan monstrueux qui baise ses pieds roses.

Des aiguilles, du fil, des boîtes demi-closes,
Les laines de Milet, peintes de pourpre et d'or,
Emplissent un panier près du rouet quit dort.

Cependant, odieux, effroyables, énormes,
Dans le fond du palais, vingt fantômes difformes,
Vingt monstres tout sanglant, qu'on ne voit qu'à demi,
Errent en foule autour du rouet endormi:
Le lion néméen, l'hydre affreuse de Lerne,
Cacus, le noir brigand de la noire caverne,
Le triple Géryon, et les typhons des eaux
Qui le soir à grand bruit soufflent dans les roseaux;
De la massure au front tous ont l'empreinte horrible,
Et tous, sans approcher, rôdant d'un air terrible,
Sur le rouet, où pend un fil souple et lié,
Fixent de loin dans l'ombre un œil humilié.

One of those who nailed Jesus Christ to the cross,
And threw, on his naked back, a vile piece of cloth,
Tore a handful of hair from his peaceful forehead
Entirely soaked in his bloody sweat, and said,
'I am going to show this to Caiaphas today!'
And clutching it tightly, this man went away.
Night had come: the whole street was sombre and black.
The man was walking – then stopped dead in his tracks:
Stunned, pale, struck with visions he could not understand,
And trembling! He held rays of sunlight in his hand.

The Spinning Wheel of Omphale

It's in the atrium, the ivory spinning wheel.
The wheel is white; the distaff black and cochineal.
The distaff is ebony, laid with lapis and jet.
It's in the atrium on an elegant carpet.

An Aeginean hand sculpted there, on its base,
Europa, from whose plea a god turns away his face.
The white bull carries her off. With a fear she can't disguise,
Europa screams in horror as she lowers her eyes
At the monstrous ocean that is kissing her feet.

A few needles, some thread, a box with a broken seal,
And Milesian wool, dyed in purple and gold,
Fill up a basket near the sleeping spinning wheel.

Meanwhile, enormous, frightening, invidious,
Twenty shapeless monsters from the depths of the palace,
Twenty blood-stained monsters that one can barely see,
Wander in a crowd around the wheel that's gone to sleep:
The hydra of Lerna, the Nemean lion,
Cacus – the thief who hid in his lair, Geryon
With his triple body, and every water sprite
That whistles its warnings into reeds at twilight.
They all wear a club's horrible imprint on their foreheads,
And they all, without approaching, like vultures, prowl or reel
In shadowy circles near the bundle of limp threads,
And fix their humbled eyes on the ivory spinning wheel.

Tu vois cela d'ici. Des ocres et des craies;
Plaines où les sillons croisent leurs milles raies,
Chaumes à fleur de terre et que masque un buisson;
Quelques meules de foin debout sur le gazon;
De vieux toits enfumant le paysage bistre;
Un fleuve qui n'est pas le Gange ou le Caystre,
Pauvre cours d'eau normand troublé de sels marins;
À droite, vers le nord, de bizarres terrains
Pleins d'angles qu'on dirait façonnés à la pelle;
Voilà les premiers plans; une ancienne chapelle
Y mêle son aiguille, et range à ses côtés
Quelques ormes tortus, aux profils irrités,
Qui semblent, fatigués du zéphyr qui s'en joue,
Faire une remonstrance au vent qui les secoue.
Une grosse charrette, au coin de ma maison,
Se rouille; et devant moi, j'ai le vaste horizon
Dont la mer bleue emplit toutes les échancrures;
Des poules et des coqs, étalant leurs dorures,
Causent sous ma fenêtre, et les greniers des toits
Me jettent, par instants, des chansons en patois.
Dans mon allée habite un cordier patriarche,
Vieux qui fait bruyamment tourner sa roue, et marche
À reculons, son chanvre autour des reins tordu.
J'aime ces flots où court le grand vent éperdu;
Les champs à promener tout le jour me convient;
Les petits villageois, leur livre en main, m'envient,
Chez le maître d'école où je me suis logé,
Comme un grand écolier abusant d'un congé.
Le ciel rit, l'air est pur; tout le jour, chez mon hôte,
C'est un doux bruit d'enfants épelant à voix haute;
L'eau coule, un verdier passe; et, moi, je dis: Merci!
Merci, Dieu tout-puissant! – Ainsi je vis; ainsi,
Paisible, heure par heure, à petit bruit j'épanche
Mes jours, tout en songeant à vous, ma beauté blanche!
J'écoute les enfants jaser, et par moment,
Je vois en pleine mer passer superbement,
Au-dessus des pignons du tranquille village,
Quelque navire ailé qui fait un long voyage,
Et fuit, sur l'Océan, par tous les vents traqué,
Qui, naguère, dormait au port, le long du quai,

Letter

You can see that from here. All ochres and chalk-whites.
A plain of furrows chequered by a thousand stripes.
Thatch-huts, level with the ground, a bush can hide.
Scattered stacks of hay standing off to one side.
Roofs of ancient homes spewing smoke all the while.
A river that is neither the Ganges nor the Nile –
A Norman stream troubled by tidal salts and sand.
On the right, toward the north, some bizarre strips of land
Full of angles you might say fashioned with a spade.
These make up the foreground. A chapel in a glade
Prods a pack of crooked elms with its steeple point,
Then aligns them nearby, bending branches out of joint,
While they shake their leaves, wearied by the zephyr's play,
And seem to reproach the winds that make them sway.
In one of the corners of my house, a large cart
Sits rusting. In front, I possess the greater part
Of a sky whose every notch touches the sea.
Hens and roosters ruffling their golden tails erect
Converse under my window, and the lofts above me
Throw down bits and pieces of songs in dialect.
A rope-maker lives down the street, an older man,
A patriarch, who turns his wheel noisily and can
Be seen walking backwards with hemp tied round his back.
I love the waves sudden gusts of wind will attack
And walking in this country suits me perfectly.
The little village children, books in hand, envy me
For I lodge at the schoolmaster's house, and walk past
As though I were a high-school student skipping class.
The sky laughs; the air is pure; the day's noise is at most
The sound of children spelling in the house of my host.
The water runs; a finch passes; 'Thank you!' I say,
'Thank you, my God!' I live this way. And in this way,
In quiet peace, hour after hour, I spend
My days thinking of you, my lover and my friend.
I listen to the children chatter; now and then
I see some wingèd sail passing by on the sea
Above the gabled roofs of this old, tranquil town –
A ship that has made a long voyage, hunted down
By winds on the ocean, continuing to flee,
A ship that was formerly sleeping on the quay,

Et que n'ont retenu, loin des vagues jalouses,
Ni les pleurs des parents, ni l'effroi des épouses,
Ni le sombre reflet des écueils dans les eaux,
Ni l'importunité des sinistres oiseaux.

Paroles dans l'ombre

Elle disait: C'est vrai, j'ai tort de vouloir mieux;
Les heures sont ainsi très-doucement passées;
Vous êtes là; mes yeux ne quittent pas vos yeux,
Où je regarde aller et venir vos pensées.

Vous voir est un bonheur; je ne l'ai pas complet.
Sans doute, c'est encor bien charmant de la sorte!
Je veille, car je sais tout ce qui vous déplaît,
À ce que nul fâcheux ne vienne ourvrir la porte;

Je me fais bien petite, en mon coin, près de vous;
Vous êtes mon lion, je suis votre colombe;
J'entends de vos papiers le bruit paisible et doux;
Je ramasse parfois votre plume qui tombe;

Sans doute, je vous ai; sans doute, je vous voi.
La pensée est un vin dont les rêveurs sont invres,
Je le sais; mais, pourtant, je veux qu'on songe à moi.
Quand vous êtes ainsi tout un soir dans vos livres,

Sans relever la tête et sans me dire un mot,
Une ombre reste au fond de mon cœur qui vous aime;
Et, pour que je vous voie entièrement, il faut
Me regarder un peu, de temps en temps, vous-même.

And which, far away from where the jealous surf lulls,
Nothing has held back, not a spouse's anxious pleas,
Nor parents, nor the dark reflections of the reefs,
Nor the shrill insistence of the sinister gulls.

Words Spoken in the Shadows

She would say: 'It's true; I am wrong to want more.
The hours are passed very sweetly this way.
You are there. My eyes never leave your eyes in which
I watch your thoughts come and go the whole day.

To see you is happiness; I can never be full.
And doubtless all of this only charms me the more!
I stand guard, because I know what disturbs you:
No annoying person can open your door.

I make myself small in my corner next to you.
You are my lion and I am your dove.
I listen to the peaceful-sweet rustle of your papers;
I pick up your pen now and then when it falls.

Doubtless I possess you; you're there for me to see.
Thought intoxicates dreamers like looks.
I know. But I also want you to dream of me.
And when you are sitting all evening in your books

Hardly lifting your head, without saying one word,
A shadow falls over my loving heart again,
Because, if I'm to see you completely, you must
Look at me a little yourself now and then.'

Écrit au bas d'un crucifix

Vous qui pleurez, venez à ce Dieu, car il pleure.
Vous qui souffrez, venez à lui, var il guérit.
Vous qui tremblez, venez à lui, car il sourit.
Vous qui passez, venez à lui, car il demeure.

«L'enfant, voyant l'aïeule à filer occupée ...»

L'enfant, voyant l'aïeule à filer occupée,
Veut faire une quenouille à sa grande poupée.
L'aïeule s'assoupit un peu; c'est le moment.
L'enfant vient par derrière, et tire doucement
Un brin de la quenouille où le fuseau tournoie,
Puis s'enfuit triomphante, emportant avec joie
La belle laine d'or que le safran jaunit,
Autant qu'en pourrait prendre un oiseau pour son nid.

Magnitudo Parvi

Le jour mourait; j'étais près des mers, sur la grève.
Je tenais par la main ma fille, enfant qui rêve,
        Jeune esprit qui se tait!
La terre, s'inclinant comme un vaisseau qui sombre,
En tourant dans l'espace allait plongeant dans l'ombre;
        La pâle nuit montait.

La pâle nuit levait son front dans les nuées;
Les choses s'effaçaient, blêmes, diminuées,
        Sans forme et sans couleur;
Quand il monte de l'ombre, il tombe de la cendre;
On sentait à la fois la tristesse descendre
        Et monter la douleur.

Written on the Bottom of a Crucifix

You who are crying, come to *this* God, for he cries.
You who are suffering, come to him, because he cures.
You who are trembling, come to him, because he smiles.
You who are passing, come to him, for he endures.

'Seeing her grandmother occupied spinning wool ...'

Seeing her grandmother occupied spinning wool,
The child looks for something her big doll might use.
The grandmother sits back – not a moment to lose.
The child comes from behind, and shakes loose with a pull
A strand of the distaff from where the spindle lies,
Then runs away in triumph, clasping to her chest
The pretty gold wool orange-stained with saffron dyes,
The way a bird might take some string to build its nest.

Magnitudo Parvi

The day was dying; I was near the ocean shore.
I held my daughter by the hand, a dreaming child
        As quiet as a sigh.
The earth, tilting upward like a foundering ship,
Revolving in space, plunged itself into darkness;
        The pale night climbed the sky.

The pale night lifted its face into the clouds;
Things were dissolving, diminished, colourless
        In the moon's distant eyes.
When night falls, or rises from the ashes at day's end,
All at once one senses sadness descend
        And anxiety rise.

Ceux dont les yeux pensifs contemplent la nature
Voyaient l'urne d'en haut, vague rondeur obscure,
      Se pencher dans les cieux,
Et verser sur les monts, sur les campagnes blondes,
Et sur les flots confus pleins de rumeurs profondes,
      Le soir silencieux!

Les nuages rampaient le long des promontoires;
Mon âme, où se mêlaient ces ombres et ces gloires,
      Sentait confusément
De tout cet océan, de toute cette terre,
Sortir sous l'œil de Dieu je ne sais quoi d'austère,
      D'auguste et de charmant!

J'avais à mes côtés ma fille bien-aimée.
La nuit se répandait ainsi qu'une fumée.
      Rêveur, ô Jéhovah,
Je regardais en moi, les paupières baissées,
Cette ombre qui se fait aussi dans nos pensées
      Quand ton soleil s'en va!

Soudain l'enfant bénie, ange au regard de femme,
Dont je tenais la main et qui tenait mon âme,
      Me parla, douce voix,
Et, me montrant l'eau sombre et la rive âpre et brune,
Et, deux points lumineux qui tremblaient sur la dune:
      – Père, dit-elle, vois,

Vois donc, là-bas, où l'ombre aux flancs des coteaux rampe,
Ces feux jumeaux briller comme une double lampe
      Qui remuerait au vent!
Quels sont ces deux foyers qu'au loin la brume voile?
– L'un est un feu de pâtre et l'autre est une étoile;
      Deux mondes, mon enfant!

Everyone whose eyes like to contemplate nature
Watched the urn above, vague, round, and obscure,
    Lean down and spread its light,
Pouring on the mountains, on the blond distances
And the waves, deep, resonant, confused as heaven is,
    The silence of the night.

The clouds crept across and down the promontories.
My soul, blending shadows and its waves with the sea's,
    Vaguely sensed the sky clear –
Issuing from all of this ocean and this earth,
And under God's eye, something luminous, august
    Enchanting and austere.

My beloved child was with me at my side.
The night was spreading out like smoke. I looked inside
    The way a dreamer does,
With lowered eyes, oh God! through the waves the wind tossed
At the darkness which also forms within our thoughts
    When your sun vanishes.

Suddenly the child, angel with a woman's look,
Whose hand I held and who was holding my soul,
    Turned in the evening air,
And pointing at the water, at the dusk-coloured shore,
And the fiery points that trembled on the dune,
    Said, 'Papa, over there,

Look, where those shadows are crawling on the hills,
Look at those fires that shine like a lamp
    And glow on the water.
What are those two lights the fog veils in the distance?'
'The one's a shepherd's fire and the other a star,
    Different worlds, my daughter!'

Aujourd'hui (1843–1855)

'Oh! je fus comme fou dans le premier moment ...'

Oh! je fus comme fou dans le premier moment,
Hélas! et je pleurai trois jours amèrement.
Vous tous à qui Dieu prit votre chère espérance,
Pères, mères, dont l'âme a souffert ma souffrance,
Tout ce que j'éprouvais, l'avez-vous éprouvé?
Je voulais me briser le front sur le pavé;
Puis je me révoltais, et, par moments, terrible,
Je fixais mes regards sur cette chose horrible,
Et je n'y croyais pas, et je m'écriais: Non!
– Est-ce que Dieu permet de ces malheurs sans nom
Qui font que dans le cœur le désespoir se lève? –
Il me semblait que tout n'était qu'un affreux rêve,
Qu'elle ne pouvait pas m'avoir ainsi quitté,
Que je l'entendais rire en la chambre à côté,
Que c'était impossible enfin qu'elle fût morte,
Et que j'allais la voir entrer par cette porte!

Oh! que de fois j'ai dit: Silence! elle a parlé!
Tenez! voici le bruit de sa main sur la clé!
Attendez! elle vient! laissez-moi, que j'écoute!
Car elle est quelque part dans la maison sans doute!

«Elle avait pris ce pli dans son âge enfantin ...»

Elle avait pris ce pli dans son âge enfantin
De venir dans ma chambre un peu chaque matin;
Je l'attendais ainsi qu'un rayon qu'on espère;
Elle entrait, et disait: «Bonjour, mon petit père»;
Prenait ma plume, ouvrait mes livres, s'asseyait
Sur mon lit, dérangeait mes papiers, et riait,
Puis soudain s'en allait comme un oiseau qui passe.
Alors, je reprenais, la tête un peu moins lasse,
Mon œuvre interrompue, et, tout en écrivant,

Today

'I felt I had gone mad ...'

I felt I had gone mad at first: I was in a daze,
Alas! and I wept bitterly for three days.
All of you from whom God took your dearest thing,
Fathers and mothers who have felt my suffering –
All that I experienced, did you feel that too?
I wanted to kneel down and crack my head in two,
And then, like a man who's been abruptly disabused,
Grew angry, looked directly at this thing, refused
To believe it, shouting out aloud to myself, 'No!'.
Was God then really letting people undergo
Sufferings that make them fall almost to despair?
It seemed that it was all some horrible nightmare,
That my child could not have left me in this way,
That I could hear her laughing in the room across the way,
That it wasn't true she wasn't living any more,
And that, at any moment, she would walk through the door!

How many times did I say: 'Hush! I hear her voice!
Wait, she is coming! Let me listen! What's that noise?
Be still! I think I hear her turning the key!
Surely she is somewhere in the house, she has to be ...'

'She had formed this habit ...'

She had formed this habit, when she was still a child,
Of coming to my room in the morning for a while.
I'd wait for her the way one waits for dawn to break.
She would say, 'Good morning, little papa' and take
My pen, open my books, sit herself on my bed,
Scatter my papers as she laughed and shook her head,
Then fly off like a bird, with a song on her lips.
I would smile and go back to my work after that
A little less fatigued. As I wrote, or just sat,

Parmi mes manuscrits je rencontrais souvent
Quelque arabesque folle et qu'elle avait tracée,
Et mainte page blanche entre ses mains froissée
Où, je ne sais comment, venaient mes plus doux vers.
Elle aimait Dieu, les fleurs, les astres, les prés verts,
Et c'était un esprit avant d'être une femme.
Son regard reflétait la clarté de son âme.
Elle me consultait sur tout à tous moments.
Oh! que de soirs d'hiver radieux et charmants
Passés à raisonner langue, histoire et grammaire,
Mes quatre enfants groupés sur mes genoux, leur mère
Tout près, quelques amis causant au coin du feu!
J'appelais cette vie être content de peu!
Et dire qu'elle est morte! hélas! que Dieu m'assiste!
Je n'étais jamais gai quand je la sentais triste;
J'étais morne au milieu du bal le plus joyeux
Si j'avais, en partant, vu quelque ombre en ses yeux.

«Elle était pâle, et pourtant rose ...»

Elle était pâle, et pourtant rose,
Petite avec de grands cheveux.
Elle disait souvent: Je n'ose,
Et ne disait jamais: Je veux.

Le soir, elle prenait ma Bible
Pour y faire épeler sa sœur,
Et, comme une lampe paisible,
Elle éclairait ce jeune cœur.

Sur le saint livre que j'admire
Leurs yeux purs venaient se fixer;
Livre où l'une apprenait à lire,
Où l'autre apprenait à penser!

Sur l'enfant, qui n'eût pas lu seule,
Elle penchait son front charmant,
Et l'on aurait dit une aïeule,
Tant elle parlait doucement!

I'd often discover among my manuscripts
Some crazy arabesque or a scribbling of hers,
And many other pages she had folded back
On which, I don't know how, I'd compose my best verse.
She loved God, green meadows, flowers, stars, and the sun:
She was a spirit even more than a woman.
Her expressions, mirroring her soul, startled one.
Before doing things, she would ask me for advice.
How many radiant, enchanting winter nights
We spent talking history and language with each other,
My four children sitting at my knees, and their mother
Nearby, conversing at the fire with a friend!
I called that 'the little we need to be content'.
To think that she's dead! … only makes me more bereft.
I was never at ease if I sensed she was sad,
I would sulk at the most joyous ball if I had
Seen the smallest shadow in her eyes when I left.

'She was pale …'

She was pale, and yet a flushed girl too,
So small with all of her long hair.
She'd often say, 'I wouldn't dare.'
She'd never say, 'But I want to.'

She would take my Bible at night
To teach her sister how to read,
Illuminating that young heart
The way a lamp spreads gentle light.

Their pure eyes would fix themselves
On that book I esteem,
A book where the one learned how to read,
The other to think and dream.

She would lean her forehead over
The child who could not read alone:
You'd think she was a grandmother
So sweet and patient was her tone.

Elle lui disait: «Sois bien sage!»
Sans jamais nommer le démon;
Leurs mains erraient de page en page
Sur Moïse et sur Salomon,

Sur Cyrus qui vint de la Perse,
Sur Moloch et Léviathan,
Sur l'enfer que Jésus traverse,
Sur l'éden où rampe Satan!

Moi, j'écoutais... – O joie immense
De voir la sœur près de la sœur!
Mes yeux s'enivraient en silence
De cette ineffable douceur.

Et, dans la chambre humble et déserte,
Où nous sentions, cachés tous trois,
Entrer par la fenêtre ouverte
Les souffles des nuits et des bois,

Tandis que, dans le texte auguste,
Leurs cœurs, lisant avec ferveur,
Puisaient le beau, le vrai, le juste,
Il me semblait, à moi, rêveur,

Entendre chanter des louanges
Autour de nous, comme au saint lieu,
Et voir sous les doigts de ces anges
Tressaillir le livre de Dieu!

«O souvenirs! printemps! aurore! ...»

O souvenirs! printemps! aurore!
Doux rayon triste et réchauffant!
– Lorsqu'elle était petite encore,
Que sa sœur était tout enfant... –

She would say to her: 'Now be good!'
And not threaten her for what she'd done.
Their hands would go from page to page
Over Moses and Solomon,

Over Cyrus the Great of Persia,
Over Moloch, Leviathan,
Over the Hell Jesus harrowed,
The Eden Satan crawled upon.

And I would listen ... – What a joy
To see the sisters side by side!
My eyes would get drunk looking on
This ineffable delight.

And, in the humble, deserted room
Where we would hear, hidden, below
The breaths of the forest and the night
Come in through the open window,

And while I watched them as they sat
Reading that inspiring text
And mining the beautiful, the true, the just,
It seemed to me, the dreamer, that

I heard the songs of praise they sing
In holy places surround us,
And saw, beneath these angels' touch,
The book of God quivering!

'Oh spring! oh dawn! oh memories! ...'

Oh spring! oh dawn! oh memories!
Sweet, sad rays that warm things again!
– Back then when she was still so small,
Her sister an infant ... back then ... –

Connaissez-vous, sur la colline
Qui joint Montlignon à Saint-Leu,
Une terrasse qui s'incline
Entre un bois sombre et le ciel bleu?

C'est là que nous vivions. – Pénètre,
Mon cœur, dans ce passé charmant! –
Je l'entendais sous ma fenêtre
Jouer le matin doucement.

Elle courait dans la rosée,
Sans bruit, de peur de m'éveiller;
Moi, je n'ouvrais pas ma croisée,
De peur de la faire envoler.

Ses frères riaient… – Aube pure!
Tout chantait sous ces frais berceaux,
Ma famille avec la nature,
Mes enfants avec les oiseaux! –

Je toussais, on devenait brave.
Elle montait à petits pas,
Et me disait d'un air très grave:
«J'ai laissé les enfants en bas.»

Qu'elle fût bien ou mal coiffée,
Que mon cœur fût triste ou joyeux,
Je l'admirais. C'était ma fée,
Et le doux astre de mes yeux!

Nous jouions toute la journée.
O jeux charmants! chers entretiens!
Le soir, comme elle était l'aînée,
Elle me disait: «Père viens!

«Nous allons t'apporter ta chaise,
«Conte-nous une histoire, dis!» –
Et je voyais rayonner d'aise
Tous ces regards du paradis.

Alors, prodiguant les carnages,
J'inventais un conte profond
Dont je trouvais les personnages
Parmi les ombres du plafond.

Do you know the hill that connects
The town of Montlignon with Saint-Leu,
A terrace leaning down between
Woods that are dark, and skies that are blue?

It's there where we lived – penetrate,
My heart, to that enchanting past! –
Under my window I would hear
The morning playing on the grass.

She'd run soundlessly through the dew
Not to wake me early in the day,
And I would keep my casement shut
So that she wouldn't run away.

Her brothers would laugh ... – Oh pure dawn!
The songs in that bower one heard!
My family singing with nature itself,
Each child of mine with a bird!

Then I'd cough and they'd become brave;
She'd climb the stairway quickly-slow,
And say to me in a serious voice:
'I left the children below.'

Whether her hair was combed or not,
My heart joyful, or otherwise,
I'd admire her, my fairy-child,
Sweet constellation of my eyes!

We would play the entire day
Charming games and talks so dear!
Nights, since she was the oldest one,
She'd say to me, 'Papa, come here!

We are going to bring you your chair,
Tell us a story, papa please!' –
And I, content, would see their eyes
Shining, those looks of paradise.

Then, lavishing gore and feeling,
I'd invent a profound story
Whose characters I would pull down
From the shadows of the ceiling.

Toujours, ces quatres douces têtes
Riaient, comme à cet âge on rit,
De voir d'affreux géants très-bêtes
Vaincus par des nains pleins d'esprit.

J'étais l'Arioste et l'Homère
D'un poëme éclos d'un seul jet;
Pendant que je parlais, leur mère
Les regardait rire, et songeait.

Leur aïeul, qui lisait dans l'ombre,
Sur eux parfois levait les yeux,
Et moi, par la fenêtre sombre
J'entrevoyais un coin des cieux!

Veni, Vidi, Vixi

J'ai bien assez vécu, puisque dans mes douleurs
Je marche sans trouver de bras qui me secourent,
Puisque je ris à peine aux enfants qui m'entourent,
Puisque je ne suis plus réjoui par les fleurs;

Puisqu'au printemps, quand Dieu met le nature en fête,
J'assiste, esprit sans joie, à ce splendide amour;
Puisque je suis à l'heure où l'homme fuit le jour,
Hélas! et sent de tout la tristesse secrète;

Puisque l'espoir serein dans mon âme est vaincu;
Puisqu'en cette saison des parfums et des roses,
O ma fille! j'aspire à l'ombre où tu reposes,
Puisque mon cœur est mort, j'ai bien assez vécu.

Je n'ai pas refusé ma tâche sur la terre.
Mon sillon? Le voilà. Ma gerbe? La voici.
J'ai vécu souriant, toujours plus adouci,
Debout, mais incliné du côté du mystère.

And these four heads would laugh, for they
Were at that age when one likes to sit
And hear of ugly, stupid giants
Defeated by dwarfs who have wit.

I was the Homer and Ariosto
Of spontaneous song it seemed.
While I told stories, their mother
Watched them as they laughed, and dreamed.

Their grandfather, reading nearby,
Would lift his eyes toward them sometimes.
And I, looking through the windowpane,
Would glimpse a corner of the sky!

Veni, Vidi, Vixi

I have lived long enough because, when I walk along,
I've no arm to lean on, despite my misery,
Because I hardly laugh when children surround me,
Because I can't be softened by flowers or song;

Because, when Nature is laughing in the spring,
I attend the feast of this love without joy;
Because I've reached the hour when men flee the day
Alas! and feel the secret pain in everything;

Because the tranquil hope in my soul has been crushed;
Because, in this season of rose-scents and dew,
My daughter! I want to be resting with you;
Because my heart is dead, I have lived long enough.

I haven't avoided my tasks on this earth.
My furrow? There it is. And my sheaf? Next to me.
I have lived with a smile, always somewhat subdued,
Upright, but inclined toward the side of mystery.

J'ai fait ce que j'ai pu; j'ai servi, j'ai veillé,
Et j'ai vu bien souvent qu'on riait de ma peine.
Je me suis étonné d'être un objet de haine,
Ayant beaucoup souffert et beaucoup travaillé.

Dans ce bagne terrestre où ne s'ouvre aucune aile,
Sans me plaindre, saignant, et tombant sur les mains,
Morne, épuisé, raillé par les forçats humains,
J'ai porté mon chaînon de la chaîne éternelle.

Maintenant, mon regard ne s'ouvre qu'à demi;
Je ne me tourne plus même quand on me nomme;
Je suis plein de stupeur et d'ennui, comme un homme
Qui se lève avant l'aube et qui n'a pas dormi.

Je ne daigne plus même, en ma sombre paresse,
Répondre à l'envieux dont la bouche me nuit.
O Seigneur! ouvrez-moi les portes de la nuit,
Afin que je m'en aille et que je disparaisse!

«Demain, dès l'aube …»

Demain, dès l'aube, à l'heure où blanchit la campagne,
Je paritirai. Vois-tu, je sais que tu m'attends.
J'irai par la forêt, j'irai par la montagne.
Je ne puis demeurer loin de toi plus longtemps.

Je marcherai les yeux fixés sur mes pensées,
Sans rien vois au dehors, sans entendre aucun bruit,
Seul, inconnu, le dos courbé, les mains croisées,
Triste, et le jour pour moi sera comme la nuit.

Je ne regarderai ni l'or du soir qui tombe,
Ni les voiles au loin descendant vers Harfleur,
Et quand j'arriverai, je mettrai sur ta tombe
Un bouquet de houx vert et de bruyère en fleur.

I've done what I could, watching like a sentinel.
I often noticed others laughing at my pain;
I was stunned that I was an object of hatred,
Having suffered a lot and worked hard as well.

In this earthly prison where wings never soar –
Bleeding and down on my hands, I don't complain;
Dejected, used up, mocked by other human convicts –
I've carried my link of the everlasting chain.

And today my eyes are only open half-way;
I don't turn around even when my name is called;
I am full of stupor and ennui, like a man
Who wakes before dawn without having slept at all.

I don't even deign, in my dark listlessness,
To answer the envious whose mouths are severe.
Oh Lord, open up for me the gates of the abyss,
So that I may go off somewhere and disappear!

'Tomorrow, at dawn ...'

Tomorrow, at dawn, when the fields bleach in the sun,
I will set out. I know it's me you're waiting for.
I will pass through the forest and pass by the mountains:
I can't be separated from you any more.

I will walk with my eyes fixed only on my thoughts,
Without a sideways glance, strange and solitary,
For my back will be bent and my hands will be crossed
In sadness, and the day will be like night to me.

I won't look at the gold of evening as it falls,
Nor the sails in the distance descending on Harfleur,
And when I arrive, I'll put flowers on your tomb,
A bouquet of holly and some heather that's in bloom.

À Villequier

Maintenant que Paris, ses pavés et ses marbres,
Et sa brume et ses toits sont bien loin de mes yeux;
Maintenant que je suis sous les branches des arbres,
Et que je puis songer à la beauté des cieux;

Maintenant que du deuil qui m'a fait l'âme obscure
    Je sors, pâle et vainqueur,
Et que je sens la paix de la grande nature
    Qui m'entre dans le cœur;

Maintenant que je puis, assis au bord des ondes,
Ému par ce superbe et tranquille horizon,
Examiner en moi les vérités profondes
Et regarder les fleurs qui sont dans le gazon;

Maintenant, ô mon Dieu! que j'ai ce calme sombre
    De pouvoir désormais
Voir de mes yeux la pierre où je sais que dans l'ombre
    Elle dort pour jamais;

Maintenant qu'attendri par ces divins spectacles,
Plaines, forêts, rochers, vallons, fleuve argenté,
Voyant ma petitesse et voyant vos miracles,
Je reprends ma raison devant l'immensité;

Je viens à vous, Seigneur, père auquel il faut croire;
    Je vous porte, apaisé,
Les morceaux de ce cœur tout plein de votre gloire
    Que vous avez brisé;

Je vien à vous, Seigneur! confessant que vous êtes
Bon, clément, indulgent et doux, ô Dieu vivant!
Je conviens que vous seul savez ce que vous faites,
Et que l'homme n'est rien qu'un jonc qui tremble au vent;

Je dis que le tombeau qui sur les morts se ferme
    Ouvre le firmament;
Et que ce qu'ici-bas nous prenons pour le terme
    Est le commencement;

At Villequier

Now that the monuments of Paris and its streets,
Its fog and its buildings, are far from my eyes;
And now that I am under the branches of trees,
And can dream of the landscape's beauty, and the sky's;

Now that, victorious and pale, I feel my grief
      About to depart,
And I sense the peace and the vastness of nature
      Entering my heart;

Now that I am able, sitting on this shore
And moved by this dazzling but calm horizon,
To examine the truths inside me once more
And look at the flowers, the grass, and the sun;

Now that, my God! I feel this dark quiet
      Knowing I can never
See again the stone in the shadow of which
      She will sleep forever;

Now that I am softened by these divine scenes,
Plains, rocks, valleys, woods, streams – blue and silvery,
And sensing my smallness and seeing your works
I feel my mind healing in this immensity;

I come to you, oh Lord, in whom I must believe,
      Carrying a token
Of your glory in all the pieces of my heart
      You have torn and broken;

I come to you, Lord! confessing that you
Are good, mild, gentle, merciful, indulgent,
And I admit that you alone know what you do,
And we are all rushes that shake in the wind;

I grant that the tomb sealing death from the air
      Opens the firmament,
And what we consider down here as the end
      Is the beginning there;

Je conviens à genoux que vous seul, père auguste,
Possédez l'infini, le réel, l'absolu;
Je conviens qu'il est bon, je conviens qu'il est juste
Que mon cœur ait saigné, puisque Dieu l'a voulu!

Je ne résiste plus à tout ce qui m'arrive
            Par votre volonté.
L'âme de deuils en deuils, l'homme de rive en rive,
            Roule à l'éternité.

Nous ne voyons jamais qu'un seul côté des choses;
L'autre plonge en la nuit d'un mystère effrayant.
L'homme subit le joug sans connaître les causes.
Tout ce qu'il voit est court, inutile et fuyant.

Vous faites revenir toujours la solitude
            Autour de tous ses pas.
Vous n'avez pas voulu qu'il eût la certitude
            Ni la joie ici-bas!

Dès qu'il possède un bien, le sort le lui retire.
Rien ne lui fut donné, dans se rapides jours,
Pour qu'il s'en puisse faire une demeure, et dire:
C'est ici ma maison, mon champ et mes amours!

Il doit voir peu de temps tout ce que ses yeux voient;
            Il vieillit sans soutiens.
Puisque ces choses sont, c'est qu'il faut qu'elles soient;
            J'en conviens, j'en conviens!

Le monde est sombre, ô Dieu! l'immuable harmonie
Se compose des pleurs aussi bien que des chants;
L'homme n'est qu'un atome en cette ombre infinie,
Nuit où montent les bons, où tombent les méchants.

Je sais que vous avez bien autre chose à faire
            Que de nous plaindre tous,
Et qu'un enfant qui meurt, désespoir de sa mère,
            Ne vous fait rien, à vous!

Je sais que le fruit tombe au vent qui le secoue,
Que l'oiseau perd sa plume et la fleur son parfum;
Que la création est une grande roue
Que ne peut se mouvoir sans écraser quelqu'un;

I admit, on my knees, it is you I should trust,
That you alone possess the real, the infinite;
I admit it was good, I admit it was just
That my heart bled because you wanted it!

I no longer resist anything that occurs
          Because of your will, to me.
We roll from grief to grief, and drift from shore to shore
          Toward your eternity.

We never see more than one side of things;
The other is sunk in dark mysteries.
We submit to the yoke without knowing the cause
And everything is brief and futile, and flees.

You always make solitude follow our steps
          No matter where we go.
You never wanted us to have certitude
          Or joy here below!

Whatever we have is soon taken away.
Nothing is given us forever from above
Such that we can make a dwelling here and say:
'This is my home, and my land, and my love.'

We won't see for long whatever we see
          And time will not relent.
Since that's how things are and how they must be;
          I consent, God, I consent!

The world is dark, Lord, and your harmony
Is composed as much of tears as it is of song.
Man is an atom in this infinity
Where the good men ascend and the wicked ones fall.

I know you have many other things to do
          Besides pitying us,
And that a dead child, a mother's distress
          Isn't much to you.

I know that fruit falls when winds shake the bough,
That birds lose their feathers and flowers their scent,
That nature's a vast wheel that doesn't move
Without crushing *some*one in its descent;

Les mois, les jours, les flots des mers, les yeux qui pleurent,
      Passent sous le ciel bleu;
Il faut que l'herbe pousse et que les enfants meurent;
      Je le sais, ô mon Dieu!

Dans vos cieux, au delà de la sphère des nues,
Au fond de cet azur immobile et dormant,
Peut-être faites-vous des choses inconnues
Où la douleur de l'homme entre comme élément.

Peut-être est-il utile à vos desseins sans nombre
      Que des êtres charmants
S'en aillent, emportés par le toubillon sombre
      Des noirs événements.

Nos destins ténébreux vont sous des lois immenses
Que rien ne déconcerte et que rien n'attendrit.
Vous ne pouvez avoir de subites clémences
Qui dérangerait le monde, ô Dieu, tranquille esprit!

Je vous supplie, ô Dieu! de regarder mon âme,
      Et de considérer
Qu'humble comme un enfant et doux comme une femme,
      Je viens vous adorer!

Considérez encor que j'avais, dès l'aurore,
Travaillé, combattu, pensé, marché, lutté,
Expliquant la nature à l'homme qui l'ignore,
Éclairant toute chose avec votre clarté;

Que j'avais, affrontant la haine et la colère,
      Fait ma tâche ici-bas,
Que je ne pouvais pas m'attendre à ce salaire,
      Que je ne pouvais pas

Prévoir que, vous aussi, sur ma tête qui ploie
Vous appensantiriez votre bras triomphant,
Et que, vous qui voyiez comme j'ai peu de joie,
Vous me reprendriez si vite mon enfant!

Qu'une âme ainsi frappée à se plaindre est sujette,
      Que j'air pu blasphémer,
Et vous jeter mes cris comme un enfant qui jette
      Une pierre à la mer!

That the months and the days, ocean waves, teary eyes,
        Pass by here below,
That the grass has to grow and children die:
        I know, my God, I know!

Far beyond the sphere of clouds, in your heaven,
In the depths of this dormant and slumbering blue,
Perhaps you effect unimaginable things
Which our grief, like an element, enters into.

Perhaps there is something you plan that depends
        On beings as sweet as these
That have gone away, carried off by the winds
        Of sinister events.

Our fates are subject to the most stringent laws
Which nothing can disturb and nothing make mild.
Reversals aren't allowed, or clemencies that would
Upset the balance, tranquil spirit, uncaused cause!

I implore you, my God, to look at my soul
        As well as consider how,
Humbly, like a child, and gently, like a woman,
        I come to praise you now.

Consider furthermore how I have, since the dawn,
Worked, wrestled, thought, walked, and struggled to explain
All of creation to men who weren't aware,
Bringing things to light and goodness in your name;

How, confronting hate and anger, I've fulfilled
        My duty here below;
That I could not have known that this would happen,
        That I could not have known

That you would allow your triumphant arm
To fall on a head that did not expect the wound,
Or that you, who see how little joy I have,
Would take my child away from me so soon!

That I might have blasphemed, bent under the blow,
        Or wallowed in self-pity,
Throwing curses at you like a child who throws
        A stone into the sea!

Considérez qu'on doute, ô mon Dieu! quand on souffre,
Que l'œil qui pleure trop finit par s'aveugler,
Qu'un être que son deuil plonge au plus noir du gouffre,
Quand il ne vous voit plus, ne peut vous contempler,

Et qu'il ne se peut pas que l'homme, lorqu'il sombre
       Dans les afflictions,
Ait présente à l'esprit la sérénité sombre
       Des constellations!

Aujourd'hui, moi qui fus faible comme une mère,
Je me courbe à vos pieds devant vos cieux ouverts.
Je me sens éclairé dans ma douleur amère
Par un meilleur regard jeté sur l'univers.

Seigneur, je reconnais que l'homme est en délire
       S'il ose murmurer;
Je cesse d'accuser, je cesse de maudire,
       Mais laisser-moi pleurer!

Hélas! laissez les pleurs couler de ma paupière,
Puisque vous avez fait les hommes pour cela!
Laissez-moi me pencher sur cette froide pierre
Et dire à mon enfant: Sens-tu que je suis-là?

Laissez-moi lui parler, incliné sur ses restes,
       Le soir, quand tout se tait,
Comme si, dans sa nuit rouvrant ses yeux célestes,
       Cet ange m'écoutait!

Hélas! vers le passé tournant un œil d'envie,
Sans que rien ici-bas puisse m'en consoler,
Je regarde toujours ce moment de ma vie
Où je l'ai vue ouvrir son aile et s'envoler!

Je verrai cet instant jusqu'à ce que je meure,
       L'instant, pleurs superflus!
Où je criai: L'enfant que j'avais tout à l'heure,
       Quoi donc! je ne l'ai plus!

Ne vous irritez pas que je sois de la sorte,
O mon Dieu! cette plaie a si longtemps saigné!
L'angoisse dans mon âme est toujours la plus forte,
Et mon cœur est soumis, mais n'est pas résigné.

Consider, my God, that we doubt when we suffer,
That eyes can go blind from crying in despair,
That anyone who sinks into grief's blackest pit,
Can't pray because he can't see you from there;

That it's not possible for those who can't see
            Past their affliction
To maintain, in their souls, that dark serenity
            Of the stars and the sun!

Now I, who once was as weak as a mother,
Kneel at your heaven to bless you, not curse:
For I feel illumined in my bitter sorrow
By a better look cast over your universe.

Oh Lord, only those whose minds are abused
            Would murmur, or deny.
I don't curse you now; I no longer accuse;
            But please, Lord, let me cry!

Alas! Allow the tears to flow from my eyes
Since you have made it so we can't keep them clear.
Let me lean over the cold, senseless stone
And say to my child, 'Can you feel that I'm here?'

Let me talk to her, bent over her remains
            In night's tranquillity,
As if, awake or stirring in *her* endless night,
            She were listening to me!

Turning an envious eye to the past,
Though nothing can console me, come what may,
I'm always looking at that moment of my life
When I saw her open her wings and fly away!

And I will see this moment until the day I die,
            The moment (useless remorse!)
When I cried, 'The girl I had a minute ago,
            What, I have her no more?'

Don't be angry if I seem to be so blind,
My God! The wound has been bleeding so long!
The pain in my soul is every bit as strong,
My heart submits now, but it isn't resigned.

Ne vous irritez pas! fronts que le deuil réclame,
Mortels sujets aux pleurs,
Il nous est malaisé de retirer notre âme
De ses grandes douleurs.

Voyez-vous, nos enfants nos sont bien nécessaires,
Seigneur; quand on a vu dans sa vie, un matin,
Au milieu des ennuis, des peines, des misères,
Et de l'ombre que fait sur nous notre destin,

Apparaître un enfant, tête chère et sacrée,
Petit être joyeux,
Si beau, qu'on a cru voir s'ouvrir à son entrée
Une porte des cieux;

Quand on a vu, seize ans, de cet autre soi-même
Croître la grâce aimable et la douce raison,
Lorsqu'on a reconnu que cet enfant qu'on aime
Fait le jour dans notre âme et dans notre maison,

Que c'est la seule joie ici-bas qui persiste
De tout ce qu'on rêva,
Considérez que c'est une chose bien triste
De le voir qui s'en va!

Mors

Je vis cette faucheuse. Elle était dans son champ.
Elle allait à grands pas moissonnant et fauchant,
Noir squelette laissant passer le crépuscule.
Dans l'ombre où l'on dirait que tout tremble et recule,
L'homme suivait des yeux les lueurs de la faulx.
Et les triomphateurs sous les arcs triomphaux
Tombaient; elle changeait en désert Babylone,
Le trône en échafaud et l'échafaud en trône,
Les roses en fumier, les enfants en oiseaux,
L'or en cendre, et les yeux des mères en ruisseaux.
Et les femmes criaient: — Rends-nous ce petit être.
Pour le faire mourir, pourquoi l'avoir fait naître? —

Don't be angry! Those whom sorrows rack
        Are apt to cry and complain;
We find it difficult to pull our souls back
        From such an ancient pain.

Oh Lord, how necessary children are for us!
And when, one of life's grey mornings, one sees
Amid sorrow, suffering, pain, and ominous
Shadows that are spreading over our destinies,

A child appear, whose head is dear and blessed,
        A little joyous creature,
So beautiful we thought we saw clouds in heaven
        Opening to greet her;

When, for sixteen years, one has seen
This other self, growing in grace, become whole,
When one discovers that the child one loves
Is the sun of one's life and the fire of one's soul,

That it is the one enduring happiness
        Of all we dream down here –
Consider how sad a thing it is for us
        To watch it disappear!

Mors

I have seen that reaper. She was out in her field,
Mowing down and harvesting. Everything would yield
To her, black skeleton whom the twilight passed through.
In that gloom from which one draws back, or struggles to,
Men watched the glintings of her scythe – for she marches.
And conquerors, under their triumphal arches,
Fell down. She was changing Babylon into groans,
Thrones into scaffolds, and scaffolds into thrones,
Roses into dung heaps, and children into dreams,
Gold into ash, and eyes of mothers into streams.
Then a woman cried: 'Give us back our little one!
To make him die an infant, why give life to our son?'

Ce n'était qu'un sanglot sur terre, en haut, en bas;
Des mains aux doigts osseux sortaient des noirs grabats;
Un vent froid bruissait dans les linceuls sans nombre;
Les peuples éperdus semblaient sous la faulx sombre
Un troupeau frissonnant qui dans l'ombre s'enfuit;
Tout était sous ses pieds deuil, épouvante et nuit.
Derrière elle, le front baigné de douces flammes,
Un ange souriant portait la gerbe d'âmes.

Le Mendiant

Un pauvre homme passait dans le givre et le vent.
Je cognai sur ma vitre; il s'arrêta devant
Ma porte, que j'ouvris d'une façon civile.
Les ânes revenaient du marché de la ville,
Portant les paysans accroupis sur leurs bâts.
C'était le vieux qui vit dans une niche au bas
De la montée, et rêve, attendant, solitaire,
Un rayon du ciel triste, un liard de la terre,
Tendant les mains pour l'homme et les joignant pour Dieu.
Je lui criai: «Venez vous réchauffer un peu.
»Comment vous nommez-vous?» Il me dit: «Je me nomme
»Le pauvre.» Je lui pris la main: «Entrez, brave homme.»
Et je lui fis donner une jatte de lait.
Le viellard grelottait de froid; il me parlait,
Et je lui répondais, pensif et sans l'entendre.
«Vos habits sont mouillés,» dis-je, «il faut les étendre
»Devant la cheminée.» Il s'approcha du feu.
Son manteau, tout mangé de vers, et jadis bleu,
Étalé largement sur la chaude fournaise,
Piqué de mille trous par la lueur de braise,
Couvrait l'âtre, et semblait un ciel noir étoilé.
Et, pendant qu'il séchait ce haillon désolé
D'où ruisselait la pluie et l'eau des fondrières,
Je songeais que cet homme était plein de prières,
Et je regardais, sourd à ce que nous disions,
Sa bure où je voyais des constellations.

The sob went up, below, but it remained earth-bound.
Hands with bony fingers reached up from underground.
An icy wind whistled through the shrouds and made them writhe.
The shivering people underneath the deadly scythe
Were like a flock fleeing in the dark without relief.
Her feet trampled everything: horror, night, and grief.
Behind her, smiling, bathed in flames like mild coals,
An angel was carrying a sheaf of new souls.

The Beggar

A poor man passed by in the wind and the frost.
I rapped on my window; he stopped and looked lost
In front of the door I opened, then turned around.
The mules were coming back from the market in town,
With peasants on their saddles and bought goods in tow.
The man, I knew, lived in that hut just below
The hill, and, ageing, dreamed of things that had the worth
Of sun from sad heavens, or pennies from the earth –
He joined his hands for God and opened them for men.
I shouted: 'Come in here and warm yourself my friend.'
'What's your name?' I asked him. He answered, 'There are some
Who call me the poor one.' I said: 'Enter, *brave homme.*'
I made him take a bowl of hot milk and some tea.
The man was shivering with cold; he talked to me
And I answered back without listening to him.
'Your clothes are drenched,' I said, 'you should really spread them
In front of the chimney.' He went up to the fire.
His coat, completely eaten by worms, was like wire,
A blue cloth now faded, which – pinpricked with holes
Suddenly appearing in the light of the coals –
Covered the hearth, resembling a starry sky.
The moment he spread his tattered coat out to dry
From which I saw puddle water drip here and there,
I thought to myself, 'This man is full of prayer,'
And stared, deaf to words and lost in meditations,
At his sackcloth in which I saw constellations.

Paroles sur la dune

Maintenant que mon temps décroit comme un flambeau,
            Que mes tâches sont terminées;
Maintenant que voici que je touche au tombeau
            Par les deuils et par les années,

Et qu'au fond de ce ciel que mon essor rêva,
            Je vois fuir, vers l'ombre entraînées,
Comme le tourbillon du passé qui s'en va,
            Tant de belles heures sonnées;

Maintenant que je dis: – Un jour, nous triomphons;
            Le lendemain, tout est mensonge! –
Je suis triste, et je marche au bord des flots profonds,
            Courbé comme celui qui songe.

Je regarde, au-dessus du mont et du vallon,
            Et des mers sans fin remuées,
S'envoler, sous le bec du vautour aquilon,
            Toute la toison des nuées;

J'entends le vent dans l'air, la mer sur le récif,
            L'homme liant la gerbe mûre;
J'écoute et je confronte en mon esprit pensif
            Ce qui parle à ce qui murmure;

Et je reste parfois couché sans me lever
            Sur l'herbe rare de la dune,
Jusqu'à l'heure où l'on voit apparaître et rêver
            Les yeux sinistres de la lune.

Elle monte, elle jette un long rayon dormant
            À l'espace, au mystère, au gouffre;
Et nous nous regardons tous les deux fixement,
            Elle qui brille et moi qui souffre.

Où donc s'en sont allés mes jours évanouis?
            Est-il quelqu'un qui me connaisse?
Ai-je encor quelque chose en mes yeux éblouis,
            De la clarté de ma jeunesse?

Words on the Dunes

Now that time is growing short like a torch
      And I've no duties in arrears,
And now that I am already touching the tomb
      With all my mourning and my years;

Now that I can see, soaring through the heavens' depths
      Toward which my soul desired to fly,
The departing and dwindling whirlwind of the past,
      Its loveliest hours, go by;

Now that I can say: 'One day we are triumphant;
      The next day everything's a lie!'
I walk along this shore that bears the breakers' brunt
      Like a dreamer, wondering why.

I look and I see, above the valley and the cliff
      And the countless waves the wind crowds,
Scattering under the storm's vulture beak,
      All of the fleeces of the clouds;

I hear the air's winds, and water on the rocks,
      A man tying sheaves with a string;
I listen, and confront, in my meditative soul,
      What speaks to what's murmuring.

And I remain there, stretched out on my back
      In the scattered grass of the dune,
Till the hour when one sees, dreaming in the black,
      The sinister eyes of the moon.

She rises and throws out a long, sleeping ray
      Into space, the abyss, mystery;
She in her brightness and I in my pain
      Stare at each other fixedly.

Where have all of my vanished days gone?
      Does anyone really know me?
Do I *still* retain something in my dazzled eyes,
      A spark of my youth's energy?

Tout s'est-il envolé? Je suis seul, je suis las;
      J'appelle sans qu'on me réponde;
O vents! ô flots! ne suis-je aussi qu'un souffle, hélas!
      Hélas! ne suis-je aussi qu'une onde?

Ne verrai-je plus rien tout ce que j'aimais?
      Au dedans de moi le soir tombe.
O terre, dont la brume efface les sommets,
      Suis-je le spectre, et toi la tombe?

Ai-je donc vidé tout, vie, amour, joie, espoir?
      J'attends, je demande, j'implore;
Je penche tout à tout mes urnes pour avoir
      De chacune une goutte encore!

Comme le souvenir est voisin du remord!
      Comme à pleurer tout nous ramène!
Et que je te sens froide en te touchant, ô mort,
      Noir verrou de la porte humaine!

Et je pense, écoutant gémir le vent amer,
      Et l'onde aux plis infranchissables;
L'été rit, et l'on voit sur le bord de la mer
      Fleurir le chardon bleu des sables.

Mugitusque boum

Mugissement des bœufs, au temps du doux Virgile,
Comme aujourd'hui, le soir, quand fuit la nuit agile,
Ou, le matin, quand l'aube aux champs extasiés
Verse à flots la rosée et le jour, vous disiez:
«Mûrissez, blés mouvants! prés, emplissez-vous d'herbes!
»Que la terre, agitant son panache de gerbes,
»Chante dans l'onde d'or d'une riche moisson!
»Vis, bête; vis, caillou; vis, homme; vis, buisson!
»À l'heure où le soleil se couche, où l'herbe est pleine
»Des grands fantômes noirs des arbres de la plaine
»Jusqu'aux lointains coteaux rampant et grandissant,
»Quand le brun laboureur des collines descend

Has it all flown away? I'm alone. I call out.
            No one responds to my scream.
Oh winds! oh billows! am I only a breath?
            Am I, alas, only a stream?

Will I never see anything I loved again?
            The night within spreads its gloom.
Oh earth, whose summits the fog is effacing,
            Am I then the ghost, you the tomb?

Have I emptied it all – life, love, joy, and hope?
            I'm waiting; I ask; I implore.
One after the other, I lift my urns to drink
            A drop from each once more!

Oh how our memories are neighbours of remorse!
            How everything makes us weep more!
Oh, how cold I feel touching you, oh Death,
            Black bolt on humanity's door!

So I dream, listening to winds groan and roar
            And waves wrinkle toward the land.
Summer is laughing, and you can see, on the shore,
            Blue thistle blooming in the sand.

Mugitusque Boum

The mooing of the cows in Virgil's time, like today,
At evening, when the night drifts down, or when the day
Is breaking, pouring waves of its sunlight and its dew
On the meadows below, you are trying to say:
'Ripen, moving wheat! Turn green, open fields!
And earth, as you bend your feathered sheaves in the wind,
Sing on the rolling surge of gold your harvest yields!
Live, beasts! Live, pebbles! Live, bushes! Live, men!
When the sun is setting and the landscape fills
With shadowy phantoms of the trees and the hills
Lengthening across the expanding distances,
When the worker, returning home, notices

»Et retourne à son toit d'où sort une fumée,
»Que la soif de revoir sa femme bien-aimée
»Et l'enfant qu'en ses bras hier il réchauffait,
»Que ce désir, croissant à chaque pas qu'il fait,
»Imite dans son cœur l'allongement de l'ombre!
»Êtres! choses! vivez! sans peur, sans deuil, sans nombre!
»Que tout s'épanouisse en sourirer vermeil!
»Que l'homme ait le repos et le bœuf le sommeil!
»Vivez! croissez! semez le grain à l'aventure!
»Qu'on sente frissonner dans toute la nature,
»Sous la feuille des nids, au seuil blanc des maisons,
»Dans l'obscur tremblement des profonds horizons,
»Un vaste emportement d'aimer, dans l'herbe verte,
»Dans l'antre, dans l'étang, dans la clairière ouverte,
»D'aimer sans fin, d'aimer toujours, d'aimer encor,
»Sous la sérénité des sombres astres d'or!
»Faites tressailler l'air, le flot, l'aile, la bouche,
»O palpitations du grand amour farouche!
»Qu'on sente le baiser de l'être illimité!
»Et paix, vertu, bonheur, espérance, bonté,
»O fruits divins, tombez des branches éternelles!»

Ainsi vous parliez, voix, grandes voix solennelles;
Et Virgile écoutait comme j'écoute, et l'eau
Voyait passer le cygne auguste, et le bouleau
Le vent, et le rocher l'écume, et le ciel sombre
L'homme … O nature! abîme! immensité de l'ombre!

«Je payai le pêcheur qui passa son chemin …»

Je payai le pêcheur qui passa son chemin,
Et je pris cette bête horrible dans ma main;
C'était un être obscur comme l'onde en apporte,
Qui, plus grand, serait hydre, et, plus petit, cloporte;
Sans forme comme l'ombre, et comme Dieu, sans nom.
Il ouvrait une bouche affreuse; un noir moignon
Sortait de son écaille; il tâchait de me mordre;
Dieu, dans l'immensité formidable de l'ordre,
Donne une place sombre à ces spectres hideux.

The smoke rising up from his chimney, and when
His desire to see his beloved wife again
And the child whom he warmed in his arms yesterday
Increases – may this longing, growing on his way,
Imitate within him the shadows' lengthening!
Creatures, be fearless, numberless. May everything
Expand to a smile, red-lipped and fresh as air!
Multiply and live! Scatter seeds everywhere!
May humans have repose and the oxen a rest!
May everyone shiver – under leaves of a nest,
In nature, on a home's white threshold, in the sun,
Within the vague tremoring below the horizon –
With the fury of love – in the grass, in the shade,
In the caves, in the ponds, in a clearing, in a glade –
To love again and always, to love endlessly
Under the dark, gilded stars' serenity!
May love's palpitations and intense quivering
Set the air – and waves, wings, and mouths – trembling!
May the universe feel the supreme being's kiss!
May peace, hope, virtue, and good will and happiness,
Divine fruits, fall from an everlasting bough!'

That is how you spoke and are trying to speak now.
And Virgil listened as I listen. Flowing by,
The water watched the noble swan, the beech tree
The wind, the rock the foam, and the sombre sky
Man ... Oh abyss! nature! night's immensity!

'I paid the fisherman ...'

I paid the fisherman who passes by my house,
Then took that horrible creature in my hands.
It was something the waves bring to birth, and would have been
A hydra if larger; if smaller, a louse –
As formless as a shadow and as nameless as God.
It opened its disgusting mouth; its scaly sides
Were speckled with black stumps. It tried to bite my hand.
In the deep expanse of the cosmos, God provides
A dark and sombre place for these hideous things.

Il tâchait de me mordre, et nous luttions tous deux;
Ses dents cerchaient mes doigts qu'effrayait leur approche;
L'homme que me l'avait vendu tourna la roche;
Comme il disparaissait, le crabe me mordit;
Je lui dis: «Vis! et sois beni, pauvre maudit!»
Et je le rejetai dans la vague profonde,
Afin qu'il allât dire à l'océan qui gronde,
Et qui sert au soleil de vase baptismal,
Que l'homme rend le bien au monstre pour le mal.

Pasteurs et troupeaux

À Madame Louise C.

Le vallon où je vais tous les jours est charmant,
Serein, abandonné, seul sous le firmament,
Plein de ronces en fleurs; c'est un sourire triste.
Il vous fait oublier que quelque chose existe,
Et, sans le bruit des champs remplis de travailleurs,
On ne saurait plus là si quelqu'un vit ailleurs.
Là, l'ombre fait l'amour; l'idylle naturelle
Rit; le bouvreuil avec le verdier s'y querelle,
Et la fauvette y met de travers son bonnet;
C'est tantôt l'aubépine et tantôt le genêt;
De noirs granits bourrus, puis des mousses riantes;
Car Dieu fait un poëme avec des variantes;
Comme le vieil Homère, il rabâche parfois,
Mais c'est avec les fleurs, les monts, l'onde et les bois!
Une petite mare est là, ridant sa face,
Prenant des airs de flot pour la fourmi qui passe,
Ironie étalée au milieu du gazon,
Qu'ignore l'océan grondant à l'horizon.
J'y rencontre parfois sur la roche hideuse
Un doux être; quinze ans, yeux bleus, pieds nus, gardeuse
De chèvres, habitant, au fond d'un ravin noir,
Un vieux chaume croulant qui s'étoile le soir;
Ses sœurs sont au logis et filent leur quenouille;
Elle essuie aux roseaux ses pieds que l'étang mouille;
Chèvres, brebis, béliers, paissent; quand, sombre esprit,

It tried to bite my hand, and we wrestled together.
Its teeth sought my fingers that fled their approach.
The fisherman who sold it to me disappeared
Behind a rock, and when he had gone it bit me.
I said, 'Be blessed and live, you cursed little thing!'
And then threw it back into the wide open sea
So that it might report to the large and grumbling
Ocean, that baptismal font of the sun,
That man returns good to a beast for evil done.

Shepherds and Flocks

To Madame Louise C.

The valley where I go every day is pure enchantment:
Serene, alone, abandoned beneath the firmament,
And filled with brambles in bloom. It is a sad smile.
It makes you forget things exist for a while.
If it weren't for the sound of the field workers there,
You wouldn't know life were going on anywhere.
For there, shadows make love; nature's pastoral
Laughs; the different finches love to quarrel;
And warblers put a word in when they're out of sorts.
Sometimes it's the hawthorn and sometimes the milkworts,
The cliffs, then the mosses that make the difference.
For God composes a long poem with variants,
And like old Homer, he repeats himself now and then,
Only it's with flowers, forests, waves, or a mountain!
There's a small pool there: when it wrinkles its surface
It looks like a tidal wave to ants that go past –
An irony that keeps spreading out with the wind
Of which the distant sea remains ignorant.
Sometimes there, on the high rock, I happen upon
A young girl – fifteen, barefoot, blue eyes, guardian
Of all the goats, who lives within a dark ravine
In a cottage through whose roof pricks of starlight can be seen.
Her sisters are at home spinning wool so time will pass;
She wipes her feet, wet from the pond, on reed grass.
Goats, ewes, and rams graze there. When I suddenly

J'apparais, le pauvre ange a peur, et me sourit;
Et moi, je la salue, elle étant l'innocence.
Ses agneaux, dans le pré plein de fleurs qui l'encense,
Bondissent, et chacun, au soleil s'empourprant,
Laisse aux buissons, à qui la bise le reprend,
Un peu de sa toison, comme un flocon d'écume.
Je passe, enfant, troupeau, s'effacent dans la brume;
Le crépuscule étend sur les longs sillons gris
Ses ailes de fantôme et de chauve-souris;
J'entends encore au loin dans la plaine ouvrière
Chanter derrière moi la douce chevrière,
Et, là-bas, devant moi, le vieux gardien pensif
De l'écume, du flot, de l'algue, du récif,
Et des vagues sans trêve et sans fin remuées,
Le pâtre promontoire au chapeau de nuées,
S'accoude et rêve au bruit de tous les infinis,
Et, dans l'ascension des nuages bénis,
Regarde se lever la lune triomphale,
Pendant que l'ombre tremble, et que l'âpre rafale
Disperse à tous les vents avec son souffle amer
La laine des moutons sinistres de la mer.

«J'ai cueilli cette fleur pour toi …»

J'ai cueilli cette fleur pour toi sur la colline.
Dans l'âpre escarpement qui sur le flot s'incline,
Que l'aigle connaît seul et peul seul approcher,
Paisible, elle croissait aux fentes du rocher.
L'ombre baignait les flancs du morne promontoire;
Je voyais, comme on dresse au lieu d'une victoire
Un grand arc de triomphe éclatant et vermeil,
À l'endroit où s'était englouti le soleil,
La sombre nuit bâtir un porche de nuées.
Des voiles s'enfuyaient, au loin diminuées;
Quelques toits, s'éclairant au fond d'un entonnoir,
Semblaient craindre de luire et de se laisser voir.
J'ai cueilli cette fleur pour toi, ma bien-aimée.
Elle est pâle, et n'a pas de corolle embaumée.
Sa racine n'a pris sur la crête des monts

Appear, she is frightened, but then smiles at me.
And I wave to her – for, to me, she's innocence.
Her lambs, out pasturing in fields where flowers' scents
Incite them, are jumping, and, as the sun descends,
Leave bits of fleece upon each bush they rub against
Which gusts of wind carry off like light flakes of foam.
I pass by: the flock melt into the fog in which they roam.
The twilight is spreading out its bat and phantom wings
Over the billows that are always wrinkling.
I can still hear the goatherd singing in the distance
In fields that were bristling with work behind me.
And over there, in front, the old, pensive guardian
Of the foam, the surf, the sea-weed, and the rocks that lie hidden
In waves that are rolling relentlessly in and out –
The shepherd-promontory with his hat of cloud
Rests on his elbows, dreaming of infinities,
And as the clouds begin to rise up with the breeze
Meditates on the triumphant moon shining there
While the shadows are trembling, and the sharp, salt air
Gusts in bitter breaths, scattering to the lee
The wool of all the sinister sheep of the sea.

'I gathered this flower for you on the hill ...'

I gathered this flower for you on the hill.
It was growing peacefully among the rocks that spill
From the escarpment that leans over the sea
Which only eagles know and only they can approach.
Shadows were bathing the sides of the promontory
When I saw – as when on the field of victory a crowd
Raises an arch with a fiery glow –
The sombre night erect a portico of cloud
At the point where the sun was vanishing below.
Sails fled or faded far away into the scene.
A few roofs, as they caught the last light from above,
Seemed afraid to shine or to let themselves be seen.
I gathered this flower for you there, my love;
It is pale and doesn't have a fragrant bouquet.
Its roots haven't taken anything from the summit

Que l'amère senteur des glauques goëmons;
Moi, j'ai dit: «Pauvre fleur, du haut de cette cime,
«Tu devais t'en aller dans cet immense abîme
«Où l'algue et le nuage et les voiles s'en vont.
«Va mourir sur un cœur, abîme plus profond.
«Fane-toi sur ce sein en qui palpite un monde.
«Le ciel, qui te créa pour t'effeuiller dans l'onde,
«Te fit pour l'océan, je te donne à l'amour.»
Le vent mêlait les flots; il ne restait du jour
Qu'une vague lueur, lentement effacée.
Oh! comme j'étais triste au fond de ma pensée
Tandis que je songeais, et que le gouffre noir
M'entrait dans l'âme avec tous les frissons du soir!

«O strophe du poëte …»

O strophe du poëte, autrefois, dans les fleurs,
Jetant mille baisers à leurs mille couleurs,
Tu jouais, et d'avril tu pillais la corbeille;
Papillon pour la rose et pour la ruche abeille,
Tu semais de l'amour et tu faisais du miel;
Ton âme bleue était presque mêlée au ciel;
Ta robe était d'azur et ton œil de lumière;
Tu criais aux chansons, tes sœurs: «Venez! chaumière,
»Hameau, ruisseau, forêt, tout chante. L'aube a lui!»
Et, douce, tu courais et tu riais. Mais lui,
Le sévère habitant de la blême caverne
Qu'en haut le jour blanchit, qu'en bas rougit l'Averne,
Le poëte qu'ont fait avant l'heure vieillard
La douleur dans la vie et le drame dans l'art,
Lui, le chercheur du gouffre obscur, le chasseur d'ombres,
Il a levé la tête un jour hors des décombres,
Et t'a saisie au vol dans l'herbe et dans les blés,
Et, malgré tes effrois et tes cris redoublés,
Toute en pleurs, il t'a prise à l'idylle joyeuse;
Il t'a ravie aux champs, à la source, à l'yeuse,
Aux amours dans les bois près des nids palpitants;
Et maintenant, captive et reine en même temps,
Prisonnière au plus noir de son âme profonde,
Parmi les visions qui flottent comme l'onde,

Except the bitter smell and the weeds' greenish-grey.
I said then: 'Poor flower, you are going to plummet
From this rocky parapet into the abyss
Where the seaweed, the clouds, and the sails disappear.
Die instead on a heart – a gulf deeper than this.
Wither on a breast in which a world palpitates.
Although the sky created you to shed your petals here
And gave you to the sea, I will give you to my love.'
The wind stirred the waves; what remained of the day
Was only a glimmer that was fading away.
How my mind turned and could not be set right
As long as I was dreaming, and the shadowy abyss
Was entering my soul with the shivering night!

'Strophe of the poet ...'

Strophe of the poet, formerly you'd let loose
A thousand kisses on the flowers' thousand hues,
And pillage April's garden wherever you'd go.
With sweetness you would make and with love you would sow
Butterflies for roses and bees for honeycombs.
You blue soul would mingle with the heavens and roam.
Your clothes were azure and your eyes made out of light.
You'd shout to songs, your sisters: 'Fly here and alight!
The hamlets, streams, and forests sing. The sun dawns on the sea!'
And you would run and laugh in delight. But then he,
The grim inhabitant of the cavern of woe
The sun, above, bleaches, and hell turns red below,
The poet whom the theatre and life's mysteries
Have made an old man before his time – but then he,
The shadow-chaser, searcher of the pit and the skies,
Lifted his head up from out of the debris,
And seized you, in spite of your fears and your cries,
Among the lonely meadows and the wheat as he flew.
He took you from the idyll in tears. He kidnapped you
Away from the holly and the source where you were,
From the nests, from the fields, from the woods you'd walk through.
And now, queen and captive at once, prisoner
Within the blackest depths of his bottomless soul,
Among all the visions that hover near and pass

Sous son crâne à la fois céleste et souterrain,
Assise, et t'accoudant sur un trône d'airain,
Voyant dans ta mémoire, ainsi qu'une ombre vaine
Fuir l'éblouissement du jour et de la plaine,
Par le maître gardée, et calme, et sans espoir,
Tandis que, près de toi, les drames, groupe noir,
Des sombres passions feuillettent le registre,
Tu rêves dans sa nuit, Proserpine sinistre.

«*Un spectre m'attendait …*»

Un spectre m'attendait dans un grand angle d'ombre,
Et m'a dit:
         – Le muet habite dans le sombre.
L'infini rêve, avec un visage irrité.
L'homme parle et dispute avec l'obscurité,
Et la larme de l'œil rit du bruit de la bouche.
Tout ce qui vous emporte est rapide et farouche.
Sais-tu pourquoi tu vis? sais-tu pourquoi tu meurs?
Les vivants orageux passent dans les rumeurs,
Chiffres tumultueux, flots de l'océan Nombre.
Vous n'avez rien à vous qu'un souffle dans de l'ombre;
L'homme est à peine né, qu'il est déjà passé,
Et c'est avoir fini que d'avoir commencé.
Derrière le mur blanc, parmi les herbes vertes,
La fosse obscure attend l'homme, lèvres ouvertes.
La mort est le baiser de la bouche tombeau.
Tâche de faire un peu de bien coupe un lambeau
D'une bonne action dans cette nuit qui gronde,
Ce cera ton linceul dans la terre profonde.
Beaucoup s'en sont allés qui ne reviendront plus
Qu'à l'heure de l'immense et lugubre reflux;
Alors, on entendra des cris. Tâche de vivre;
Crois. Tant que l'homme vit, Dieu pensif lit son livre;
L'homme meurt quand Dieu fait au coin du livre un pli.
L'espace sait, regarde, écoute. Il est rempli
D'oreilles sous la tombe, et d'yeux dans les ténèbres.
Les morts, ne marchant plus, dressent leur pieds funèbres;
Les feuilles sèches vont et roulent sous les cieux.
Ne sens-tu pas souffler le vent mystérieux?

Under his infernal and celestial skull,
Seated, elbows resting on a throne made of brass,
Watching all the brilliance of the day slowly flee
Vague, vain, and shadow-like, inside your memory,
Guarded by the master, and calm and without hope –
While next to you the dramas, a terrifying group,
Flip through the sombre passions' register unseen –
You dream within his night like a dark Proserpine.

'A shade was waiting …'

A shade was waiting in the darkness near a glow.
It said:
      'The speechless dwells in the blackness below.
Infinity dreams with a scowl on its face.
Men converse and argue with the darkness of the place;
A mouth's response is mocked by a tear in the eye.
Do you know why you live? Do you know why you die?
Everything that moves you is sudden and intense.
Tempestuous souls pass into a sigh –
Numerals on the ocean of Numbers and Events.
As soon as you are born you're already undone;
It is to have finished to say you have begun.
The only thing you have is a shadowy breath.
Behind the white wall, in the lawn's verdant bloom,
A grave-plot awaits with open lips until Death
Arrives with a kiss from the mouth of the tomb.
Try to do some good, go and cut a little shred
Of goodness in this night that grumbles and churns:
That will be your shroud in the earth's quiet bed.
Many have departed who will now not return
Until that hour of the sad ebbing back.
You will hear laments then. Believe. Try to live.
God reads a living man's book from front to back.
A man dies when God bends a corner of a page.
Space knows and watches. It is full in every age
Of ears under tombs, and of eyes in the black.
The dead, no longer walking, extend their feet back.
The withered leaves revolve beneath the heavens and spin.
Can't you feel the breath of the mysterious wind?'

Un jour, le morne esprit, le prophète sublime
        Qui rêvait à Patmos,
Et lisait, frémissant, sur le mur de l'abîme
        De si lugubres mots,

Dit à son aigle: «O monstre! il faut que tu m'emportes.
        Je veux vois Jéhovah.»
L'aigle obéit. Des cieux ils franchirent les portes;
        Enfin, Jean arriva;

Il vit l'endroit sans nom dont nul archange n'ose
        Traverser le milieu,
Et ce lieu redoutable était plein d'ombre, à cause
        De la grandeur de Dieu.

Éclaircie

L'Océan resplendit sous sa vaste nuée.
L'onde, de son combat sans fin exténuée,
S'assoupit, et, laissant l'écueil se reposer,
Fait de toute la rive un immense baiser.
On dirait qu'en tous lieux, en même temps, la vie
Dissout le mal, le deuil, l'hiver, la nuit, l'envie,
Et que le mort couché dit au vivant debout:
Aime! et qu'une âme obscure, épanouie en tout,
Avance doucement sa bouche vers nos lèvres.
L'être, éteignant dans l'ombre et l'extase ses fièvres,
Ouvrant ses flancs, ses seins, ses yeux, ses cœurs épars,
Dans ses pores profonds reçoit de toutes parts
La pénétration de la sève sacrée.
La grande paix d'en haut vient comme une marée.
Le brin d'herbe palpite aux fentes du pavé;
Et l'âme a chaud. On sent que le nid est couvé.
L'infini semble plein d'un frisson de feuillée.
On croit être à cette heure où la terre éveillée
Entend le bruit que fait l'ouverture du jour,

'One day the solemn spirit ...'

One day the solemn spirit, the prophet who is
         Dreaming in Patmos,
And trembling, reading all the devastating words
         Written on the wall of the abyss,

Said to his eagle: 'Monster, take me away.
         I want to see God.'
The eagle obeyed. It flew through heaven's gates.
         Finally, John arrived.

He saw the place angels rarely ever see
         Let alone pass through,
And this imposing place was shadowed, due
         To God's immensity.

Clearing

The ocean is glittering beneath its swarming throes.
The surf, worn out by its continuous war,
Grows still, as if allowing the rocks some repose,
And makes a vast kiss out of the length of the shore.
You'd almost say that life, at once and everywhere in sight,
Were dissolving evil, envy, grief, the winter, and the night;
That the dead lying round were saying to the living:
Love! – and that some soul who is dispersed in everything
Were inching her lips peacefully toward ours.
Dousing her fevers in shadows and elation,
And opening her sides, her breasts, her scattered hearts,
This being is receiving the penetration
Of sacred sap through every one of her pores.
Heaven's peace rises like the tide from ocean floors.
Blades of grass in pavement cracks quiver with unrest.
And the soul feels hot. Something's brooding on a nest.
Infinity seems filled with the rustling of leaves.
The earth is awake at this hour and one believes
It's listening to the day as it opens from above,

Le premier pas du vent, du travail, de l'amour,
De l'homme, et le verrou de la porte sonore,
Et le hennissement du blanc cheval aurore.
Le moineau d'un coup d'aile, ainsi qu'un fol esprit,
Vient taquiner le flot monstrueux qui sourit;
L'air joue avec la mouche et l'écume avec l'aigle;
Le grave laboureur fait ses sillons et règle
La page où s'écrira le poëme des blès;
Des pêcheurs sont là-bas sous un pampre attablés;
L'horizon semble un rêve éblouissant où nage
L'écaille de la mer, la plume du nuage,
Car l'Océan est l'hydre et le nuage oiseau.
Une lueur, rayon vague, part du berceau
Qu'une femme balance au seuil d'une chaumière,
Dore les champs, les fleurs, l'onde, et devient lumière
En touchant un tombeau qui dort près du clocher.
Le jour plonge au plus noir du gouffre, et va chercher
L'ombre, et la baise au front sous l'eau sombre et hagarde.
Tout est doux, calme, heureux, apaisé; Dieu regarde.

Nomen, Numen, Lumen

Quand il eut terminé, quand les soleils épars,
Éblouis, du chaos montant de toutes parts,
Se furent tous rangés à leur place profonde,
Il sentit le besoin de se nommer au monde;
Et l'être formidable et serein se leva;
Il se dressa sur l'ombre et cria: JÉHOVAH!
Et dans l'immensité ces septs lettres tombèrent;
Et ce sont, dans les cieux que nos yeux réverbèrent,
Au-dessus de nos fronts tremblants sous leur rayon,
Les septs astres géants du noir septentrion.

To the first steps of wind, and of work, and of love,
To men, to the bolts being pulled from creaking doors
And the white dawn breaking through the neighing of its horse.
A sparrow flutters like a maddened spirit as it tries
To tease the monstrous surf with the beating of a wing.
The foam plays with eagles and the air with the flies.
A worker is ploughing the fields and drawing lines
On the page on which the wheat will write its poem.
The fishermen are sitting over there by some vines.
The skyline is dreamlike, enormous, dazzling
Where the scales of the sea and the clouds' feathers swim,
For the sea is a hydra, each cloud a bird's wing.
A gleam, a faint ray that shoots from the cradle
A woman balances on a cottage threshold
Glazes the flowers, fields, and waves, then turns to gold
When striking a grave near the church it sinks behind.
The day plunges into the sea, and tries to find
Its shadow, kisses it through the surf and is gone.
Everything is quiet, mild, appeased: God looks on.

Nomen, Numen, Lumen

And when he had finished, when the sky's scattered suns,
The fires of chaos climbing from all directions,
Were arranged permanently in their rows,
He felt the need to name himself to the world below.
Then the tranquil being stood up and cried aloud:
'Jehovah,' leaning over the darkness and the clouds,
And these seven letters fell into the expanse.
They became, in skies reverberating in the air
Far above our foreheads trembling in their rays,
The seven giant stars of the northern Great Bear.

À Celle qui est restée en France

I

Mets-toi cur ton séant, lève tes yeux, dérange
Ce drap glacé qui fait des plis sur ton front d'ange,
Ouvre tes mains, et prends ce livre: il est à toi.

Ce livre où vit mon âme, espoir deuil, rêve, effroi,
Ce livre qui contient le spectre de ma vie,
Mes angoisses, mon aube, hélas! de pleurs suivie,
L'ombre et son ouragan, la rose et son pistil,
Ce livre azuré, triste, orageux, d'où sort-il?
D'où sort le blême éclair qui déchire la brume?
Depuis quatre ans, j'habite un tourbillon d'écume;
Ce livre en a jailli. Dieu dictait, j'écrivais;
Car je suis paille au vent: Va! dit l'esprit. Je vais.
Et, quand j'eus terminé ces pages, quand ce livre
Se mit à palpiter, à respirer, à vivre,
Une église des champs que le lierre verdit,
Dont la tour sonne l'heure à mon néant, m'a dit:
Ton cantique est fini; donne-le-moi, poëte.
Je le réclame, a dit la forêt inquiète;
Et le doux pré fleuri m'a dit: Donne-le-moi.
La mer, en le voyant frémir, m'a dit: Pourquoi
Ne pas me le jeter, puisque c'est une voile!
C'est à moi qu'appartient cet hymne, a dit l'étoile.
Donne-le-nous, songeur, ont crié les grands vents.
Et les oiseaux m'ont dit: Vas-tu pas aux vivants
Offrir ce livre, éclos si loin de leurs querelles?
Laisse-nous l'emporter dans nos nids sur nos ailes!
Mais le vent n'aura point mon livre, ô cieux profonds!
Ni la sauvage mer, livrée aux noirs typhons,
Ouvrant et referment ses flots, âpres embûches;
Ni la verte forêt qu'emplit un bruit de ruches;
Ni l'église où le temps fait tourner son compas;
Le pré ne l'aura pas, l'astre ne l'aura pas;
L'oiseau ne l'aura pas; qu'il soit aigle ou colombe,
Les nids ne l'auront pas; je le donne à la tombe.

To the One Who Stayed Behind in France

I

Sit up in your bed and raise your eyes; throw aside
That cold sheet wrinkling your angelic face.
Stretch out your hands and take this book: it is yours.

This book where my soul lives, its hopes, dreams, and wars,
This book containing the spectre of my years,
My struggles, my dawns, alas! followed by my tears,
The shadow and its storm, the rose, its pistil, the air,
This book – tempestuous and azured – comes from where?
Where does the lightning bolt that cuts through fog come from?
I have lived four years in an eddy of foam.
This book came from it. God spoke to me, I wrote.
For I'm a wind-blown straw. God said, 'Go!' And I went.
And when I had finished these pages, when this book
Began to palpitate, and to breathe, live, and look,
A country church whose walls the ivy settled in
And whose clock tolled the hour of my oblivion
Said to me, 'Your song has ended, give it to me.'
'We have claims on it,' said the forest's anxious trees,
And the meadow: 'Why not give it to me instead?'
Watching it shake, the ocean turned to me and said:
'Why don't you throw it to me, since it's a sail!'
And the stars in heaven said, 'This hymn belongs to us.'
'Oh dreamer, why not us?' the four winds cried and wailed.
And the birds questioned me: 'Why *are* you giving this
To men, when it hatched far from their quarrellings?
Allow us to bring it to our nests on our wings!'
But the wind will not receive this book, nor the breeze,
Nor the savage and hurricane-buffeted seas
That open and close their waves like hunting traps;
Nor the forests humming with the murmur of bees;
Nor the church where clock hands divide and collapse.
It isn't for the meadows; and it's not for the stars;
It isn't for the birds – eagles, doves, no matter whom –
And it isn't for their nests: I give it to the tomb.

Autrefois, quand septembre en larmes revenait,
Je partais, je quittais tout ce qui me connaît,
Je m'évadais; Paris s'effaçait; rien, personne!
J'allais, je n'étais plus qu'une ombre qui frissonne,
Je fuyais, seul, sans voirs, sans penser, sans parler,
Sachant bien que j'irais où je devais aller;
Hélas! je n'aurais pu même dire: Je souffre!
Et, comme subissant l'attraction d'un gouffre,
Que le chemin fût beau, pluvieux, froid, mauvais,
J'ignorais, je marchais devant moi, j'arrivais.
O souvenirs! ô forme horrible des collines!
Et, pendant que la mère et la sœur, orphelines,
Pleuraient dans la maison, je cherchais le lieu noir
Avec l'avidité morne du désespoir;
Puis j'allais au champ triste à côté de l'église;
Tête nue, à pas lents, les cheveux dans la bise,
L'œil aux cieux, j'approchais; l'accablement soutient;
Les arbres murmuraient: C'est le père qui vient!
Les ronces écartaient leurs branches desséchées;
Je marchais à travers les humbles croix penchées,
Disant je ne sais quels doux et funèbres mots;
Et je m'agenouillais au milieu des rameaux
Sur la pierre qu'on voit blanche dans la verdure.
Pourquoi donc dormais-tu d'une façon si dure
Que tu n'entendais pas lorsque je t'appelais?

Et les pêcheurs passaient en traînant leur filets,
Et disaient: Qu'est-ce donc que cet homme qui songe?
Et le jour, et le soir, et l'ombre qui s'allonge,
Et Vénus, qui pour moi jadis étincela,
Tout avait disparu que j'étais encor là.
J'étais là, suppliant celui qui nous exauce;
J'adorais, je laissais tomber sur cette fosse,
Hélas! où j'avais vu s'évanouir mes cieux,
Tout mon cœur goutte à goutte en pleurs silencieux;
J'effeuillais de la sauge et de la clématite;
Je me la rappelais quand elle était petite,
Quand elle m'apportait des lys et des jasmins,
Ou quand elle prenait ma prume dans ses mains,
Gaie, et riant d'avoir de l'encre à ses doigts roses;
Je respirais les fleurs sur cette cendre écloses,

Before, when September would return with its tears.
I'd set out, leaving everything behind that knew me.
I'd escape; Paris faded; there was nothing and no one.
I would go. No more than a quivering shadow,
I fled, without seeing, thinking, speaking, alone,
Knowing I was travelling to where I had to go.
I couldn't even say 'I am suffering from this!'
As if attracted to the depths of an abyss,
I didn't even know if it was rainy or clear,
Or cold. I walked before myself. Soon I drew near.
Oh memories! Sinister contours of the hills!
And while her mother and her sister were at prayer
Or crying at home, I would look for that place
With all the gloomy eagerness that comes from despair.
I would go to that field that was nearby the church,
Hat in hand, with slow steps, hair blowing in the breeze.
I'd approach looking up, grief-supported. The trees
Would murmur around me: 'It's her father!' The mosses
Looked up; and the brambles parted their branches.
I walked among the humble and the bent-over crosses
Repeating I don't know what sweet or mournful words.
And I would kneel down amid branches without birds
On stones shining white among the dark greenery.
Why are you sleeping such a deep and endless sleep
That you don't seem to hear me when I call your name?

The fishermen would drag their nets past, whispering:
'Who or what is that dreamy man?' And everything –
The day, the evening, lengthening shadows, the sea,
And Venus, who always used to sparkle for me –
Would vanish the moment when I arrived there.
I was there, imploring the one who hears our prayers;
And worshipping, allowing my entire heart
To fall, drop by drop, in silent, salty tears
On the grave where I saw my heaven disappear!
I stripped bits of leaves off the clematis and sage,
I remembered when she, at a much younger age,
Would bring bouquets of lilies and jasmines to me,
When she'd take my pen in her little hands with glee,
And laugh at the ink that would spill on her nails.
I breathed in the flowers that grew out of that moss,

Je fixais mon regard sur ces froids gazons verts,
Et par moments, ô Dieu, je voyais, à travers
La pierre du tombeau, comme une fleur d'âme!

Oui, jadis, quand cette heure en deuil qui me réclame
Tintait dans le ciel triste et dans mon cœur saignant,
Rien ne me retenait, et j'allais; maintenant,
Hélas…! – O fleuve! ô bois! vallons dont je fus l'hôte,
Elle sait, n'est-ce pas? que ce n'est pas ma faute
Si, depuis ces quatres ans, pauvre cœur sans flambeau,
Je ne suis pas allé prier sur son tombeau!

III

Ainsi, ce noir chemin que je faisais, ce marbre
Que je contemplais, pâle, adossé contre un arbre,
Ce tombeau sur lequel mes pieds pouvaient marcher,
La nuit, que je voyais lentement approcher,
Ces ifs, ce crépuscule avec ce cimetière,
Ces sanglots, qui du moins tombaient sur cette pierre,
O mon Dieu, tout cela, c'était donc du bonheur!

Dis, qu'as-tu fait pendant tout ce temps-là? – Seigneur,
Qu'a-t-elle fait? – Vois-tu la vie en vos demeures?
À quelle horloge d'ombre as-tu compté les heures?
As-tu sans bruit parfois poussé l'autre endormi?
Et t'es-tu, m'attendant, réveillée à demi?
T'es-tu, pâle, accoudée à l'obscure fenêtre
De l'infini, cherchant dans l'ombre à reconnaître
Un passant, à travers le noir cercueil mal joint,
Attentive, écoutant si tu n'entendais point
Quelqu'un marcher vers toi dans l'éternité sombre?
Et t'es-tu recouchée ainsi qu'un mât qui sombre,
En disant: Qu'est-ce donc? mon père ne vient pas!
Avez-vous tous les deux parlé de moi tout bas?

Que de fois j'ai choisi, tout mouillés de rosée,
Des lys dans mon jardin, des lys dans ma pensée!
Que de fois j'ai cueilli de l'aubépine en fleur!
Que de fois j'ai, là-bas, cherché la tour d'Harfleur,
Murmurant: C'est demain que je pars! et, stupide,
Je calculais le vent et la voile rapide,

I fixed my regard on those cold, verdant lawns,
And at times, oh my God, I would see there, across
The tombstone, a light, like the soul's, flashing by!

Yes before, when this grief-filled hour and this day
Would call me, tolling in my heart and the sky,
Nothing held me back; I would go; but today,
Alas! – oh river, forests, valleys where I'd halt –
She knows, doesn't she? that it hasn't been my fault
If, these four years that have passed away so soon,
I haven't gone and prayed at the foot of her tomb!

III

And so that sombre road I would take, and that stone
I would go and contemplate, leaning on a tree,
That marble on top of which I could walk alone,
The evening I would watch as it drew nearer me,
Those yews, those shadows in the graveyard at day's end,
That tombstone my tears could at least trickle toward,
All of that, oh my God, that was happiness then?

What have you been doing all this time? Tell me. – Lord,
What has she been doing? – In your life do you see ours?
With what shadow-clock have you been counting the hours?
Have you nudged that soul sleeping near you now and then?
Have you, waiting up for me, half opened your eyes?
Have you propped your elbows up again and again
At infinity's pane, and tried to recognize
Someone who was passing by your ill-jointed coffin?
Have you been looking out and listening often
For souls walking near in that dark eternity?
Have you, like a foundering ship, sunk back again
And asked: 'What has happened? Will he *ever* come then?'
Have both of you been talking down there about me?

How often I have picked the lilies I could find
In my garden – the dew-drenched lilies of my mind!
How often I've collected hawthorn blooms for her!
How often I've looked for the tower of Harfleur
Murmuring, 'Tomorrow I will set out to sea!'
I'd calculate the wind and the ship's velocity –

Puis ma main s'ouvrait triste, et je disais: Tout fuit!
Et le bouquet tombait, sinistre, dans la nuit!
Oh! que de fois, sentant qu'elle devait m'attendre,
J'ai pris ce que j'avais dans le cœur de plus tendre
Pour en charger quelqu'un qui passerait par là!

Lazare ouvrit les yeux quand Jésus l'appela;
Quand je lui parle, hélas! pourquoi les ferme-t-elle?
Où serait donc le mal quand de l'ombre mortelle
L'amour violerait deux fois le noir secret,
Et quand, ce qu'un dieu fit, un père le ferait?

IV

Que ce livre, du moins, obscur message, arrive,
Murmure, à ce silence, et, flot, à cette rive!
Qu'il y tombe, sanglot, soupir, larme d'amour!
Qu'il entre en ce sépulcre où sont entrés un jour
Le baiser, la jeunesse, et l'aube, et la rosée,
Et le rire adoré de la fraîche épousée,
Et la joie, et mon cœur, qui n'est pas ressorti!
Qu'il soit le cri d'espoir qui n'a jamai menti,
Le chant de deuil, la voix du pâle adieu qui pleure,
Le rêve dont on sent l'aile qui nous effleure!
Qu'elle dise: Quelqu'un est là; j'entends du bruit!
Qu'il soit comme le pas de mon âme en sa nuit!

Ce livre, légion tournoyante et sans nombre
D'oiseaux blancs dans l'aurore et d'oiseaux noirs dans l'ombre,
Ce vol de souvenirs fuyants à l'horizon,
Cet essaim que je lâche au seuil de ma prison,
Je vous le confie, air, souffles, nuée, espace!
Que ce fauve océan qui me parle à voix basse,
Lui soit clément, l'épargne et le laisse passer!
Et que le vent ait soin de n'en rien disperser,
Et jusqu'au froid caveau fidèlement apporte
Ce don mystérieux de l'absent à la morte!

O Dieu! puisqu'en effet, dans ces sombres feuillets,
Dans ces strophes qu'au fond de vos cieux je cueillais,
Dans ces chants murmurés comme un épithalame
Pendant que vour tourniez les pages de mon âme,

Then my hand would open and I'd say, 'Nothing lasts!'
And the bouquet fell, sinister, out of my grasp.
How often, feeling she was waiting in despair,
I'd gather up my tenderest feelings to ask
Someone who was going that way to take them there!

When Jesus called Lazarus he opened his eyes.
When I call her, alas! why does *she* keep hers closed?
What harm would there be if love were to break through
The dark enigma of life a second time,
If, what a god has done, a father were to do?

IV

May this book at least arrive where I used to go before –
A murmur in that silence, a wave upon that shore!
May it fall there – with its sobs, and its sighs and loving tears –
May it enter the tomb where that day long ago
Youth and kisses entered, and the dew, and dawn's glow,
And the laughter of the new bride adored by her friends,
And joy, and her father's heart that hasn't left it since!
May it be the clarion of hope that doesn't lie,
The song of grief, the voice of a tearful good-bye,
The dream whose fearful wing one senses slice the air!
May she say: 'Wait, I hear a noise! Someone's there!'
And may it be the steps of my soul in her night!

This book, this wheeling and gigantic flight
Of white birds in the morning and of black birds at night,
This flock of memories at the edge of my vision,
This swarm I release at the door of my prison –
I entrust it – air, breaths, clouds and space – all to you!
And may the savage ocean whose voice always grumbles,
Be merciful to it and allow it to pass through!
May the wind take care not to scatter things at least,
And faithfully carry this mysterious gift
Sent from the absent person to the deceased!

My God! Because, among these leaflets bound as one,
In these strophes gathered in the depths of your sky,
In these lines sung like an epithalamion
While you turned the pages of my soul with a sigh;

Puisque j'ai, dans ce livre, enregistré mes jours,
Mes maux, mes deuils, mes cris dans les problèmes sourds,
Mes amours, mes travaux, ma vie heure par heure;
Puisque vous ne voulez pas encor que je meure,
Et qu'il faut bien pourtant que j'aille lui parler;
Puisque je sens le vent de l'infini souffler
Sur ce livre qu'emplit l'orage et le mystère;
Puisque j'ai versé là toutes vos ombres, terre,
Humanité, douleur, dont je suis le passant;
Puisque de mon esprit, de mon cœur, de mon sang,
J'ai fait l'âcre parfum de ces versets funèbres,
Va-t-en, livre, à travers les ténèbres!
Fuis vers la brume où tout à pas lents est conduit!
Oui, qu'il vole à la fosse, à la tombe, à la nuit,
Comme une feuille d'arbre ou comme une âme d'homme!
Qu'il roule au gouffre où va tout ce que la voix nomme!
Qu'il tombe au plus profond du sépulcre hagard,
À côté d'elle, ô mort! et que là, le regard,
Près de l'ange qui dort, lumineux et sublime,
Le voie épanoui, sombre fleur de l'abîme!

V

O doux commencements d'azur qui me trompiez,
O bonheurs! je vous ai durement expiés;
J'ai le droit aujourd'hui d'être, quand la nuit tombe,
Un de ceux qui se font écouter de la tombe,
Et qui font, en parlant aux morts blêmes et seuls,
Remuer lentement les plis noirs des linceuls,
Et dont la parole, âpre ou tendre, émeut les pierres,
Les grains dans les sillons, les ombres dans les bières,
La vague et la nuée, et devient une voix
De la nature, ainsi que la rumeur des bois.
Car voilà, n'est-ce pas, tombeaux? bien des années
Que je marche au milieu des croix infortunées,
Échevelé parmi les ifs et les cyprès,
L'âme au bord de la nuit, et m'approchant tout près;
Et que je vais, courbé sur le cercueil austère,
Questionnant le plomb, les clous, le ver de terre
Qui pour moi sort des yeux de la tête de mort,
Le squelette qui rit, le squelette qui mord,
Les mains aux doigts noueux, les crânes, les poussières,
Et les os des genoux qui savent des prières!

Because, in this book, I have recorded my days,
My loves and my projects, every hour gone by,
My ills, my sorrows, fruitless questions we all raise;
Because, up to now, you have not wished me to die
And yet I nevertheless need to speak with her;
Because I feel the breath of infinity stir
Over this volume of storms and mystery;
Because I have poured all of your humanity –
Earth, pain, and shadows – I have witnessed into it;
Because I've distilled the bitter perfume of these lines
With all of my heart and my blood and my mind –
Oh book, traverse the darkness and find the infinite!
Fly toward the smoke where things are lead by slow steps!
May this book fly away to the night's lowest depths
Like the leaf of a tree – or the soul of a man!
May it roll where whatever is named spends its days!
May it fall to the bottom of the grave itself and land
Next to her, oh Death! and down there, may the Gaze,
Beside the sleeping angel, sublime and luminous,
Look at her astonished, sombre bloom in that abyss!

V

Oh sweet beginnings of the heavens' lying blue!
Oh happinesses! I have expiated you
Painfully. Today I have the right, when evening falls,
To be one of those whom the tomb will listen to,
And who, when they talk to the pale and lonely dead,
Make the folds of winding sheets rustle in their beds,
And whose speech, hard or tender, somehow moves the stones,
The dust in the whirlwinds, the shadows in the tombs,
The waves and the clouds – and becomes another voice
Of nature, the breath of the wind, a forest noise.
For it's been – am I not right, tomb? – many years now
Since I have walked in the middle of the crowd
Of crosses, cypresses, and yew trees on that lawn,
And – bending over the coffin, head bowed,
Dishevelled, drawing near, and anxious – since I've gone
To question everything: the nails, the wood, the lead,
The worm crawling out of the sockets of Death's head,
Skeletons who laugh, skeletons who grind their teeth,
The knotty-fingered hands and the dusty skulls there,
And the bones of the knees so familiar with prayer!

Hélas! j'ai fouillé tout. J'ai voulu voir le fond.
Pourquoi le mal en nous avec le bien se fond,
J'ai voulu savoir. J'ai dit: Que faut-il croire?
J'ai creusé la lumière, et l'aurore, et la gloire,
L'enfant joyeux, la vierge et sa chaste frayeur,
Et l'amour, et la vie, et l'âme – fossoyeur.

Qu'ai-je appris? J'ai, pensif, tout saisi sans rien prendre;
J'ai vu beaucoup de nuit et fait beaucoup de cendre.
Qui sommes-nous? que veut dire ce mot: Toujours?
J'ai enseveli, songes, espoirs, amours,
Dans la fosse que j'ai creusée en ma poitrine.
Qui donc a la science? où donc est la doctrine?
Oh! que ne suis-je encor le rêveur d'autrefois,
Qu s'égarait dans l'herbe, et les prés, et les bois,
Qui marchait souriant, le soir, quand le ciel brille,
Tenant la main petite et blanche de sa fille,
Et qui, joyeux, laissant luire le firmament,
Laissant l'enfant parler, se sentait lentement
Emplir de cet azur et de cette innocence!

Entre Dieu qui flamboie et l'ange qui l'encense,
J'ai vécu, j'ai lutté, sans crainte, sans remord.
Puis ma porte soudain s'ouvrit devant la mort,
Cette visite brusque et terrible de l'ombre.
Tu passes en laissant le vide et le décombre,
O spectre! tu saisis mon ange et tu frappas.
Un tombeau fut dès lors le but de tous mes pas.

VI

Je ne puis plus reprendre aujourd'hui dans la plaine
Mon sentier d'autrefois qui descend vers la Seine;
Je ne puis plus aller où j'allais; je ne puis,
Pareil à la laveuse assise au bord du puits,
Que m'accouder au mur de l'éternel abîme;
Paris m'est éclipsé par l'énorme Solime;
La haute Notre-Dame à présent, qui me luit,
C'est l'ombre ayant deux tours, le silence et la nuit,
Et laissant des clartés trouer ses fatals voiles;
Et je vois sur mon front un panthéon d'étoiles;
Si j'appelle Rouen, Villequier, Caudebec,

I have searched everything! I wished to see the core.
I questioned my beliefs and wanted to know more.
To know why, when good is in us, evil is near,
I tunnelled through the dawn and glory, light and waves,
The bliss of the infant and the virgin's chaste fear,
Love, life, the soul itself – I tunnelled and dug graves.

What have I learned? I've seized it all and grasped nothing.
I've seen a lot of night and I've made a lot of dust.
Who are we? What does 'forever' mean? And 'must'?
I have buried everything – my dreams, hopes, and loves –
Inside of the grave I have carved out of my chest.
Who has knowledge then? Where can doctrine be found?
I am no longer the old dreamer who stood
Or wandered in the grass, the meadows, and the woods,
And walked, smiling, when stars shone on the water,
Holding the white, tiny hand of his daughter,
And who, rejoicing, letting all the firmament ignite,
And letting the child talk, would gradually sense
Himself filling up with that sky and innocence!

I lived without remorse or fear and drew each breath
Between the God who blazes and the angel's spark.
Suddenly my door opened up in front of Death –
A brusque and terrifying visit from the dark.
You pass by and leave behind debris and a void,
Oh shade! You seized and struck my angel from your depths.
Since then a tomb has been the goal of all my steps.

VI

And now I can no longer walk that path again,
My trail of former times leading down to the Seine;
I can't go where I used to; I can't very well –
Like the washerwoman at the edge of the well –
Do anything but sit and stare at the abyss.
Jerusalem has put my Paris in eclipse.
The tall Notre-Dame which at one time was my light
Is shadowed with two towers, silence and the night
Letting shafts of brightness pierce its fatal veils now.
I can see a pantheon of stars on my brow.
If I call out *Rouen, Villequier,* and *Caudebec,*

Toute l'ombre me crie: Horeb, Cédron, Balbeck!
Et, si je pars, m'arrête à la première lieue,
Et me dit: Tourne-toi vers l'immensité bleue!
Et me dit: Les chemins où tu marchais sont clos.
Penche-toi sur les nuits, sur les vents, sur les flots!
À quoi penses-tu donc? que fais-tu, solitaire?
Crois-tu donc sous tes pieds avoir encor la terre?
Où vas-tu de la sorte et machinalement?
O songeur! penche-toi sur l'être et l'élément!
Écoute la rumeur des âmes dans les ondes!
Contemple, s'il te faut de la cendre, les mondes;
Cherche au moins la poussière immense, si tu veux
Mêler de la poussière à tes sombres cheveux,
Et regarde, en dehors de ton propre martyre,
Le grand néant, si c'est le néant qui t'attire!
Sois tout à ces soleils où tu remonteras!
Laisse là ton vil coin de terre. Tends les bras,
O proscrit de l'azur, vers les astres patries!
Revois-y refleurir tes aurores flétries;
Deviens le grand œil fixe ouvert sur le grand tout.
Penche-toi sur l'énigme où l'être se dissout,
Sur tout ce qui naît, vit, marche, s'éteint, succombe,
Sur tout le genre humain et sur toute la tombe!

Main mon cœur toujours saigne et du même côté.
C'est en vain que les cieux, les nuits, l'éternité,
Veulent distraire un âme et calmer un atome.
Tout l'éblouissement des lumières du dôme
M'ôte-t-il une larme? Ah! l'étendue a beau
Me parler, me montrer l'universel tombeau,
Les soirs sereins, les bois rêveurs, la lune amie;
J'écoute, et je reviens à la douce endormie.

VII

Des fleurs! oh! si j'avais des fleurs! si je pouvais
Aller semer des lys sur ces deux froids chevets!
Si je pouvais couvrir de fleurs mon ange pâle!
Les fleurs sont l'or, l'azur, l'émeraude, l'opale!
Le cercueil au milieu des fleurs veut se coucher;
Les fleurs aiment la mort, et Dieu les fait toucher
Par leur racine aux os, par leur parfum aux âmes!

The shadows shout back *Horeb, Cedron,* and *Balbeck!*
If I go out, I stop at the very first place
And say, 'Look up at the immensity of space!'
Or else, 'All the roads you are walking on are closed!
Lean your head over the nights, winds, and waves!
What are you thinking then – and doing, lonely one?
So you think the earth is under your feet, and the sun
Above? Where *do* you go and gaze without seeing?
Oh dreamer, lean over the elements of being!
Listen to the whispering souls in sea-swirls!
If ash is what you need, contemplate the worlds.
At least search out the massive spheres if you care
To mix dust into your dishevelled head of hair,
And look about, away from your own martyrdom,
At nothingness, if you are attracted by that!
Give yourself and climb to the sun from which you've come!
Leave you vile corner of this earth. Break your bars,
Azure's exile, stretch your arms out toward the stars!
Watch your withered dawns bloom again there, and become
The mammoth eye that opens on the universe.
Lean toward the enigma where all beings disperse,
And all things are born, live and walk, fade, succumb –
Lean toward the entire human race and its tomb!'

But my heart is still bleeding hard from the same side.
It's in vain that the night, eternity, the sky,
Want to calm an atom or distract a man's soul.
All the dazzling light of the firmament's dome,
Does it dry up one tear? The expanse of the whole
Speaks to me and shows me the universal tomb,
The peaceful nights, the woods, the pale friend of the sun:
I listen, then return to my sweet sleeping one.

VII

Oh flowers! Oh, if I had flowers and could go
And plant some lilies on those frozen beds below,
If I could place flowers over my angel's head,
Flowers coloured gold, azure, opal, emerald!
Coffins wish to sleep among the flowers, their friends.
Flowers love death, and God himself makes them touch
Bones through their roots, and the soul through their scents!

Puisque je ne le puis, aux lieux que nous aimâmes,
Puisque Dieu ne veut pas nous laisser revenir,
Puisqu'il nous fait lâcher ce qu'on croyait tenir,
Puisque le froid destin, dans ma geôle profonde,
Sur la première porte en scelle une seconde,
Et, sur le père triste et sur l'enfant qui dort,
Ferme l'exil après avoir fermé la mort,
Puisqu'il est impossible à présent que je jette
Même un brin de bruyère à sa fosse muette,
C'est bien le moins qu'elle ait mon âme, n'est-ce pas?
O vent noir dont j'entends sur mon plafond le pas!
Tempête, hiver, qui bats ma vitre de ta grêle!
Mers, nuits! et je l'ai mise en ce livre pour elle!

Prends ce livre; et dis-toi: Ceci vient du vivant
Que nous avons laissé derrière nous, rêvant.
Prends. Et quoique de loin, reconnais ma voix, âme!
Oh! ta cendre est le lit de mon reste de flamme;
Ta tombe est mon espoir, ma charité, ma foi;
Ton linceul toujours flotte entre la vie et moi.
Prends ce livre, et fais-en sortir un divin psaume!
Qu'entre tes vagues mains il devienne fantôme!
Qu'il blanchisse, pareil à l'aube qui pâlit,
À mesure que l'œil de mon ange le lit,
Et qu'il s'évanouisse, et flotte, et disparaisse,
Ainsi qu'un âtre obscur qu'un souffle errant caresse,
Ainsi qu'une lueur qu'on voit passer le soir,
Ainsi qu'un tourbillon de feu de l'encensoir,
Et que, sous ton regard éblouissant et sombre,
Chaque page s'en aille en étoiles dans l'ombre!

VIII

Oh! quoi que nous faissions et quoi que nous disions,
Soit que notre âme plane au vent des visions,
Soit qu'elle se cramponne à l'argile natale,
Toujours nous arrivons à ta grotte fatale,
Gethsémani, qu'éclaire une vague lueur!
O rocher de l'étrange et funèbre sueur!
Cave où l'esprit combat le destin! ouverture
Sur les profonds effrois de la sombre nature!
Antre d'où le lion sort rêveur, en voyant

Because I can't do this, because I am impelled
To stay away, and God doesn't wish us to return,
Because we must let go of what we once believed we held,
Because fate itself seals a second door upon
The first door of my prison buried in these depths,
And, on the saddened father and the sleeping child,
Closes Exile's door, having closed already Death's,
Because, at this moment, it's impossible to throw
Even a slender stalk of heather on her tomb,
My soul is certainly the least she should have, no?
Black wind whose step I hear above, storms that blur
Or pummel with hailstones my window like a drum,
Seas, nights – and I have put it in this book for her!

Take this book; and say to yourself: 'This must have come
From someone whom we left behind us in a dream.'
Take it. And no matter how distant I may seem,
Recognize my voice. For your ashes hold my flame;
Your tomb is my faith and my hope, my charity;
Your shroud is always floating between life and me.
Take this book and make a holy psalm of your own
So this becomes a shadow in your shadowy hands!
May it turn white the way the morning pales and clears
For as long as it holds my angel's interest,
And may it float up, then fade away and disappear
Like a hearth which a wandering breath will caress,
Like a light one sees pass at night and leave a trace,
Like a brazier flame a sudden gust of wind blows back –
And may each page, under your dark and dazzling gaze
Fly away, sparkling with stars, into the black!

VIII

Whatever we do and whatever we say,
Whether our soul is soaring over vision's sea,
Whether it is clinging fast to its native clay,
We always arrive at your cave, Gethsemane,
Illuminated by a vague and eerie flare!
Oh rock of strange funereal sweat! Cavern where
The spirit battles destiny itself! Opening
Onto dark nature's most profound anxieties,
Cave which the lion exits dreaming when he sees

Quelqu'un de plus sinistre et de plus effrayant,
La douleur, entrer, pâle, amère, échevelée!
O chute! asile! ô seuil de la trouble vallée
D'où nous apercevons nos ans fuyants et courts,
Nos propres pas marqués dans la fanges des jours,
L'échelle où le mal pèse et monte, spectre louche,
L'âpre frémissement de la palme farouche,
Les degrés noirs tirant en bas les blancs degrés,
Et les frissons aux front des anges effarés!

Toujours nous arrivons à cette solitude,
Et, là, nous nous taisons, sentant la plénitude!

Paix à l'Ombre! Dormez! dormez! dormez! dormez!
Êtres, groupes confus lentement transformés!
Dormez, les champs! dormez, les fleurs! dormez, les tombes!
Toits, murs, seuils des maisons, pierres des catacombes,
Feuilles au fond des bois, plumes au fond des nids,
Dormez! dormez, brins d'herbe, et dormez, infinis!
Calmez-vous, forêt, chêne, érable, frêne, yeuse!
Silence sur la grande horreur religieuse,
Sur l'Océan qui lutte et qui ronge son mors,
Et sur l'apaisement insondable des morts!
Paix à l'obscurité muette et redoutée!
Paix au doute effrayant, à l'immense ombre athée,
À toi, nature, cercle et centre, âme et milieu,
Fourmillement de tout, solitude de Dieu!
O générations aux brumeuses haleines,
Reposez-vous! pas noirs qui marchez dans les plaines!
Dormez, vous qui saignez; dormez, vous qui pleurez!
Douleurs, douleurs, douleurs, fermez vos yeux sacrés!
Tout est religion et rien n'est imposture.
Que sur toute existence et toute créature,
Vivant du souffle humain ou du souffle animal,
Debout au seuil du bien, croulante au bord du mal,
Tendre ou farouche, immonde ou splendide, humble ou grande,
La vaste paix des cieux de toutes parts descende!
Que les enfers dormants rêvent les paradis!
Assoupissez-vous, flots, mers, vents, âmes, tandis
Qu'assis sur la montagne en présence de l'Être,
Précipice où l'on voit pêle-mêle apparaître
Les créations, l'astre et l'homme, les essieux
De ces chars de soleil que nous nommons les cieux,

Someone more sinister and more frightening –
Sorrow – enter, bitter and dishevelled and pale!
Asylum, pit, valley next to which others pale,
From where we can perceive our short and fleeing years,
The footsteps we print in the days' dirt and mire,
The wild palm quivering with anger and with fear,
The ladder on which evil tests its weight, and climbs higher,
The stairway's black steps pulling down all the white,
The trembling foreheads of angels gripped in fright!

We always come alone to the edge of this pit,
And fall silent, sensing the abundance in it.

Peace to the Spirit! Go to sleep now! Go to sleep!
Confused groups and beings that are slowly transformed!
Go to sleep, all you fields! Go to sleep flowers, homes,
And roofs, walls, thresholds, stones and graves, catacombs!
Feathers in birds' nests and leaves that fall from trees,
Go to sleep! Sleep, grass! Go to sleep, infinities!
Calm yourselves oak, holly, ash, and maple leaf!
Silence on the horror of religious belief,
On the ocean that struggles and champs at the bit,
On the calm of the dead, fathomless and infinite!
Peace to the speechless, dreaded dark the nights exude!
Peace to fearful doubt and atheism's shadow,
To you, nature, circle and centre, soul and marrow,
Teeming swarm of everything and God's solitude!
Repose, generations whose breaths will never cease!
Oh black steps who walk across the fields, rest in peace!
Go to sleep, you who bleed; go to sleep, you who cry!
Oh sorrows, sorrows, sorrows, close and rest your holy eyes!
Everything is sacred and nothing is deceit.
May heaven's vast peace – on the creatures nature bore
And who, whether animal or human, live and breathe
Upright on Good's threshold, tottering on Evil's shore,
Tender or ferocious, giant, splendid; humble, great –
Descend from every corner of the sky and the sun!
May the sleeping hells dream of paradises now!
May seas, winds, and souls drift asleep, while the one
Seated in the presence of Being on a height –
A precipice from which, pell-mell, come into sight
Creatures, planets, men, and the axles of those cars
Of suns we like to call the heavens and the stars,

Les globes, fruits, vermeils des divines ramées,
Les comètes d'argent dans un champ noir semées,
Larmes blanches du drap mortuaire des nuits,
Les chaos, les hivers, ces lugubres ennuis,
Pâle, ivre d'ignorance, ébloui de ténèbres,
Voyant dans l'infini s'écrire des algèbres,
Le contemplateur, triste et meurtri, mais serein,
Mesure le problème aux murailles d'airain,
Cherche à distinguer l'aube à travers les prodiges,
Se penche, frémissant, au puits des grands vertiges,
Suit de l'œil des blancheurs qui passent, alcyons,
Et regarde, pensif, s'étoiler de rayons,
De clartés, de lueurs, vaguement enflammés,
Le gouffre monstrueux plein d'énormes fumées.

The globes, vermilion fruit hanging on divine boughs,
The silver comets sown in a black field like seeds,
The white tears of night's spreading mortuary shroud,
The chaoses, the winters, those lugubrious ennuis –
Pale and drunk with ignorance, dazzled by the scene,
Staring at the numbers traced upon infinities,
The contemplator, bruised and saddened, but serene,
Measures the problem on walls made out of brass,
Follows the halcyons and whitish flares that pass,
Distinguishes the dawn across the precipice,
Leans, shivering, above the well of dizziness,
And watches pensively – as it fills up with stars,
Brilliant flashes, lights enflamed with different hues –
The monstrous abyss out of which the darkness spews.

From *Les Chansons des rues et des bois* (1865)

Saison des semailles. Le soir.

C'est le moment crépusculaire.
J'admire, assis sous un portail,
Ce reste de jour dont s'éclaire
La dernière heure du travail.

Dans les terres, de nuit baignées,
Je contemple, ému, les haillons
D'un vieillard qui jette à poignées
La moisson future aux sillons.

Sa haute silhouette noire
Domine les profonds labours.
On sent à quel point il doit croire
À la fuite utile des jours.

Il marche dans la plaine immense,
Va, vient, lance la graine au loin,
Rouvre sa main, et recommence,
Et je médite, obscur témoin,

Pendant que, déployant ses voiles,
L'ombre, où se mêle une rumeur,
Semble élargir jusqu'aux étoiles
Le geste auguste du semeur.

«Les enfants lisent, troupe blonde ...»

Les enfants lisent, troupe blonde;
Ils épellent, je les entends;
Et le maître d'école gronde
Dans la lumière du printemps.

From *Songs of the Streets and the Woods*

Sowing Season. Evening.

It is the twilight hour now.
I sit beneath a gate and admire
The day's remains the final hour
Of fieldwork seems to set on fire.

Across the fields half bathed with night
I contemplate the tattered form
Of an old man throwing fistfuls of
The future crop into an earth still warm.

His immense black silhouette
Dominates the work and the sun's last rays.
One senses how much he must believe
In the useful passing of the days.

Walking in this expansive plain,
He comes and goes, flings the grain out straight,
Opens his hand and starts again,
While I, his witness, meditate

In shadows settling ever lower
Into which some vague sounds blend,
Making the star-filled night enlarge
The solemn gestures of the sower.

'The troop of children read and spell ...'

The troop of children read and spell.
I am listening to them outside.
The schoolmaster keeps scolding them
In the clear springtime light.

J'aperçois l'école entr'ouverte;
Et je rôde au bord des marais;
Toute la grande saison verte
Frisonne au loin dans les forêts,

Tout rit, tout chante; c'est la fête
De l'infini que nous voyons;
La beauté des fleurs semble faite
Avec la candeur des rayons.

J'épelle aussi, moi; je me penche
Sur l'immense livre joyeux.
O champs, quel vers que la pervenche!
Quelle strophe que l'aigle, ô cieux!

Mais, mystère! rien n'est sans tache.
Rien! – Qui peut dire par quels nœuds
La végétation rattache
Le lys chaste au chardon hargneux?

Tandis que là-bas siffle un merle,
La sarcelle, des roseaux plats
Sort, ayant au bec une perle;
Cette perle agonise, hélas!

C'est le poisson qui, tout à l'heure,
Poursuivait l'aragne, courant
Sur sa bleue et vague demeure,
Sinistre monde transparent.

Un coup de fusil dans la haie,
Abois d'un chien; c'est le chasseur.
Et pensif, je sens une plaie
Parmi toute cette douceur.

Et, sous l'herbe pressant la fange,
Triste passant de ce beau lieu,
Je songe au mal, énigme étrange,
Faute d'orthographe de Dieu.

Roaming along the marsh's shore,
I can see the open school.
All of the verdant season is
Shivering into the forest's core.

Everything laughs: infinity
Celebrates right before our eyes.
The flowers' beauty seems composed
Of the sun's brightness, and the sky's.

I, too, am spelling now. I lean
Over this world, this poem in disguise.
Fields, what a line the periwinkle is!
What a stanza the eagle is, oh Skies!

But nothing is without a stain.
Nothing! – Who can say through what ties
The vegetation binds again
The spiteful thistles to the lilies?

While blackbirds whistle over there,
A teal flies out of the grass
Carrying a pearl in its beak:
That pearl is suffering, alas!

It is the poison a moment ago
The spider sprayed as it uncurled
Itself over its blue and vague
Sinister and transparent world.

A rifleshot in the hedges,
A dog barks: the hunter is near.
All the while I can feel a wound
Beneath this sweetness, a kind of fear.

Sad passerby of this beautiful place,
I walk across grass pushing through the sod,
Thinking of that strange enigma, evil,
The spelling mistake of God.

La Méridienne du lion

Le lion dort, seul sous sa voûte.
Il dort de ce puissant sommeil
De la sieste, auquel s'ajoute,
Comme un poids sombre, le soleil.

Les déserts, qui de loin écoutent,
Respirent; le maître est rentré.
Car les solitudes redoutent
Ce promeneur démesuré.

Son souffle soulève son ventre;
Son œil de brume est submergé,
Il dort sur le pavé de l'antre,
Formidablement allongé.

La paix est sur son grand visage,
Et l'oubli même, car il dort.
Il a l'altier sourcil du sage
Et l'ongle tranquille du fort.

Midi sèche l'eau des citernes;
Rien du sommeil ne le distrait;
Sa gueule ressemble aux cavernes,
Et sa crinière à la foret.

Il entrevoit des monts difformes,
Des Ossas et des Pélions,
À travers les songes énormes
Que peuvent faire les lions.

Tout se tait sur la roche plate
Où ses pas tout à l'heure erraient.
S'il remuait sa grosse patte,
Que de mouches s'envoleraient!

The Lion's Midday Sleep

The lion sleeps inside his vault
His soundless sleep, the deepest one
Of midday, made still more profound
By the warming weight of the sun.

The deserts, listening far away,
Exhale: the master's back again.
Even the solitudes are scared
When the lion strolls from his den.

His eyes appear submerged in haze.
With every breath, his side inflates.
Spread out on the floor of his cave,
His body's bulk intimidates.

Yet there is peace on his large face;
Even some forgetfulness shows.
He has a wise man's wrinkled brow,
A strong man's talons in repose.

Noon is drying out the cisterns;
Nothing distracts him from his rest.
His jaws are like a cavern mouth;
His mane resembles a forest.

He can make out the blurry forms
Of Pelions and Ossas that stream
In and out of the immensities
That lions are able to dream.

The rock is hushed, as if in awe:
No echoes of his footsteps' patter.
Were he to lift his massive paw,
How many flies would scatter!

From *L'Année Terrible* (1872)

«*J'entreprend de conter l'année …*»

J'entreprends de conter l'année épouvantable,
Et voilà que j'hésite, accoudé sur ma table.
Faut-il aller plus loin? dois-je continuer?
France! ô deuil! voir un astre aux cieux diminuer!
Je sens l'ascension lugubre de la honte.
Morne angoisse! un fléau descend, un autre monte.
N'importe. Poursuivons. L'histoire en a besoin.
Ce siècle est à la barre et je suis son témoin.

Du Haut de la muraille de Paris

À la nuit tombante

L'Occident était blanc, l'Orient était noir;
Comme si quelque bras sorti des ossuaires
Dressait un catafalque aux colonnes du soir,
Et sur le firmament déployait deux suaires.

Et la nuit se fermait ainsi qu'une prison.
L'oiseau mêlait sa plainte au frisson de la plante.
J'allais. Quand je levai mes yeux vers l'horizon,
Le couchant n'était plus qu'une lame sanglante.

Cela faisait penser à quelque grand duel
D'un monstre contre un dieu, tous deux de même taille;
Et l'on eût dit l'épée effrayante du ciel
Rouge et tombée à terre après une bataille.

(Novembre, 1870)

From *The Horrific Year*

'*I'm setting out to narrate that horrific year ...*'

I'm setting out to narrate that horrific year.
I hesitate, elbows on my table – out of fear?
Should I go further? Should I continue now?
France – what grief! – to see a star fade and go down!
I can feel the dismal ascension of disgrace.
Agony! one scourge goes, another shows its face.
No matter. Let's go on. We must do history's business.
This century is on trial and I am its witness.

On Top of Paris's Ramparts

At nightfall

The western sky was white; the eastern was all black –
As if some arm, rising from a charnel house, were bent
On erecting a catafalque on evening's columns
And unfurling two shrouds across the firmament.

The night was being shut like the door of a cell.
Plants shook, birds lamented as the light began to fade.
I went away. When I looked up again, night fell:
The setting sun had shrunken to a blood-stained blade.

It all made one think of some momentous duel
Between a monster and God, giants equal in size.
One would have sworn that heaven's terrifying sword
Was red, having fallen from some battle of the skies.

(November, 1870)

1er Janvier

Enfant, on vous dira plus tard que le grand-père
Vous adorait; qu'il fit de son mieux sur la terre,
Qu'il eut fort peu de joie et beaucoup d'envieux,
Qu'au temps où vous étiez petits il était vieux,
Qu'il n'avait pas de mots bourrus ni d'airs moroses,
Et qu'il vous a quittés dans la saison des roses;
Qu'il est mort, qu c'était un bonhomme clément;
Que, dans l'hiver fameux du grand bombardement,
Il traversait Paris tragique et plein d'épées,
Pour vous porter des tas de jouets, des poupées,
Et des pantins faisant mille gestes bouffons;
Et vous serez pensifs sous les arbres profonds.

(Janvier, 1871)

Lettre à une femme

(Par ballon monté, 10 janvier)

Paris terrible et gai combat. Bonjour, madame.
On est un peuple, on est un monde, on est une âme.
Chacun se donne à tous et nul ne songe à soi.
Nous sommes sans soleil, sans appui, sans effroi.
Tout ira bien pourvu que jamais on ne dorme.
Schmitz fait des bulletins plats sur la guerre énorme;
C'est Eschyle traduit par le père Brumoy.
J'ai payé quinze francs quatre œufs frais, non pour moi,
Mais pour mon petit George et ma petite Jeanne.
Nous mangeons du cheval, du rat, de l'ours, de l'âne.
Paris est si bien pris, cerné, muré, noué,
Gardé, que notre ventre est l'arche de Noé;
Dans nos flancs toute bête, honnête ou mal famée,
Pénètre, et chien et chat, le mammon, le pygmée,
Tout entre, et la souris rencontre l'éléphant.
Plus d'arbres; on les coupe, on les scie, on les fend;
Paris sur ses chenets met les Champs-Élysées.

1 January

Some day they will tell you that your grandfather adored
You completely; that he did his best here; you'll be told
That he had little joy, and that many envied him;
That, when you were little, he was already old;
That he never had black moods, nor a harsh word to say;
That he left you in the season of the roses one day;
That he's dead; that he was merciful, even to hard men;
That, in the winter of the great siege and bombardment,
He walked through Paris, tragic barricaded town,
To bring you a pile of toys to play with – dolls to squeeze
And jumping jacks which make a thousand gestures like a clown –
And you will stop and think awhile beneath the deep trees.

(January, 1871)

Letter to a Woman

(Via balloon sent up, January 10)

Horrific, festive Paris is at war. Greetings, friend.
We are one world, we are one soul, we are one end.
Everyone gives everything; no thought is selfish here.
We have no sun, nothing to lean on, and no fear.
All will be well, provided we don't ever sleep.
Schmitz's war reports are so dull they make you weep.
It's Aeschylus translated by the eighteenth-century.
I paid fifteen francs for four eggs – not for me,
But for my George and my Jeannine. Our daily fare?
We are eating horse and rat and donkey, even bear.
Paris is so well barricaded, guarded, dark,
Surrounded, that our stomachs resemble Noah's ark.
Every creature, well- or ill-regarded, worse than that,
Pours into our bodies: mammoth, pygmy, dog and cat.
Everything goes in: mice meet elephants in there.
Trees are being cut down, chopped up, split up. None is spared.
The Champs-Élysées has been tossed onto the flames.

On a l'onglée aux doigts et le givre aux croisées.
Plus de feu pour sécher le linge des lavoirs,
Et l'on ne change plus de chemise. Les soirs
Un grand murmure sombre abonde au coin des rues,
C'est la foule; tantôt ce sont des voix bourrues,
Tantôt des chants, parfois de belliqueux appels.
La Seine lentement traîne des archipels
De glaçons hésitants, lourds, où la canonnière
Court, laissant derrière elle une écumante ornière.
On vit de rien, on vit de tout, on est content.
Sur nos tables sans nappe, où la faim nous attend,
Une pomme de terre arrachée à sa crypte
Est reine, et les oignons sont dieux comme en Égypte.
Nous manquons de charbon, mais notre pain est noir.
Plus de gaz; Paris dort sous un large éteignoir;
À six heures du soir, ténèbres. Des tempêtes
De bombes font un bruit monstrueux sur nos têtes.
D'un bel éclat d'obus j'ai fait mon encrier.
Paris assassiné ne daigne pas crier.
Les bourgeois sont de garde autour de la muraille;
Ces pères, ces maris, ces frères qu'on mitraille,
Coiffés de leurs képis, roulés dans leurs cabans,
Guettent, ayant pour lit la planche de leurs bancs.
Soit. Moltke nous canonne et Bismarck nous affame.
Paris est un héros, Paris est une femme;
Il sait être vaillant et charmant; ses yeux vont,
Souriant et pensifs, dans le grand ciel profond,
Du pigeon qui revient au ballon qui s'envole.
C'est beau: le formidable est sorti du frivole.
Moi, je suis là, joyeux de ne voir rien plier.
Je dis à tous d'aimer, de lutter, d'oublier,
De n'avoir d'ennemi que l'ennemi; je crie:
Je ne sais plus mon nom, je m'appelle Patrie!
Quant aux femmes, soyez très fière, en ce moment
Où tout penche, elles sont sublimes simplement.
Ce qui fit la beauté des Romaines antiques,
C'étaient leurs humbles toits, leurs vertus domestiques,
Leurs doigts que l'âpre laine avait faits noirs et durs,
Leurs courts sommeils, leur calme, Annibal près des murs,
Et leurs maris debout sur la porte Colline.
Ces temps sont revenus. La géante féline,
La Prusse tient Paris, et, tigresse, elle mord
Ce grand cœur palpitant du monde à moité mort.

We've numbness in our fingers and frost on our panes.
No fires to dry our clothes or wash with anymore.
We wear the same shirts every day now. In this war
Dark murmurs permeate each neighbourhood at night.
It's the crowd; sometimes voices that are itching to fight,
Sometimes song, sometimes shouting, loud and bellicose.
The Seine is slowly dragging archipelagoes
Of hesitant ice chunks, through which the gunboats snake
Leaving a foamy track behind them in their wake.
We live on nothing and on everything, as if impervious.
On our linenless tables, where hunger waits for us,
A potato, torn from its crypt (the frozen sod),
Is queen and, as in Egypt, every onion is a god.
We don't have any coal, but our bread is always black;
No lamp gas; as if Paris were snuffed out by the attack,
Darkness at six o'clock at night. Tempestuous
Bombings make a terrifying noise on top of us.
I made my inkwell from the shrapnel of a bomb.
Assassinated Paris doesn't cry out in alarm.
All the bourgeois are keeping guard along the walls.
These fathers, husbands, brothers, shelled with bombs and cannon balls,
Wrapped in their cloaks and wearing kepis, gaze ahead,
Watching and waiting, with a bench plank for a bed.
So be it. Moltke shells us; Bismarck starves us; we won't bow.
Paris is a hero and a woman. It knows how
To be brave and charming through it all, and its eyes,
Smiling and thoughtful, search the depths of the skies
For pigeons returning and balloons sent on their way.
The frivolous gives birth to the incredible today.
And I am there, glad to see that nothing's yielded yet,
Telling everyone to love, to fight, and to forget,
To have one enemy, the enemy; somehow
I've lost my name; I have become 'The Homeland' now.
The women? You can be proud of them. At this time
When everything's on edge, they are simply sublime.
What made all the women of Rome especially
Beautiful was their humble roofs and their economy,
Their fingers that the rough wool had made black and hard,
Their sleeplessness, their calmness when their husbands were on guard
At the Colline gate and Hannibal was at their walls.
Those days have returned. Holding Paris in its claws,
The giant tigress, Prussia, bites into and tears apart
This dead-to-the-world yet still palpitating heart.

Eh bien, dans ce Paris, sous l'étreinte inhumaine,
L'homme n'est que Français, et la femme est Romaine.
Elles acceptent tout, les femmes de Paris,
Leur âtre éteint, leurs pieds par le verglas meurtris,
Au seuil noir des bouchers les attentes nocturnes,
La neige et l'ouragan vidant leurs froides urnes,
La famine, l'horreur, le combat, sans rien voir
Que la grande patrie et que le grand devoir;
Et Juvénal au fond de l'ombre est content d'elles.
Le bombardement fait gronder nos citadelles.
Dès l'aube, le tambour parle au clairon lointain;
La diane réveille, au vent frais du matin,
La grande ville pâle et dans l'ombre apparue;
Une vague fanfare erre de rue en rue.
On fraternise, on rêve un succès; nous offrons
Nos cœurs à l'espérance, à la foudre nos fronts.
La ville par la gloire et le malheur élue
Voit arriver les jours terribles et salue.
Eh bien, on aura froid! eh bien, on aura faim!
Qu'est cela? C'est la nuit. Et que sera la fin?
L'aurore. Nous souffrons, mais avec certitude.
La Prusse est le cachot et Paris est Latude.
Courage! on refera l'effort des jours anciens.
Paris avant un mois chassera les Prussiens.
Ensuite nous comptons, mes deux fils et moi, vivre
Aux champs, auprès de vous, qui voulez bien nous suivre,
Madame, et nous irons en mars vous en prier
Si nous ne sommes pas tués en février.

And so, in this inhuman embrace, left alone,
The men are only French, but the women are of Rome.
They accept everything and let what is suffice:
Hearths without fire, feet bruised by pavement ice,
Butchers on the threshold, night attacks in waves and turns,
The wind and the snowstorms pouring out their frozen urns,
Fighting, famine, dread, not being able to see
Anything except a great nation and great duty;
And Juvenal's ghost is glad, wherever he is.
Bombings make the walls groan inside our fortresses.
Drums answer bugles from the moment that dawn breaks.
In the cold, morning air, the reveille sounds and wakes
The giant city, pale and draped in shadows like a sheet.
A fanfare wanders as though lost from street to street.
We fraternize, we dream of our victory, we expose
Our hearts to hope, our bodies to the cannon's heavy blows.
Elected by misfortune and by glory, the city
Greets each horrific day with equanimity.
So we'll be cold? we will go hungry then, my friend?
What are cold and hunger? Only night. Where will it end?
In dawn. We are enduring with a kind of certainty.
Prussia is the prison-house; Paris, the escapee.
We will bring back the old resolve. Have no doubt:
We will expel the Prussians before the month is out.
Then we, my sons and I, would like to live near you
In the country, where we'll see you, and you can visit too,
Madame: we'll invite you there in March and be merry,
If we haven't in the meantime been killed in February.

From *L'Art d'être grand-père* (1877)

Fenêtres ouvertes

LE MATIN. – EN DORMANT

J'entends des voix. Lueurs à travers ma paupière.
Une cloche est en branle à l'église Saint-Pierre.
Cris des baigneurs. Plus près! plus loin! non, par ici!
Non, par là! Les oiseaux gazouillent, Jeanne aussi.
Georges l'appelle. Chant des coqs. Une truelle
Racle un toit. Des chevaux passent dans la ruelle.
Grincement d'une faulx qui coupe le gazon.
Chocs. Rumeurs. Des couvreurs marchent sur la maison.
Bruits du port. Sifflement des machines chauffées.
Musique militaire arrivant par bouffées.
Brouhaha sur le quai. Voix françaises. Merci.
Bonjour. Adieu. Sans doute il est tard, car voici
Que vient tout près de moi chanter mon rouge-gorge.
Vacarme de marteaux lointains dans une forge.
L'eau clapote. On entend haleter un steamer.
Une mouche entre. Souffle immense de la mer.

Jeanne endormie (*«Elle dort ...»*)

Elle dort; ses beaux yeux se rouvriront demain;
Et mon doigt qu'elle tient dans l'ombre emplit sa main;
Moi, je lis, ayant soin que rien ne la réveille,
Des journaux pieux; tous m'insultent; l'un conseille
De mettre à Charenton quiconque lit mes vers;
L'autre voue au bûcher mes ouvrages pervers;
L'autre, dont une larme humecte les paupières,
Invite les passants à me jeter des pierres;
Mes écrits sont un tas lugubre et vénéneux
Où tous les noirs dragons du mal tordent leurs nœuds;
L'autre croit à l'enfer et m'en déclare apôtre;

From *The Art of Being a Grandfather*

Open Windows

MORNING. HALF ASLEEP.

I hear voices. Lights hit my eyes and the bedroom wall.
A bell swings into motion at the church of Saint Paul.
Vacationer's shouts: 'Over here – there – no, go through,
No, around!' The birds are chirping; Jeannine chirps too.
George calls her. Cocks are crowing. A trowel suddenly
Scrapes the roof. Horses tromp up and down the alley.
The grating of a scythe as it cuts through the grass.
Shocks. Noises. Footfalls overhead when roofers pass.
Port sounds. Whistles from machines: a boat departs.
Military music arrives in spurts and starts.
Uproars on the dock. French voices: 'Merci.
Bonjour. Adieu.' It must be late for now I see
A red-breasted robin coming close to sing to me.
The pounding of hammers in a forge far-away.
Water splashing. Steamboats panting on their way.
A fly comes in. The immense breath of the sea.

Jeannine Asleep ('She's asleep …')

She's asleep. Her bright eyes will reopen tomorrow.
Her hand is holding onto my finger. She rests.
I am reading all the pious journals, taking care
Not to wake her. All insult me. One suggests
To throw whoever reads my poems into Charenton.
Another consigns them to the flames. And then there's one
With tears moistening his lids abundantly
Urging every passerby to throw a stone at me.
My writings are 'a venomous, lugubrious mess
Where Evil's black dragons twist their tails without rest'.
One says I'm 'hell's apostle', one 'the devil's brother'.

L'un m'appelle Antechrist, l'autre Satan, et l'autre
Craindrait de me trouver le soir au coin d'un bois;
L'un me tend la ciguë et l'autre me dit: Bois!
J'ai démoli le Louvre et tué les otages;
Je fais rêver au peuple on ne sait quels partages;
Paris en flamme envoie à mon front sa rougeur;
Je suis incendiaire, assassin, égorgeur,
Avare, et j'eusse été moins sombre et moins sinistre
Si l'empereur m'avait voulu faire ministre;
Je suis l'empoisonneur public, le meurtrier;
Ainsi viennent en foule autour de moi crier
Toutes ces voix jetant l'affront, sans fin, sans trêve;
Cependant l'enfin dort, et, comme si son rêve
Me disait: — Sois tranquille, ô père, et sois clément! —
Je sens sa main presser la mienne doucement.

One calls me the Antichrist, one Satan, and another
Wouldn't want to meet me at night. One holds a cup
Of hemlock out to me; another yells, 'Drink up!'
I destroyed the Louvre and I killed the hostages.
My brow is red from Paris – Paris burning, that is.
I've made people dream about who knows what kind of loot.
I'm an agitator, murderer, butcher, and, to boot,
A miser. And I would have been less stern and sinister
If the emperor had wished to make me his minister.
I poison the public; I'm the public's assassin.
That is why these voices, shrill, relentless, and harassing,
Are crowding around me to let out their screams.
But the child is sleeping, and – as if in her dreams
She were saying to me, 'Be at peace, father, and be kind!' –
I can feel her tiny hand gently squeezing mine.

From *La Légende des siècles* (1859, 1877, 1883)

La Conscience

Lorsque avec ses enfants vêtus de peaux de bêtes,
Échevelé, livide au milieu des tempêtes,
Caïn se fut enfui de devant Jéhovah,
Comme le soir tombait, l'homme sombre arriva
Au bas d'une montagne en une grande plaine;
Sa femme fatiguée et ses fils hors d'haleine
Lui dirent: — Couchons-nous sur la terre, et dormons. —
Caïn, ne dormant pas, songeait au pied des monts.
Ayant levé la tête, au fond des cieux funèbres
Il vit un œil, tout grand ouvert dans les ténèbres,
Et qui le regardait dans l'ombre fixement.
— Je suis trop près, dit-il avec un tremblement.
Il réveilla ses fils dormant, sa femme lasse,
Et se remit à fuir sinistre dans l'espace.
Il marcha trente jours, il marcha trente nuits.
Il allait, muet, pâle et frémissant aux bruits,
Furtifs, sans regarder derrière lui, sans trêve,
Sans repos, sans sommeil. Il atteignit la grève
Des mers dans le pays qui fut depuis Assur.
— Arrêtons-nous, dit-il, car cet asile est sûr.
Restons-y. Nous avons du monde atteint les bornes. —
Et, comme il s'asseyait, il vit dans les cieux mornes
L'œil à la même place au fond de l'horizon.
Alors il tressaillit en proie au noir frisson.
— Cachez-moi, cria-t-il; et, le doigt sur la bouche,
Tous ses fils regardaient trembler l'aïeul farouche.
Caïn dit à Jabel, père de ceux qui vont
Sous des tentes de poil dans le désert profond:
— Étends de ce côté la toile de la tente. —
Et l'on développa la muraille flottante;
Et, quand on l'eut fixée avec des poids de plomb:
Vous ne voyez plus rien? dit Tsilla, l'enfant blond,
La fille de ses fils, douce comme l'aurore;
Et Caïn répondit: — Je vois cet œil encore! —
Jubal, père de ceux qui passent dans les bourgs
Soufflant dans des clairons et frappant des tambours,

From *The Legend of the Centuries*

Conscience

When Cain, dishevelled, angry, in the middle of a storm,
Fleeing with his children wrapped in hides to keep warm,
Was running from Jehovah, he arrived at the base
Of a solitary mountain in the middle of a waste
As night came down and darkness gave the shadows depth.
His wife, exhausted, and his children, out of breath,
Said to him, 'Let's lie down here and go to sleep.'
Cain dreamed at the mountain's foot, unable to sleep.
Lifting his head, he looked up and saw an eye
Entirely open, in the depths of the sky,
Which stared at him fixedly from out of the night.
'I am too close,' he said, shuddering at the sight.
And so he woke his sleeping sons along with his wife
And set out again, as if fleeing for his life.
He marched for thirty nights; he marched for thirty days.
He travelled, silent, pale, afraid of noises, in a daze,
Furtively, without looking back or stopping once,
Without rest, without sleep, until he came after months
To the coast which would be the Assyrian shore.
'Let us stop here,' he said, 'This refuge is secure.
We've reached the world's limits. Let us rest – or try to.'
But as he went to sit, he glanced across the sky's blue
And saw the eye hanging in the last place he had looked.
Fear sent him into convulsions. As he shook
He shouted 'Cover me!'. With their fingers on their mouths,
All of his children watched their father's trembling hands.
Cain said to Jab, whose sons would later move about
As nomads under tasselled tents across the sands,
'Spread out the canvas of your tent over here.'
And so they put together a floating barrier.
In order to secure it, leaden weights were fastened on.
'You can see nothing now?' asked Zillah, sweet as dawn,
The blond child, daughter of his daughters and his sons.
'I still see that eye!' was Cain's terrified response.
Then Jubal, father of those men who travel from
Market towns blowing horns and banging on their drums,

Cria: — Je saurai bien construire une barrière. —
Il fit un mur de bronze et mit Caïn derrière.
Et Caïn dit: — Cet œil me regarde toujours!
Hénoch dit: — Il faut faire une enceinte de tours
Si terrible, que rien ne puisse approcher d'elle.
Bâtissons une ville avec sa citadelle.
Bâtissons une ville, et nous la fermerons. —
Alors Tubalcaïn, père des forgerons,
Construisit une ville énorme et surhumaine.
Pendant qu'il travaillait, ses frères, dans la plaine,
Chassaient les fils d'Énos et les enfants de Seth;
Et l'on crevait les yeux à quiconque passait;
Et, le soir, on lançait des flèches aux étoiles.
Le granit remplaça la tente aux murs de toiles,
On lia chaque bloc avec des nœuds de fer,
Et la ville semblait une ville d'enfer;
L'ombre des tours faisait la nuit dans les campagnes;
Ils donnèrent aux murs l'épaisseur des montagnes;
Sur la porte on grava: «Défense à Dieu d'entrer.»
Quand ils eurent fini de clore et de murer,
On mit l'aïeul au centre en une tour de pierre.
Et lui restait lugubre et hagard. — O mon père!
L'œil a-t-il disparu? dit en tremblant Tsilla.
Et Caïn répondit: — Non, il est toujours là.
Alors il dit: — Je veux habiter sous la terre
Comme dans son sépulchre un homme solitaire;
Rien ne me verra plus, je ne verrai plus rien. —
On fit donc une fosse, et Caïn dit: C'est bien!
Puis il descendit seul sous cette voûte sombre.
Quand il se fut assis sur sa chaise dans l'ombre
Et qu'on eut sur son front fermé le souterrain,
L'œil était dans la tombe et regardait Caïn.

Booz endormi

Booz s'était couché de fatigue accablé;
Il avait tout le jour travaillé dans son aire;
Puis avait fait son lit à sa place ordinaire;
Booz dormait auprès des boisseaux pleins de blé.

Said, 'I know how to build a wall.' So he designed it,
Had it made from bronze, and put Cain behind it.
But Cain said, 'The eye is still out there, hovering.'
Enoch said, 'Let's build a score of towers in a ring
So terrifying no one will dare to come close.
Let's build a city with a large gate we can close.
Let's build a city, and we'll seal him inside.'
And so the forefather of blacksmiths, Tubalcain,
Constructed an inhuman city, tall and wide.
While he was building it, his brothers on the plain
Were hunting down the children of Enosh and Seth.
They ripped out the eyes of every person they met.
And every night they fired their arrows at the stars.
Granite replaced the canvas walls. And iron bars
Were used to join the huge blocks of this citadel.
The city looked as if it were a city from hell:
Its towers caused a night to fall on outlying fields.
Its walls were like mountains. For they built them not to yield
To anything. They scrawled above its gate: 'No Gods allowed.'
And when they had finished walling in and walling out
They put Cain in the towers' most secure and guarded wing.
But he remained listless, and only seemed to stare.
'Has the eye disappeared?' asked Zillah, trembling.
Cain answered back to her, 'No. It's still there.'
And then he said to them, 'I want to live underground
Like a hermit in his tomb – in some place without sound
Where no one will see me, and I won't see them as well.'
And so they dug a ditch, and Cain replied, 'You've done well.'
Then he went down into the black crypt alone.
And when he was sitting in the darkness on his throne,
And they had sealed the vault in which he would remain,
The eye was in the tomb there and looked straight at Cain.

Boaz Asleep

Boaz lay down burdened with fatigue and the heat.
He had been threshing in his granary all day.
And then he made his bed in his usual place.
Boaz went to sleep among the bushels of wheat.

Ce vieillard possédait des champs de blés et d'orge;
Il était, quoique riche, à la justice enclin;
Il n'avait pas de fange en l'eau de son moulin;
Il n'avait pas d'enfer dans le feu de sa forge.

Sa barbe était d'argent comme un ruisseau d'avril.
Sa gerbe n'était point avare ni haineuse;
Quand il voyait passer quelque pauvre glaneuse:
– Laissez tomber exprès des épis, disait-il.

Cet homme marchait pur loin des sentiers obliques,
Vêtu de probité candide et de lin blanc;
Et, toujours du côté des pauvres ruisselant,
Ses sacs de grains semblaient des fontaines publiques.

Booz était bon maître et fidèle parent;
Il était généreux, quoiqu'il fût économe;
Les femmes regardaient Booz plus qu'un jeune homme,
Car le jeune homme est beau, mais le vieillard est grand.

Le vieillard, qui revient vers la source première,
Entre aux jours éternels et sort des jours changeants;
Et l'on voit de la flamme aux yeux des jeunes gens,
Mais dans l'œil du vieillard on voit de la lumière.

*

Donc, Booz dans la nuit dormait parmi les siens.
Près des meules, qu'on eût prises pour des décombres,
Les moissoneurs couchés faisaient des groupes sombres;
Et ceci se passait dans des temps très anciens.

Les tribus d'Israël avaient pour chef un juge;
La terre, où l'homme errait sous la tente, inquiet
Des empreintes de pieds de géants qu'il voyait,
Était mouillée encor et molle du déluge.

*

Comme dormait Jacob, comme dormait Judith,
Booz, les yeux fermés, gisait sous la feuillée;
Or, la porte du ciel s'étant entre-bâillée
Au-dessus de sa tête, un songe en descendit.

This ancient man possessed vast fields of wheat and corn.
Although he was rich, he had a love of justice still.
There wasn't any mud in the water of his mill.
There wasn't any hell in the fire of his forge.

His beard was streaked with silver, like a stream's April surface.
His sheaves were neither miserly nor filled with bitterness.
Whenever he saw a poor woman gleaning wheat
He'd say to his workers, 'Let some ears fall on purpose.'

This man walked far away from pathways choked with weed,
Clothed in a white robe and his integrity.
His sacks of grain, like public fountains, flowed plentifully,
Always spilling over on the side of those in need.

Boaz was a kind lord and loyal relative,
Generous to everyone, though prudent every time.
Women looked at Boaz more than all the young men.
For the young man is handsome, but the old is sublime.

Old men, returning to the source of life, forego
The changing days and enter changelessness again.
And though you see a fire in the eyes of young men,
In the eyes of an old man you can see a glow.

*

And so Boaz slept among his own in the evening.
The reapers lay like dark mounds piled in a row
Next to the millstones one might mistake for ruins.
And all of this took place a very long time ago.

The tribes of Israel had a judge for a leader.
Troubled by the footprints of giants in the mud
Nomadic peoples wandered with their tents across an earth
Still soft and dripping from the wake of the flood.

*

Just as Jacob slept and Judith slept, Boaz lay there
Underneath a bed of leaves and gently closed his eyes.
For when the gate of heaven opened over his head
A dream went out and drifted downwards through the skies.

Et ce songe était tel, que Booz vit un chêne
Qui, sorti de son ventre, allait jusqu'au ciel bleu;
Une race y montait comme une longue chaîne;
Un roi chantait en bas, en haut mourait un Dieu.

Et Booz murmurait avec la voix de l'âme:
«Comment se pourrait-il que de moi ceci vînt?
Le chiffre de mes ans a passé quatre-vingt,
Et je n'ai pas de fils, et je n'ai plus de femme.

«Voilà longtemps que celle avec qui j'ai dormi,
O Seigneur! a quitté ma couche pour la vôtre;
Et nous sommes encor tout mêlés l'un à l'autre,
Elle à demi vivante et moi mort à demi.

«Une race naîtrait de moi! Comment le croire?
Comment se pourrait-il que j'eusse des enfants?
Quand on est jeune, on a des matins triomphants;
Le jour sort de la nuit comme d'une victoire;

«Mais, vieux, on tremble ainsi qu'à l'hiver le bouleau;
Je suis veuf, je suis seul, et sur moi le soir tombe,
Et je courbe, ô mon Dieu! mon âme vers la tombe,
Comme un bœuf ayant soif penche son front vers l'eau.»

Ainsi parlait Booz dans le rêve et l'extase,
Tournant vers Dieu ses yeux par le sommeil noyés;
Le cèdre ne sent pas une rose à sa base,
Et lui ne sentait pas une femme à ses pieds.

*

Pendant qu'il sommeillait, Ruth, une moabite,
S'était couchée aux pieds de Booz, le sein nu,
Espérant on ne sait quel rayon inconnu,
Quand viendrait du réveil la lumière subite.

Booz ne savait point qu'une femme était là,
Et Ruth ne savait point ce que Dieu voulait d'elle.
Un frais parfum sortait des touffes d'asphodèle;
Les souffles de la nuit flottaient sur Galgala.

And in this dream Boaz saw an oak tree grow out of
The middle of his stomach and ascend into the blue.
A nation climbed upward like the links of a chain:
A king sung at the bottom and a God died above.

And Boaz started speaking to his soul in a murmur,
'How can this ever come to pass in my life?
The number of my years has now gone over eighty.
And I don't have a son. And I no longer have a wife.

It has been a long time since the one who shared my bed,
O Lord, has departed from my side and gone to yours;
And we are still very much a part of each other:
She is half-living still and half of me is dead.

How can I believe a race will yet be born from me?
How is it still possible for me to have children?
When one is young, every morning is triumphant:
The day rises up from the night like victory.

But when one is older, the winter makes one shiver.
I'm alone and old now: night will fall on me soon.
I'm already, God, bending my soul toward the tomb,
The way a thirsty bull leans his head toward the river.'

Boaz was speaking in a dream, as if drunk,
Turning his swimming eyes toward God in his sleep.
A cedar doesn't smell a rose growing near its trunk,
And Boaz didn't see the woman lying at his feet.

*

While he was sleeping there, Ruth, a Moabite,
Lay down with her breasts bared at Boaz's feet,
Hoping for some sort of unfamiliar ray
In which understanding would flare up like a light.

Boaz didn't know that a woman was there,
And Ruth didn't know what God wanted from her.
A cool scent drifted from the tufts of asphodels.
The breaths of evening floated over Galgala's hills.

L'ombre était nuptiale, auguste et solennelle;
Les anges y volaient sans doute obscurément,
Car on voyait passer dans la nuit, par moment,
Quelque chose de bleu qui paraissait une aile.

La respiration de Booz qui dormait,
Se mêlait au bruit sourd des ruisseaux sur la mousse.
On était dans le mois où la nature est douce,
Les collines ayant des lys sur leur sommet.

Ruth songeait et Booz dormait; l'herbe était noire;
Les grelots des troupeaux tombait du firmament;
Une immense bonté tombait du firmament;
C'était l'heure tranquille où les lions vont boire.

Tout reposait dans Ur et dans Jérimadeth;
Les astres émaillent le ciel profond et sombre;
Le croissant fin et clair parmi ces fleurs de l'ombre
Brillait à l'occident, et Ruth se demandait,

Immobile, ouvrant l'œil à moitié sous ses voiles,
Quel dieu, quel moisonneur de l'éternel été,
Avait, en s'en allant, négligemment jeté
Cette faucille d'or dans le champ des étoiles.

Première Rencontre du Christ avec le tombeau

En ce temps-là, Jésus était dans la Judée;
Il avait délivré la femme possédée,
Rendu l'ouïe aux sourds et guéri les lépreux;
Les prêtres l'épiaient et parlaient bas entre eux.
Comme il s'en retournait vers la ville bénie,
Lazare, homme de bien, mourut à Béthanie.
Marthe et Marie étaient ses sœurs; Marie, un jour,
Pour laver les pieds nus du maître plein d'amour,
Avait été chercher son parfum le plus rare.
Or, Jésus aimait Marthe et Marie et Lazare.
Quelqu'un lui dit: «Lazare est mort.»
                                    Le lendemain,

The darkness was nuptial, solemn, and august.
Surely there were angels flying in the glimmering,
For you could see, passing in the night now and then,
Something that was bluish and appeared to be a wing.

Boaz's breathing was as soft as a child's
And blended with the water rustling in the copse.
It was in the month when nature is mild.
The hills were adorned with lilies on their tops.

Ruth dreamed and Boaz slept. The dark grass seemed to sigh.
The flock's bells were tinkling vaguely in the breeze.
An immense goodness fell from the height of the sky;
It was at the hour when the lions drink in peace.

Everything was resting in Jerimadeth and Ur;
The stars glazed the deep sky as far as you could see.
A bright, thin crescent shone among these shadowy
Flowers of evening, and Ruth wondered to herself,

Motionless, half opening her eyes and looking far
Into the night, what reaper of eternity – what kind
Of god – had, leaving us, carelessly tossed behind
This golden sickle in the dark field of the stars.

Christ's First Encounter with the Tomb

Jesus was in Judea then. Before he left
He exorcised a woman demons had possessed.
Cured the lepers, gave back the hearing to the deaf.
The priests were watching, whispering among themselves.
As Jesus was returning to the holy city,
Lazarus, an upright man, died in Bethany.
Martha and Mary were his sisters. Once before
Mary had brought her finest perfume before
The beloved master to wash his naked feet.
For Jesus loved Lazarus, Martha, and Mary.
Someone told him, 'Lazarus is dead.'
                              The next day,

Comme le peuple était venu sur son chemin,
Il expliquait la loi, les livres, les symboles,
Et, comme Elie et Job, parlait par paraboles.
Il disait: « – Qui me suit, aux anges est pareil.
Quand un homme a marché tout le jour au soleil
Dans un chemin sans puits et sans hôtellerie,
S'il ne croit pas, quand vient le soir, il pleure, il crie;
Il est las; sur la terre il tombe haletant.
S'il croit en moi, qu'il prie, il peut au même instant
Continuer sa route avec des forces triples.» –
Puis il s'interrompit, et dit à ses disciples:
– «Lazare, notre ami, dort; je vais l'éveiller.» –
Eux dirent: – «Nous irons, maître, où tu veux aller.»
Or, de Jérusalem, où Salomon mit l'arche,
Pour gagner Béthanie, il faut trois jours de marche.
Jésus partit. Durant cette route souvent,
Tandis qu'il marchait seul et pensif en avant,
Son vêtement parut blanc comme la lumière.

Quand Jésus arriva, Marthe vint la première,
Et, tombant à ses pieds, s'écria tout d'abord:
– «Si nous t'avions eu maître, il ne serait pas mort.»
Puis reprit en pleurant: – «Mais il a rendu l'âme.
Tu viens trop tard.» Jésus lui di: – «Qu'en sais-tu femme?
Le moissonneur est seul maître de la moisson.»

Marie était restée assise à la maison.

Marthe lui cria: – «Viens, le maître te réclame.»
Elle vint. Jésus dit: – «Pourquoi pleures-tu, femme?»
Et Marie à genoux lui dit: – «Toi seul est fort.
Si nous t'avions eu, maître, il ne serait pas mort.»
Jésus reprit: – «Je suis la lumière et la vie.
Heureux celui qui voit ma trace et l'a suivie!
Qui croit en moi vivra, fût-il mort et gisant!» –
Et Thomas, appelé Didyme, était présent.

Et le Seigneur, dont Jean et Pierre suivaient l'ombre,
Dit aux juifs accourus pour le voir en grand nombre:
– «Où donc l'avez-vous mis?» – Il répondirent: «Vois,»
Lui montrant de la main, dans un champs, près d'un bois,
À côté d'un torrent qui dans les pierres coule,
Un sépulcre.

As people were gathering around him on his way,
He preached about the law, the symbols, and the scrolls.
Like Job and Elijah, he spoke in parables:
'Whoever follows me is like an angel within.
When a man has travelled in the hot sun and light
On roads without water or the shelter of an inn,
If he does not believe, he cries bitterly at night;
Exhausted, he collapses panting on the ground.
If he believes in me, at that instant let him pray:
With triple the strength he will continue on his way.'
To speak to his disciples then, he turned around:
'Lazarus is asleep. I'm going to wake him.' And although
They didn't understand him, they said that they would go
Wherever he wanted. Walking from Jerusalem
To Bethany would take about three days for them.
Jesus set out. When deep in thought, he often chose
To walk alone in front of his disciples. A burst
Of light, like an aureole, shimmered on his clothes.

When Jesus arrived, Martha came to him first,
And falling at his feet and looking upwards, she said:
'If you had been here, teacher, he wouldn't be dead.'
Then sobbing, she continued: 'He has let his spirit go.
You're too late.' Jesus answered, 'Woman, what do you know?
The harvester alone knows what the harvest will yield.'

Mary had stayed at home, looking toward the field.

Martha shouted out to her: 'The teacher's calling you.'
She came. Jesus asked her, 'Why are you crying too?'
She answered, 'You alone are strong,' then shook her head:
'If you had been here, teacher, he wouldn't be dead.'
Jesus said: 'I am the resurrection and the life.
Happy are those who recognize and follow me!
He who believes in me will live, though he be dead.'
And Thomas ('The Twin') was there, and heard what he said.

And then the Lord, whom Peter and John were following,
Said to the many Jews who came because of him,
'Where have you laid him?' They responded, 'Come and see,'
Pointing beyond a field close by a group of trees
And a stream whose pebbled waters were not running loud
At a tomb.

Et Jésus pleura.
                              Sur quoi la foule
Se prit à s'écrier: – «Voyez comme il l'aimait!
Lui qui chasse, dit-on, Satan et le soumet,
Eût-il, s'il était Dieu, comme on nous le rapporte,
Laissé mourir quelqu'un qu'il aimait de la sorte?»

Or, Marthe conduisait au sépulcre Jésus.
Il vint. On avait mis une pierre dessus.
– «Je crois en vous, dit Marthe, ainsi que Jean et Pierre;
Mais voilà quatre jours qu'il est sous cette pierre.»

Et Jésus dit: – «Tais-toi, femme, car c'est le lieu
Où tu vas, si tu crois, voir la gloire de Dieu.» –
Puis il reprit: – «Il faut que cette pierre tombe.» –
La pierre ôtée, on vit le dedans de la tombe.
Jésus leva les yeux au ciel et marcha seul
Vers cette ombre où le mort gisait dans son linceul,
Pareil au sac d'argent qu'enfouit un avare.
Et, se penchant, il dit à haute voix: «Lazare!»

Alors le mort sortit du sépulcre; ses pieds
Des bandes du linceul étaient encor liés;
Il se dressa debout le long de la muraille;
Jésus dit: – «Déliez cet homme, et qu'il s'en aille.» –
Ceux qui virent cela crurent en Jésus-Christ.

Or, les prêtres, selon qu'au livre il est écrit,
S'assemblèrent, troublés, chez le préteur de Rome;
Sachant que Christ avait ressuscité cet homme,
Et que tous avaient vu le sépulcre s'ouvrir,
Ils dirent: – «Il est temps de le faire mourir.»

Then Jesus wept.
                              Seeing which the crowd
Began to whisper, 'See how much he loved that man!
He's the one they say cast out Satan on command:
If he were really God though, would he have allowed
Someone he holds in such affection pass away?'

Martha led Jesus to the gravesite in a daze.
He followed. They had placed a stone on top of it.
Martha said, 'I believe in you like John or Peter,
But he has been beneath that rock now for four days.'

Jesus said: 'Be quiet, woman. This is the place
Where you will see the glory of God if you have faith.'
'This stone must be removed,' he said. And once the stone
Was taken out, Jesus looked to heaven while the crowd
Was staring at the tomb and Jesus walking alone
Into the darkness where the man lay in his shroud –
Like a sack of gold a miser buries in the earth.
And leaning down, he shouted, 'Lazarus, come forth!'.

The dead man came out of the tomb, though both his feet
Remained constricted by the stiffened winding sheet.
When Lazarus stood up and leaned against the wall,
Jesus said: 'Take his grave clothes off, so he can walk.'
All of those who saw this felt that Christ was God's son.

According to what's written in the scripture, every one
Of the priests assembled later at the praetor's home,
And knowing that many had seen the open tomb
And Christ raise the man, murmured under their breath,
'The time has come now to have him put to death.'

L'Hydre

Quand le fils de Sancha, femme du duc Geoffroy,
Gil, ce grand chevalier nommé l'Homme qui passe,
Parvint, la lance haute et la visière basse,
Aux confins du pays dont Ramire était roi,
Il vit l'hydre. Elle était effroyable et superbe;
Et, couchée au soleil, elle rêvait dans l'herbe.
Le chevalier tira l'épée et dit: C'est moi.
Et l'hydre, déroulant ses torsions farouches
Et se dressant, parla par une des ses bouches,
Et dit: – Pour qui viens-tu, fils de doña Sancha?
Est-ce pour moi, réponds, ou pour le roi Ramire?
– C'est pour le monstre. – Alors c'est pour le roi, beau sire.
Et l'hydre, reployant ses nœuds, se recoucha.

Mahomet

Le divin Mahomet enfourchait tour à tour
Son mulet Daïdol et son âne Yafour;
Car le sage lui-même a, selon l'occurrence,
Son jour d'entêtement et son jour d'ignorance.

Le Parricide

Un jour, Kanut, à l'heure où l'assoupissement
Ferme partout les yeux sous l'obscur firmament,
Ayant pour seul témoin la nuit, l'aveugle immense,
Vit son père Swéno, vieillard presque en démence,
Qui dormait, sans un garde à ses pieds, sans un chien;
Il le tua, disant: Lui-même n'en sait rien.
Puis il fut un grand roi.

                      Toujours vainqueur, sa vie
Par la prospérité fidèle fut suivie;

The Hydra

When the son of Doña Sancha (Duke Geoffrey's wife), Guy,
That famous knight known as 'the One who Passes By,'
Came with his visor down, lance raised, and bristling,
To the border of the country where Ramùr was the king,
He saw the hydra. It was superb and frightening.
It was dreaming in the sunlight with its gleaming scales.
The knight unsheathed his sword and shouted: 'It is I!'
The hydra then, uncoiling its ferocious tails
And opening one of its mouths, made this reply:
'Son of Doña Sancha, so renowned among men,
For whom have you come, then, for me or king Ramùr?'
'For the monster.' 'Then you've come for the king, my good sir.'
And the hydra tucked his coils in and lay down again.

Mohammed

Mohammed would take up a pitchfork at each pass
To prod his mule Daïdol, and Yafour, his ass,
Because even wise men, depending on the event,
Have days when they're stubborn, and days when they're ignorant.

The Parricide

One day, Kanut, when twilight, soft and heaven-sent,
Was closing eyes everywhere beneath the firmament,
Having only one (blind and giant) witness, night,
Seeing his old and senile father under torchlight
Asleep, without a guard or guard dog – bending low,
Murdered him, remarking, 'Even he doesn't know.'
Then he was a great king.
                              Knowing only victory,
He was accompanied by true prosperity.

Il fut plus triomphant que la gerbe des blés,
Quand il passait devant les vieillards assemblés,
Sa présence éclairait ces sévères visages;
Par la chaîne des mœurs pures et des lois sages
À son cher Danemark natal il enchaîna
Vingt îles, Fionie, Arnhout, Folster, Mona;
Il bâtit un grand trône en pierres féodales;
Il vainquit les saxons, les pictes, les vandales,
Le celte, et le borusse, et le slave aux abois,
Et les peuples hagards qui hurlent dans les bois;
Il abolit l'horreur idolâtre, et la rune,
Et le menhir féroce où le soir, à la brune,
Le chat sauvage vient frotter son dos hideux;
Il disait en parlant du grand César: Nous deux;
Une lueur sortait de son cimier polaire;
Les monstres expiraient partout sous sa colère;
Il fut, pendant vingt ans qu'on l'entendait marcher,
Le cavalier superbe et le puissant archer;
L'hydre morte, il mettait le pied sur la portée;
Sa vie, en même temps bénie et redoutée,
Dans la bouche du peuple était un fier récit;
Rien que dans un hiver, ce chasseur détruisit
Trois dragons en Écosse et deux rois en Scanie;
Il fut héros, il fut géante, il fut génie;
Le sort de tout un monde au sien semblait lié;
Quant à son parricide, il l'avait oublié.
Il mourut. On le mit dans un cercueil de pierre,
Et l'évêque d'Aarhus vint dire une prière,
Et chanter sur sa tombe un hymne, déclarant
Que Kanut était saint, que Kanut était grand,
Qu'un céleste parfum sortait de sa mémoire,
Et qu'ils le voyaient, eux, les prêtres, dans la gloire,
Assis comme un prophète à la droite de Dieu.

Le soir vint; l'orgue en deuil se tut dans le saint lieu;
Et les prêtres, quittant la haute cathédrale,
Laissèrent le roi mort dans la paix sépulcrale.
Alors il se leva, rouvrit ses yeux obscurs,
Prit son glaive, et sortit de la tombe, les murs
Et les portes étant brumes pour les fantômes;
Il traversa la mer qui reflète les dômes
Et les tours d'Altona, d'Aarhus et d'Elseneur;
L'ombre écoutait les pas de ce sombre seigneur;

He was more triumphant than a sheaf at harvest's end.
Whenever he passed the assembly of old men
Their granite faces lit up briefly and they'd pause.
Through a combination of good morals and laws
He was able to annex for the Danes Fionia,
Arnholt, Falster, Mona – twenty islands in all.
He fashioned an enormous throne from feudal bricks.
He defeated the Saxons, the Vandals, and the Picts,
Celts, Byelorussians, Slavs in ambush holding back,
And all the forest peoples who scream when they attack.
He abolished magic runes and idolatry,
The menhir where, on foggy evenings, you can see
Feral cats come to rub their backs as they pass through.
Speaking of Caesar, he would often say, 'Us two.'
His icy helmet gave off a mysterious glare.
His anger made monsters go extinct everywhere.
During the score of years he reigned and righted wrong,
He was the noble knight, the archer skilled and strong.
Having killed the hydra, he stamped out its progeny.
His life, both blessed and feared throughout the Baltic sea,
Was a proud story no one living could avoid.
In one winter alone, he hunted down and destroyed
Three dragons in Scotland and two kings in Skane.
He was a hero, a giant, a genius. In his reign
The fate of the whole world seemed linked to his own.
His parricide though? He forgot, or ceased to care.
He died. They placed him in a coffin made of stone.
The bishop of Aarhus came down to say a prayer
Over the tomb in which Kanut lay in state.
He called him a saint, said that he was truly great,
That heavenly scents would spring from his memory,
That they, the priests, already saw him in his glory,
Sitting like a prophet at the right hand of the Lord.

All the priests left the high cathedral, reassured
The dead king was resting in the peace of his grave.
Night fell. Now the silenced organ ceased to grieve.
Opening his eyes again, the king took up his sword
Then left the tomb (for spirits, solid walls are nothing more
Than mist one passes through or through which one roams).
He walked across the sea that reflects all the domes
And towers of Altona, Aarhus, and Elsenor.
The shadows listened for the footsteps of their lord.

Mais il marchait sans bruit, étant lui-même un songe;
Il alla droit au mont Savo que le temps ronge,
Et Kanut s'approcha de ce farouche aïeul,
Et lui dit: — «Laisse-moi, pour m'en faire un linceul,
O montagne Savo que la tourmente assiège,
Me couper un morceau de ton manteau de neige. – »
Le mont le reconnut et n'osa refuser.
Kanut prit son épée impossible à briser,
Et sur le mont, tremblant devant ce belluaire,
Il coupa de la neige et s'en fit un suaire;
Puis il cria: — «Vieux mont, la mort éclaire peu;
De quel côté faut-il aller pour trouver Dieu? – »
Le mont au flanc difforme, aux gorges obstruées,
Noir, triste, dans le vol éternel des nuées,
Lui dit: — «Je ne sais pas, spectre, je suis ici.» –
Kanut quitta le mont par les glaces saisi;
Et, le front haut, tout blanc dans son linceul de neige,
Il entra, par-delà l'Islande et la Norvège,
Seul dans le grand silence et dans la grande nuit;
Derrière lui le monde obscur s'évanouit;
Il se trouva, spectre, âme, roi sans royaume,
Nu, face à face avec l'immensité fantôme;
Il vit l'infini; porche horrible et reculant
Où l'éclair, quand il entre, expire triste et lent,
L'ombre, hydre dont les nuits sont les pâles vertèbres,
L'informe se mouvant dans le noir, les Ténèbres;
Là, pas d'astre; et pourtant on ne sait quel regard
Tombe de ce chaos immobile et hagard;
Pour tout bruit, le frisson lugubre que fait l'onde
De l'obscurité, sourde, effarée et profonde,
Il avança disant: — «C'est la tombe; au-delà
C'est Dieu.» – Quand il eut fait trois pas, il appela;
Mais la nuit est muette ainsi que l'ossuaire,
Et rien ne répondit; pas un pli du suaire
Ne s'émut, et Kanut avança; la blancheur
Du linceul rassurait le sépulcral marcheur;
Il allait; tout à coup, sur son livide voile
Il vit poindre et grandir comme une noire étoile;
L'étoile s'élargit lentement, et Kanut,
La tâtant de sa main de spectre, reconnut
Qu'une goutte de sang était sur lui tombée;
Sa tête, que la peur n'avait jamais courbée,
Se redressa; terrible, il regarda la nuit,

Being a dream himself, he marched on noiselessly.
Kanut went straight to Savo mountain by the sea,
And on this mountain trembling before its liege,
Said, 'Savo, peak to which the elements lay siege,
Let me cut some snow from your summit wrapped in cloud,
So that I may use it to make my funeral shroud.'
Recognizing him, the mountain dared not refuse.
Kanut took up the sword that only he could use
(His unbreakable sword) and, approaching the peak,
Cut the snow and fashioned it into a winding sheet,
Then shouted, 'Ancient mountain, death gives little insight.
In which direction should one set out for God's light?'
Brooding from within the endless spinning of the skies,
The mountain with its blocked ravines and crooked sides
Responded, 'Spirit, I am here, I do not know.'
Kanut left the mountain in the grip of so much ice.
Head high, completely white in his shroud made of snow,
He walked beyond Norway, beyond Iceland, alone,
Into the immense and silent night. The heavens cleared.
Behind him, the enigmatic world disappeared.
He found himself – spectre, soul – a kingdomless king,
Naked, face to face with a gigantic, ghostly thing –
Infinity – horrific and receding doorway
Where lighting bolts slowly and sadly fade away;
Hydras and shades for which the nights are vertebrae;
Shapeless things moving through the darkness in a daze;
Starless skies – and yet an indefinable gaze
Falls from this unmovable confusion without sound.
Instead of noise, percussive shivers made by waves
Of enigmatic darkness, muffled and profound.
He marched on, whispering, 'The tomb's here. But beyond
There is God.' He took three steps and cried aloud,
But night, deafer than a morgue, did not respond.
Motionlessness. Silence. Not one wrinkle in his shroud
Was moving. Kanut pushed on. The purity
And whiteness of his garment reassured him so that he
Could go on. Then he saw something on his shroud
Appear and grow larger – a kind of black star.
The star expanded slowly, and Kanut, reaching out
And touching it, knew (and, knowing, shook with a start)
A drop of blood had fallen from somewhere out of sight.
His head which, until then, had always kept its poise
Straightened up. Enraged, he looked out at the night

Et ne vit rien; l'espace était noir; pas un bruit;
– «En avant!» dit Kanut, levant sa tête fière;
Une seconde tache auprès de la première
Tomba, puis s'élargit; et le chef cimbrien
Regarda l'ombre épaisse et vague, et ne vit rien.
Comme un limier à suivre une piste s'attache,
Morne, il reprit sa route; une troisième tache
Tomba sur le linceul. Il n'avait jamais fui;
Kanut pourtant cessa de marcher devant lui,
Et tourna du côté du bras qui tient le glaive;
Une goutte de sang, comme à travers un rêve,
Tomba sur le suaire et lui rougit la main;
Pour la seconde fois il changea de chemin,
Comme en lisant on tourne un feuillet d'un registre,
Et se mit à marcher vers la gauche sinistre;
Une goutte de sang tomba sur le linceul;
Et Kanut recula, frémissant d'être seul,
Et voulut regagner sa couche mortuaire;
Une goutte de sang tomba sur le suaire;
Alors il s'arrêta livide, et ce guerrier,
Blême, baissa la tête et tâcha de prier;
Une goutte de sang tomba sur lui. Farouche,
La prière effrayée expirant dans sa bouche,
Il se remit en marche; et, lugubre, hésitant,
Hideux, ce spectre blanc passait; et, par instant,
Une goutte de sang se détachait de l'ombre,
Implacable, et tombait sur cette blancheur sombre.
Il voyait, plus tremblant qu'au vent le peuplier,
Ces taches s'élargir et se multiplier;
Une autre, une autre, une autre, une autre, ô cieux funèbres!
Leur passage rayait vaguement les ténèbres;
Ces gouttes, dans les plis du linceul, finissant
Par se mêler, faisaient des nuages de sang;
Il marchait, il marchait; de l'insondable voûte
Le sang continuait à pleuvoir goutte à goutte,
Toujours, sans fin, sans bruit, et comme s'il tombait
De ces pieds noirs qu'on voit la nuit pendre au gibet;
Hélas! qui donc pleurait ces larmes formidables?
L'infini. Vers les cieux, pour le juste abordables,
Dans l'océan de nuit sans flux et sans reflux,
Kanut s'avançait, pâle et ne regardant plus;
Enfin, marchant toujours comme en une fumée,
Il arriva devant une porte fermée

And saw nothing. Space was black. There was no noise.
Looking straight ahead, he shouted, 'Onward!' – in vain.
Directly in front of the first, a second stain
Fell then grew larger, and this lord who didn't scare
Looked into the thickened gloom and saw nothing there.
As a bloodhound will pause for a moment, then strain
To follow a scent, he marched on. Another stain
Fell onto his shroud. He had never run away.
Kanut stopped walking any farther then and there
And turned toward his broadsword's side to go that way.
A drop of blood, as if it had come from a nightmare,
Fell on him and stained the hand he could barely see.
For a second time he turned away and changed his stride
The way one turns the pages of a registry,
And started walking toward the left and sinister side.
A drop of blood fell onto the winding sheet then
And Kanut jumped backwards, knowing he was alone
And wishing he were back in his death bed again.
A drop of blood fell onto the shroud. He turned to stone
(All colour gone from his face) and this warrior
Lowered his head and attempted to pray.
A drop of blood fell onto him. And just as before,
He became enraged – his prayer was frightened away –
Then, hesitant and gloomy, started walking again.
This appalling ghost passed by, and, now and then,
A drop of blood detached itself from the darkness
And fell onto this sombre whiteness unappeased.
Shaking like a poplar in the wind, Kanut imagined
These stains increasing and expanding without end:
Another and another and another! – like a flood
Of red needles shining vaguely at their tops.
Trickling into folds in the winding sheet, these drops,
Mixing together, created cloudlets of blood.
He walked on. He walked on. The blood kept coming down
Drop by drop, from that vault no one can sound –
Continuously, noiselessly, as though it might
Be falling from feet hanging from a gibbet at night.
Alas! Who was shedding each formidable tear?
Infinity. Kanut advanced, trembling with fear,
Toward paradise, pale, no longer looking around,
Into the ocean of night without a sound.
Finally, walking always as though in a haze,
He came to a closed door from which the brilliant rays

Sous laquelle passait un jour mystérieux;
Alors sur son linceul il abaissa les yeux;
C'était l'endroit sacré, c'était l'endroit terrible;
On ne sait quel rayon de Dieu semble visible;
De derrière la porte on entend l'hosanna.

Le linceul était rouge et Kanut frissonna.

Et c'est pourquoi Kanut, fuyant devant l'aurore
Et reculant, n'a pas osé paraître encore
Devant le juge au front duquel le soleil luit;
C'est pourquoi ce roi sombre est resté dans la nuit,
Et, sans pouvoir rentrer dans sa blancheur première,
Sentant, à chaque pas qu'il fait vers la lumière,
Une goutte de sang sur sa tête pleuvoir,
Rôde éternellement sous l'énorme ciel noir.

Le Travail des captifs

Dieu dit au roi: «Je suis ton Dieu. Je veux un temple.»

C'est ainsi, dans l'azur où l'astre le contemple,
Que Dieu parla; du moins le prêtre l'entendit.
Et le roi vint trouver les captifs, et leur dit:
– «En est-il un de vous qui sache faire un temple?
– Non, dirent-ils. – J'en vais tuer cent pour l'exemple,
Dit le roi. Dieu demande un temple en son courroux.
Ce que Dieu veut du roi, le roi le veut de vous.
C'est juste.» –
        C'est pourquoi l'on fit mourir cent hommes.
Alors un des captifs cria: – «Sire, nous sommes
Convaincus. Faites-nous, roi, dans les environs,
Donner une montagne, et nous la creuserons.
– Une caverne? dit le roi. – Roi qui gouvernes,
Dieu ne refuse point d'entrer dans les cavernes,
Dit l'homme, et ce n'est pas une rébellion
Que faire un temple à Dieu de l'antre du lion.
– Faites,» dit le roi.

Of a strange and mysterious dawn were streaming out –
Then lowered his eyes again to look at his shroud.
This was the holy, awe-inspiring place.
You weren't sure which of God's rays shone. Behind the gates
Hosannas rose up and you could hear the angels sing.

The shroud was soaked with blood and Kanut was shivering.

And that is why Kanut, rebuffed and fleeing out of fear
From the light of the dawn, hasn't yet dared appear
Before the judge whose forehead shines forever with the sun;
That is why this dark king has remained in the night:
Because he can't be pure again, his sin can't be undone.
And sensing at every step he takes toward the light
A drop of blood falling on his head, that is why
He prowls eternally through the enormous black sky.

The Work of the Prisoners

God spoke: 'I am your God. I want a temple built for me.'

It was thus, where the stars contemplate Him, that He
(At least according to the high priest) commanded.
And so the king approached the prisoners and demanded:
'Does any one of you know how to build a temple?'
'No,' they said. 'Kill a hundred men as an example,'
Said the king. 'God is asking this in anger. And when
God asks the king, the king asks you – and that is how
It should be.'
                    That is why they killed a hundred men.
Afterwards one prisoner spoke up: 'We are now
Convinced, sire. All you have to do is look about
And find a nearby mountain: we will hollow it out.'
'A cavern?' asked the king. 'O king who reigns on high,
God does not refuse to enter caves,' the man replied.
'And great, sublime king, it is no rebellion when
Your subjects build a temple from a lion's den.'
'Then do it,' said the king.

L'homme eut donc une montagne,
Et les captifs, traînant les chaînes de leur bagne,
Se mirent à creuser ce mont, nommé Galgal;
Et l'homme était leur chef, bien qu'il fût leur égal,
Mais dans la servitude, ombre où rien ne pénètre,
On a pour chef l'esclave à qui parle le maître.

Ils creusèrent le mont Galgal profondémont.
Quand ils eurent fini, l'homme dit: — «Roi clément
Vos prisonniers ont fait ce que le ciel désire;
Mais ce temple est à vous avant d'être à Dieu, sire;
Que votre Éternité daigne venir le voir.
— J'y consens, répondit le roi. — Notre devoir,
Reprit l'humble captif prosterné sur les dalles,
Est d'adorer la cendre où marchent vos sandales;
Quand vous plaît-il de voire notre œuvre? — Sur-le-champ.»
Alors le maître et l'homme, à ses pieds se couchant,
Furent mis sous un dais sur une plate-forme;
Un puits était bouché par une pierre énorme,
La pierre fut levée, un câble hasardeux
Soutint les quatre coins du trône, et tous les deux
Descendirent au fond du puits, unique entrée
De la montagne à coups de pioches éventrée.
Quand ils furent en bas, le prince s'étonna.
«C'est de cette façon qu'on entre dans l'Etna,
C'est ainsi qu'on pénètre au trou de la Sibylle,
C'est ainsi qu'on aborde à l'Hadès immobile,
Mais ce n'est pas ainsi qu'on arrive au saint lieu.
— Qu'on monte ou qu'on descende, on va toujours à Dieu,
Dit l'architecte, ayant comme un forçat la marque;
O roi, soyez ici le bienvenu, monarque
Qui, parmi les plus grands et parmi les premiers
Rayonnez, comme un cèdre au milieu des palmiers
Règne, et comme Pathmos brille entre les Sporades.
— Qu'est ce bruit? dit le roi. — Ce sont mes camarades
Qui laissent retomber le couvercle du puits.
— Mais nous ne pourrons plus sortir. — Rois, vos appuis
Sont les astres, ô prince, et votre cimeterre
Fait reculer la foudre, et vous êtes sur terre
Le soleil, comme au ciel le soleil est le roi.
Que peut craindre ici-bas Votre Hautesse? — Quoi!
Plus d'issue! — O grand roi, roi sublime, qu'importe!
Vous êtes l'homme à qui Dieu même ouvre la porte.»

So the man had his mountain,
And the prisoners, each dragging his convict's chain,
Began to hollow out the mountain called Gesequel.
The man was their leader, although he was their equal.
For in slavery, a darkness no one penetrates or seeks,
The leader is the slave to whom the master speaks.

They hollowed out Gesequel. The work was punishing.
And when they had finished, the man said, 'Gentle king,
Your prisoners have built all that heaven could desire;
The temple is yours before God's, however, sire:
May your Highness deign to look at it and judge its beauty.'
'I will,' the king consented with a nod. 'It is our duty,'
The humble slave responded on his knees as if to God,
'To worship the dust upon which your sandals trod.
When would you like to see our work?' 'Right away.'
And so the master and the prisoner made their way
To a platform covered over by a canopy.
A boulder stoppered up the shaft they couldn't see.
The stone was pried out, and a flimsy-looking cable
Attached to the platform's four corners. Both were able
Thereby to descend into the shaft now unblocked –
The only entrance into the disemboweled rock.
Once down there, the king was more astounded than before.
'This is how you enter into Etna's molten core;
This is how you penetrate the Sibyl's secret caves
Or reach the gates of Hell which nothing ever moves,
Not how you arrive at a holy place or ground.'
'One always goes toward God, whether going up or down,'
Said the architect branded with a convict's mark.
'O king, you are welcome here. O my monarch
Who, among the greatest and the highest spread your rays,
And, like a cedar in the midst of lesser trees,
Reign – just as Patmos shines among the Sporades.'
'What is that noise?' the king asked. 'My fellow slaves
Letting the cover to the temple fall back down.'
'But then we won't be able to get out.' 'Your great renown
Is such that your levers are the stars; your scimitar
Can roll back the thunder itself; on earth you are
The sun, as the sun is king in heaven every day.
What can Your Highness fear down here?' 'Did you just say
There's no way out?' 'King, what difference does that make?
You are he to whom God Himself unlocks the gate.'

Alors le roi cria: — «Plus de jour, plus de bruit,
Tout est noir, je ne vois plus rien. Pourquoi la nuit
Est-elle dans ce temple ainsi qu'en une cave?
Pourquoi? — Parce que c'est ta tombe,» dit l'esclave.

La Rose de l'Infante

Elle est toute petite, une duègne la garde.
Elle tient à la main une rose, et regarde.
Quoi? que regarde-t-elle? Elle ne sait pas. L'eau,
Un bassin qu'assombrit le pin et le bouleau;
Ce qu'elle a devant elle; un cygne aux ailes blanches,
Le bercement des flots sous la chanson des branches,
Et le profond jardin rayonnant et fleuri.
Tout ce bel ange a l'air dans la neige pétri.
On voit un grand palais comme au fond d'une gloire,
Un parc, de clairs viviers où les biches vont boire,
Et des paons étoilés sous les bois chevelus.
L'innocence est sur elle une blancheur de plus;
Toutes ses grâces font comme un faisceau qui tremble.
Autour de cette enfant l'herbe est splendide et semble
Pleine de vrais rubis et de diaments fins;
Un jet de saphirs sort des bouches des dauphins.
Elle se tient au bord de l'eau; sa fleur l'occupe;
Sa basquine est en point de Gênes; sur sa jupe
Un arabesque, errant dans les plis du satin,
Suit les mille détours d'un fil d'or florentin.
La rose épanouie et toute grande ouverte,
Sortant du frais bouton comme d'une urne ouverte,
Charge la petitesse exquise de sa main;
Quand l'enfant, allongeant ses lèvres de carmin,
Fronce, en la respirant, sa riante narine,
La magnifique fleur, royale et pupurine,
Cache plus qu'à demi ce visage charmant,
Si bien que l'œil hésite, et qu'on ne sait comment
Distinguer de la fleur ce bel enfant qui joue,
Et si l'on voit la rose ou si l'on voit la joue.
Ses yeux bleus sont plus beaux sous son pur sourcil brun.
En elle tout est joie, enchantement, parfum;

And then the king cried out, 'No more noise, no more light!
Everything is black. I am blind now. Why the night?
Tell me why this temple is darker than a cave.'
'Why? Because this temple is your tomb,' replied the slave.

The Infanta's Rose

She's a small girl whom a duenna watches over.
She is holding a rose in her hand, and looking over
Onto what? What *is* she looking at? She doesn't know.
The water, the pool into which the pine trees throw
Their shadows, whatever is in front of her, a swan,
The lapping of the waves underneath the branches' song,
And the vast garden there, flowering and aglow.
Everything about this angel has an air of snow.
The palace seems to jut out as the sun begins to sink;
The park, the clear ponds where the red deer go to drink,
The peacocks, the trees, appear against the background light.
Innocence on her is like a deeper shade of white.
Her graces make a kind of tied and trembling fascicle.
The lawn around this child is superb and often will
Trick the eye into seeing diamonds within it.
A stream of sapphires shoots from the mouths of the dolphins.
She keeps close to the pool and her flower. Her shirt
Was sewn in Genoa. The arabesque on her skirt,
Wandering around the silken contours of each fold,
Follows all the stitches made with Florentine gold.
The rose itself is in full bloom. It seems to turn
Toward her, pouring from the bud as from an urn,
And weigh down the exquisite smallness of her hand.
And when the child cracks her cherry lips into a smile,
Wrinkling her nostrils breathing in the flower's smell,
The brilliant, purple flower, in its own majestic style,
Hides more than half of her enchanting face so well
Your eyes hesitate, and your mind no longer knows
How to tell the flower and the playing girl apart,
And whether you are looking at her cheek or her rose.
Beneath her brown eyebrows, her blue eyes look prettier.
Everything is joy, enchantments, fresh scents for her.

Quel doux regard, l'azur! et quel doux nom, Marie!
Tout est rayon; son œil éclaire et son nom prie.
Poutant, devant la vie et sous le firmament,
Pauvre être! elle se sent très grande vaguement;
Elle assiste au printemps, à la lumière, à l'ombre,
Au grand soleil couchant horizontal et sombre,
À la magnificence éclatante du soir,
Aux ruisseaux murmurants qu'on entend sans les voir,
Aux champs, à la nature éternelle et sereine,
Avec la gravité d'une petite reine;
Elle n'a jamais vu l'homme que se courbant;
Un jour, elle sera duchesse de Brabant;
Elle gouverna la Flandre ou la Sardaigne.
Elle est l'infante, elle a cinq ans, elle dédaigne.
Car les enfants des rois sont ainsi; leurs front blancs
Portent un cercle d'ombre, et leurs pas chancelants
Sont des commencements de règne. Elle respire
Sa fleur en attendant qu'on lui cueille un empire.
Et son regard, déjà royal, dit: C'est à moi.
Il sort d'elle un amour mêlé d'un vague effroi.
Si quelqu'un, la voyant si tremblante et si frêle,
Fût-ce pour la sauver, mettait la main sur elle,
Avant qu'il eût pu faire un pas ou dire un mot,
Il aurait sur le front l'ombre de l'échafaud.

La douce enfant sourit, ne faisant autre chose
Que de vivre et d'avoir dans la main une rose,
Et d'être là devant le ciel, parmi les fleurs.

Le jour s'éteint; les nids chuchotent, querelleurs;
Les pourpres du couchant sont dans les branches d'arbre;
La rougeur monte au front des déesses de marbre
Qui semblent palpiter sentant venir la nuit;
Et tout ce qui planait redescend; plus de bruit,
Plus de flamme; le soir mystérieux recueille
Le soleil sous la vague et l'oiseau sous la feuille.

Pendant que l'enfant rit, cette fleur à la main,
Dans le vaste palais catholique romain
Dont chaque ogive semble au soleil une mitre,
Quelqu'un de formidable est derrière la vitre;
On voit d'en bas une ombre, au fond d'une vapeur,
De fenêtre en fenêtre errer, et l'on a peur;

What a sweet name, Marie! And what a sweet, sky-blue gaze!
Everything is light: her eyes shine; her name prays.
And yet, in the face of life in this terrestrial state,
Poor creature! she vaguely senses she is very great.
She's involved in the spring, in the darkness and the light,
In the large sun's setting, in the coming of the night,
In the evening's magnificent burst and brilliancy,
In the murmuring streams one hears but doesn't see,
In the fields, in a nature so eternal and serene –
All with the importance of a tiny little queen.
She's never seen a man who wasn't bowing or bent.
One day she will become the duchess of Brabant.
Flanders and Sardinia will be among her reigns.
She's a child; she is five years old; she disdains.
For princes' children are all like that; their bright heads
Are crowned in shadows, and their first uncertain steps
Mark the beginnings of their rule. She sniffs her flower,
Waiting for someone to pluck an empire for her.
Love mixed with a vague fear are all that you can see.
Her already regal gaze says *That belongs to me.*
If someone, noticing she was trembling or hurt,
(Even to save or comfort) laid a finger on her,
He would have the guillotine's shadow on his head
Before he could take a single step or say one word.

The sweet child smiles, not doing anything more
Than living, holding onto the rose as before,
And standing there among the flowers and the sky.

The day comes to an end; nests quarrel and sigh.
The setting sun lights up the branches of the trees.
Its redness fills the faces of the statues, and one sees
Goddesses blush, as though they sensed the coming night.
Everything which rose up redescends. No more light;
No more noise; the enigmatic scene receives
The sun beneath its water, and the birds beneath its leaves.

But while the child's laughing with her flower in her hands,
Within the dark recesses of the palace's expanse
Where every pointed arch looks like a mitre in the sun,
Something dreadful waits behind the glass; and yet one
Only sees – as in a dusky mist – a shade
Wandering between windows. And one is afraid.

Cette ombre au même endroit, comme en un cimetière,
Parfois est immobile une journée entière;
C'est un être effrayant qui semble ne rien voir;
Il rôde d'une chambre à l'autre, pâle et noir;
Il colle aux vitraux blancs son front lugubre, et songe;
Spectre blême! Son ombre aux feux du soir s'allonge;
Son pas funèbre est lent, comme un glas de beffroi;
Et c'est la Mort, à moins que ce ne soit le Roi.

C'est lui; l'homme en qui vit et tremble le royaume.
Si quelqu'un pouvait voir dans l'œil de ce fantôme
Debout en ce moment l'épaule contre un mur,
Ce qu'on apercevrait dans cet abîme obscur,
Ce n'est pas l'humble enfant, le jardin, l'eau moirée
Reflétant le ciel d'or d'une claire soirée,
Les bosquets, les oiseaux se becquetant entre eux,
Non: au fond de cet œil comme l'onde vitreux,
Sous ce fatal sourcil qui dérobe à la sonde
Cette prunelle autant que l'océan profonde,
Ce qu'on distinguerait, c'est, mirage mouvant,
Tout un vol de vaisseaux en fuite dans le vent,
Et dans l'écume, au pli des vagues, sous l'étoile,
L'immense tremblement d'une flotte à la voile,
Et, là-bas, sous la brume, une île, un blanc rocher,
Écoutant sur les flots ces tonnerres marcher.

Telle est la vision qui, dans l'heure où nous sommes,
Emplit le froid cerveau de ce maître des hommes;
Et qui fait qu'il ne peut rien voir autour de lui.
L'armada, formidable et flottant point d'appui
Du levier dont il va soulever tout un monde,
Traverse en ce moment l'obscurité de l'onde;
Le roi dans son esprit la suit des yeux, vainqueur,
Et son tragique ennui n'a plus d'autre lueur.

Philippe Deux était une chose terrible.
Iblis dans le Koran et Caïn dans la Bible
Sont à peine aussi noirs qu'en son Escurial
Ce royal spectre, fils du spectre impérial.
Philippe Deux était le Mal tenant la glaive.
Il occupait le haut du monde comme un rêve.
Il vivait: nul n'osait le regarder; l'effroi
Faisait une lumière étrange autour du roi;

Just as in a graveyard, this shadow doesn't stir
An entire day sometimes, and it never turns its back.
It is a creature which appears to stare and stare
And see nothing. It prowls from room to room, pale and black.
It glues its ghostly head onto the window pane and dreams.
Its fearful shadow lengthens in the evening's glowing beams.
Its gait is heavy, ringing as a large bell would ring.
It must be Death itself, unless it is the king.

It is he: the man in whom the kingdom lives and fears.
If you could see his phantom eyes when he appears
Standing with his shoulder up against a wall –
If you could look into this murky abyss,
You wouldn't see the child there, the garden, and all
Of the water reflecting the evening in its bliss,
Nor the hedges, nor the birds cooing to each other,
No: inside his eyes as glassy as sea water,
Underneath his eyebrows which mask what is within
(Ocean-like) from probing gazes, you can see
A moving mirage: thronging vessels in a sea
Fleeing in front of or speeding with the wind,
A flotilla at full sail plunging through the swell,
Beneath the stars, into the foams and wrinklings,
And an island over there – that white rock – in the haze
Listening to these thunderings over the waves.

At this moment, such is the vision or the whim
That fills the cold brain of this master of men,
And makes it so he can see nothing around him.
The armada, fulcrum of the lever with which he
Will lift up an entire world to show his might,
Is already ploughing through the darkness of the sea.
The king follows it with his mind's eye, a victor,
And his tragic boredom has no other source of light.

Philip the Second was a terrifying thing.
Neither the Bible's Cain nor the Koran's Iblis
Were quite as black as this spectre-like king –
This Philip, son of an imperial spectre.
Philip was Evil itself, wielding its sword.
Like a nightmare, he stood on the summit of the world.
While he lived, no one dared to look at him; and fear
Caused a strange light to shine on him when he appeared.

On tremblait rien qu'à voir passer ses majordomes;
Tant il se confondait, aux yeux troublés des hommes,
Avec l'abîme, avec les astres du ciel bleu!
Tant semblait grande à tous son approche de Dieu!
Sa volonté fatale, enfoncée, obstinée,
Était comme un crampon mis sur la destinée;
Il tenait l'Amérique et l'Inde, il s'appuyait
Sur l'Afrique, il régnait sur l'Europe, inquiet
Seulement du côté de la sombre Angleterre;
Sa bouche était silence et son âme mystère;
Son trône était de piège et de fraude construit;
Il avait pour soutien la force de la nuit;
L'ombre était le cheval de sa statue équestre.
Toujours vêtu de noir, ce Tout-Puissant terrestre
Avait l'air d'être en deuil de ce qu'il existait;
Il ressemblait au sphinx qui digère et se tait;
Immuable; étant tout, il n'avait rien à dire.
Nul n'avait vu ce roi sourire; le sourire
N'étant pas plus possible à ces lèvres de fer
Que l'aurore à la grille obscure de l'enfer.
S'il secouait parfois sa torpeur de couleuvre,
C'était pour assister le bourreau dans son œuvre,
Et sa prunelle avait pour clarté le reflet
Des bûchers sur lesquels par moments il soufflait.
Il était redoutable à la pensée, à l'homme,
À la vie, au progrès, au droit, dévot à Rome;
C'était Satan régant au nom de Jésus-Christ;
Les choses qui sortaient de son nocturne esprit
Semblaient un glissement sinistre de vipères.
L'Escurial, Burgos, Aranjuez, ses repaires,
Jamais n'illuminaient leurs livides plafonds;
Pas de festins, jamais de cour, pas de bouffons;
Les trahisons pour jeu, l'autodafé pour fête.
Les rois troublés avaient au-dessus de leur tête
Ses projets dans la nuit obscurément ouverts;
Sa rêverie était un poids sur l'univers;
Il pouvait et voulait tout vaincre et tout dissoudre;
Sa prière faisait le bruit sourd d'un foudre;
De grands éclairs sortaient de ses songes profonds.
Ceux auxquels il pensait disaient: Nous étouffons.
Et les peuples, d'un bout à l'autre de l'empire,
Tremblaient, sentant sur eux ces deux yeux fixes luire.

You trembled just seeing his stewards in the hall.
That's how grand his nearness to God seemed to all!
That is how much he was confused in men's eyes
With the bottomless abyss, with the stars of blue skies!
His fatal will – deep within and holding stubbornly –
Was like a large clamp thrust down on destiny.
The Indies and America were his; he had a piece
Of Africa; he had Europe; he was not quite at ease
Only with England on this side of the sea.
His mouth was silence and his soul a mystery.
His throne was built upon fraud and intrigue.
He possessed the force of night, with which he was in league.
Darkness itself was the statue of his horse.
Always dressed in black, this All-Powerful force
Appeared as if he mourned the fact of his existence.
He was like the Sphinx, taking all things in in silence.
Changeless. Being everything, what had he to say?
No one had seen this king smile; for a ray
Of hope on iron lips was no more possible
Than dawn breaking over the black gates of hell.
He shakes off his snake-like torpor with a jerk
Only to assist the executioner with his work.
And all of the sparkles in his eyes reflect the pyre
He blows on now and again so it burns higher.
He was the enemy of thought, and of the home,
Of life, of law, of progress. Though devoted to Rome,
He was Satan reigning in the name of Jesus Christ.
Everything which crept from his teeming brain at night
Seemed a pack of slithering vipers more than men.
Aranjuez, the Escurial, and Burgos – all his dens
Never had their dark ceilings lit with chandeliers.
No celebrations, no clowns, no courtiers:
Treason was the only game; the feast, autodafé.
Kings became troubled, being threatened every day
By all the secret projects he released at night.
His dreams weighed on the universe. And in his might
He could and wished to crush everything and push it under.
His prayers made a sound as deafening as thunder.
Lightning bolts issued from his dreams. When he'd awake
Those he merely thought about felt they would suffocate.
And nations of the empire came from everywhere
Trembling, sensing the fixity of his stare.

Charles fut le vautour, Philippe est le hibou.

Morne en son noir pourpoint, la toison d'or au cou,
On dirait du destin la froide sentinelle;
Son immobilité commande; sa prunelle
Luit comme un soupirail de caverne; son doigt
Semble, ébauchant un geste obscur que nul ne voit,
Donner un ordre à l'ombre et vaguement l'écrire.
Chose inouïe! il vient de grincer un sourire.
Un sourire insondable, impénétrable, amer.
C'est que la vision de son armée en mer
Grandit de plus en plus dans sa sombre pensée;
C'est qu'il la voit voguer par son dessein poussée,
Comme s'il était là, planant sous le zénith;
Tout est bien; l'océan docile s'aplanit,
L'armada lui fait peur comme au déluge l'arche;
La flotte se déploie en bon ordre de marche,
Et, les vaisseaux grandant les espaces fixés,
Échiquier de tillacs, de ponts, de mâts dressés,
Ondule sur les eaux comme une immense claie.
Ces vaisseaux sont sacrés; les flots leur font la haie;
Les courants, pour aider ces nefs à débarquer,
Ont leur besogne à faire et n'y sauraient manquer;
Autour d'elles la vague avec amour déferle,
L'écueil se change en port, l'écume tombe en perle.
Voici chaque galère avec son gastadour;
Voilà ceux de l'Escaut, voilà ceux de l'Adour;
Les cent mestres de camp et les deux connétables;
L'Allemagne a donné ses ourques redoutables,
Naples ses brigantins, Cadix ses galions,
Lisbonne ses marins, car il faut des lions.
Philippe se penche, et, qu'importe l'espace!
Non seulement il voit, mais il entend. On passe,
On court, on va. Voici le cri des porte-voix,
Le pas des matelots courant sur les pavois,
Les moços, l'amiral appuyé sur son page,
Les tambours, les sifflets des maîtres d'équipage,
Les signaux pour la mer, l'appel pour les combats,
Le fracas sépulchral et noir du branle-bas.
Sont-ce des cormorans? sont-ce des citadelles?
Les voiles font un vaste et sourd battement d'ailes;
L'eau gronde, et tout ce groupe énorme vogue, fuit,
Et s'enfle et roule avec un prodigieux bruit.

Charles was the vulture; Philip is the owl.

In black, with a gold chain round his neck like a towel...
You'd say he was the sentinel of destiny.
His stillness commands. And the pupils in each eye
Light up like air holes in a cave. His finger seems
To trace in some obscure gesture nobody sees
An order to the shadows, scrawling it on air.
The unheard of happens! He has just cracked a smile,
Inscrutable and bitter, as if something held it there:
It is a vision of his army, all the while
Advancing, growing larger in the darkness of his mind.
That's because it glides along, propelled by his design.
As if he were present, he can see his vessels scud
Effortlessly along. The docile ocean flattens out.
The fleet astounds the water like the Ark in the Flood.
All ships are perfectly deployed and move about
Within the positions they're assigned to protect.
It is a chessboard of decks and upright masts
Bobbing on the water like a massive fishing net.
His ships are sacred: waves line up and let them pass.
The currents, helping them disembark and keep their form,
Have their assigned tasks they won't fail to perform.
Waves break almost lovingly around the sterns in swirls.
Reefs change into harbours, foam and spindrift into pearls.
Look at each commander atop each man-of-war:
Here are those from Escaut; over there those from Adour;
One hundred post captains; two High Constables.
Germany supplies its ourques for the alliance,
Cadix its galleons, Naples brigantines,
And Lisbon its seamen – for one must have some lions.
Philip leans forward now (What does distance matter?)
And not only sees but can hear the sailors scatter
Hurrying to their posts. Alarms and trumpet blasts:
Sounds of sailors running on the decks and climbing masts,
The cabinboys, the admiral giving orders to his page,
The drums, the boatswain's whistles, sudden calls to engage
The enemy, signals for attack sent on their way,
The black and funereal noise of disarray.
Are they vultures? fortresses? One hears shudderings.
The topsails make a deafening sound like flapping wings.
The water growls, and this huge flotilla buoys
Itself up, and glides, rolling with a thunderous noise.

Et le lugubre roi sourit de voir groupées
Sur quatre cents vaisseaux quatrevingt mille épées.
O rictus du vampire assouvissant sa faim!
Cette pâle Angleterre, il la tient donc enfin!
Qui pourrait la sauver? Le feu va prendre aux poudres.
Philippe dans sa droite a la gerbe des foudres;
Qui pourrait délier ce faisceau dans son poing?
N'est-il pas le seigneur qu'on ne contredit point?
N'est-il pas l'héritier de César? le Philippe
Dont l'ombre immense va du Gange au Pausilippe?
Tout n'est-il pas fini quand il a dit: Je veux!
N'est-ce pas lui qui tient la victoire aux cheveux?
N'est-ce pas lui qui lance en avant cette flotte,
Ces vaisseaux effrayants dont il est le pilote
Et que la mer charrie ainsi qu'elle le doit?
Ne fait-il pas mouvoir avec son petit doigt
Tous ces dragons ailés et noirs, essaim sans nombre?
N'est-il pas, lui, le roi? n'est-il pas l'homme sombre
À qui ce tourbillon de monstres obéit?

Quand Béit-Cifresil, fils d'Abdallah-Béit,
Eut creusé le grand puits de la mosquée, au Caire,
Il y grava: «Le ciel est à Dieu; j'ai la terre.»
Et, comme tout se tient, se mêle et se confond,
Tous les tyrans n'étant qu'un seul despote au fond,
Ce que dit ce sultan jadis, ce roi le pense.

Cependant, sur le bord du bassin, en silence,
L'infante tient toujours sa rose gravement,
Et, doux ange aux yeux bleus, la baise par moment.
Soudain un souffle d'air, une de ces haleines
Que le soir frémissant jette à travers les plaines,
Tumultueux zéphyr, effleurant l'horizon,
Trouble l'eau, fait frémir les joncs, met un frisson
Dans les lointains massifs de myrte et d'asphodèle,
Vient jusqu'au bel enfant tranquille, et, d'un coup d'aile,
Rapide, et secouant même l'arbre voisin,
Effeuille brusquement la fleur dans le bassin.
Et l'infante n'a plus dans la main qu'une épine.
Elle se penche, et voit sur l'eau cette ruine;
Elle ne comprend pas; qu'est-ce que donc? Elle a peur;
Et la voilà qui cherche au ciel avec stupeur
Cette brise qui n'a pas craint de lui déplaire.

The gloomy king smiles to himself to see aboard
His four hundred vessels, some eighty-thousand swords.
A vampire's open mouth, about to devour!
Finally he will have England when they land!
Who can save her now? One spark ignites the powder.
Philip holds the sheaf of lightning bolts in his right hand.
And who can loosen this tied bundle from his fist?
Isn't he the master no one ever contradicts?
Doesn't he descend from Caesar's line? This Philip who
Casts a shadow stretching from the Ganges to the Po?
Aren't things decided when he says: 'I want it so'?
Isn't he the one who holds success by the throat?
Isn't it he who put this very fleet afloat?
These terrifying ships he steered across the ocean?
These vessels which the sea, as it should, helps on their way?
Didn't his little finger set all this in motion,
All of these black, wingèd dragons poised to kill?
And isn't he the king? Must not these monsters obey
This enigmatic man who bends the whole world to his will?

When the son of Abdallah Bei-it, Bei-it Cifresil,
Had dug the great well for Cairo's mosque, he placed a sign
In front which said: 'The sky belongs to God; the earth is mine.'
And since all things connect to each other, mix, and blend,
All tyrants merge into one despot in the end,
And this king believes what that sultan boasted then.

Meanwhile, in silence at the pool's edge once again,
The infanta is still holding onto her rose
And, like a blue-eyed angel, kisses it now and then.
Suddenly, one of those gusts the evening throws
Across the plains, setting all the air trembling,
Turns violent as it passes over the horizon,
Disturbs the water, makes the rushes shake as well
As the distant plateaus fringed with asphodel,
Makes its way to the child, so serene and beautiful,
And then, in a wing's beat, strikes the nearby tree
And strips all the petals of the rose into the pool.
Now the child only has a thorn in her hand.
She looks at the destruction and does not understand
What has happened (What *is* this then?) for she is afraid.
She looks at the heavens, searching them in a blur
For the wind gust which doesn't seem to mind displeasing her.

Que faire? le bassin semble plein de colère;
Lui, si clair tout à l'heure, il est noir maintenant;
Il a des vagues; c'est une mer bouillonnant;
Toute la pauvre rose est éparse sur l'onde;
Ses cent feuilles, que noie et roule l'eau profonde,
Tournoyant, naufrageant, s'en vont de tous côtés
Sur mille petits flots par la brise irrités;
On croit voir dans un gouffre une flotte qui sombre.
– «Madame, dit la duègne avec sa face d'ombre
À la petite fille étonnée et rêvant,
Tout sur terre appartient aux princes, hors le vent.»

Après la Bataille

Mon père, ce héros au sourire si doux,
Suivi d'un seul housard qu'il aimait entre tous
Pour sa grande bravoure et pour sa haute taille,
Parcourait à cheval, le soir d'une bataille,
Le champ couvert de morts sur qui tombait la nuit.
Il lui sembla dans l'ombre entendre un faible bruit.
C'était un espagnol de l'armée en déroute
Qui se traînait sanglant sur le bord de la route,
Râlant, brisé, livide, et mort plus qu'à moitié,
Et qui disait: – À boire, à boire par pitié! –
Mon père, ému, tendit à son housard fidèle
Une gourde de rhum qui pendait à sa selle,
Et dit: – Tiens, donne à boire à ce pauvre blessé. –
Tout à coup, au moment où le housard baissé
Se penchait vers lui, l'homme, une espèce de maure,
Saisit un pistolet qu'il étreignait encore,
Et vise au front mon père en criant: Caramba!
Le coup passa si près que le chapeau tomba
Et que le cheval fit un écart en arrière.
– Donne-lui tout de même à boire, dit mon père.

But what can she do? The pool itself seems full of rage.
Its once crystal surface now turns black and shadowy.
Waves break across it. It's a boiling sea.
The entire rose is dispersed across the pool,
And its one hundred petals which the water scatters round,
Twisting and flying everywhere, are quickly drowned
In thousands of wavelets stirred up by the wind.
You'd swear you saw a fleet there sinking in the swirl.
'My lady,' the duenna says from shade she's hidden in,
And turning toward the dreaming and astonished little girl,
'Everything on earth belongs to kings, except the wind.'

After the Battle

My father, that warrior with a reassuring smile,
Followed by a lone hussar he loved especially
For his great courage and extraordinary size,
Was riding through a battlefield on which you could see
The dead on whom the night was slowly coming down.
My father thought he heard a cry. He turned around
And saw a Spaniard from the routed troops revive,
Who, coughing, broken, pale, and more dead than alive,
Was dragging himself along the road from which they'd come
Imploring: 'A drink please, have pity if you have some!'
My father was moved. He took out a gourd of rum
Hanging from his saddle, and passed it to his aide.
'Give the man a drink!' he said. The huge hussar obeyed –
Or tried to. No sooner had the aide gone to alight
To give the man the drink, when he, a kind of Moor,
Lifted up the pistol which he still held onto tight,
Aimed it at my father's forehead, fired, and swore.
The shot passed so close to him his horse vaulted back,
And the hat he was wearing was knocked from his head.
'Give him a drink anyway,' my father said.

J'avais vingt ans, j'étais criblé de coups de lance,
On me porta sanglant et pâle à l'ambulance.
On me fit un lit d'herbe, on me déshabilla.
J'avais sur moi des vers; j'étais, dans ce temps-là,
Poète, comme Horace amoureux de Barine.
Les lances qui m'avaient fort piqué la poitrine
Avaient aussi troué mes quatrains à Chloris.
Tout manquait; on n'est pas soigné comme à Paris
Dans ces vieilles forêts du pays de Thuringe;
Le chirugien dit: – Nous n'avons pas de linge.
Il lut mes vers et dit: – C'est un païen, je crois.
La sœur de charité fit un signe de croix.
Et le docteur reprit: – Pas de linge: que faire? –
Ah! cette guerre était grande, et je la préfère
À votre paix. Quel temps! je suis un des témoins.
J'ai des grades de plus et des cheveux de moins,
Le vieux général songe au jeune capitaine,
Et l'envie. Ah! l'aurore est charmante, et lointaine! –
Donc je perdais mon sang, j'étais évanoui.
J'étais jeune, blessé, mourant, mais vivant; oui,
Très vivant! Le docteur disait: – La mort est sûre
Si l'on ne parvient pas à bander la blessure;
Du linge! ou dans une heure il est mort! – Cependant
Il partit. La bataille autour de nous grondant,
Pleine de chocs, de meurtre et d'ombre, et des haleines
De l'immense agonie éparse dans les plaines,
L'appelait de sa voix formidable au secours;
On ne donne aux blessés que des instants très courts.
J'étais seul, et mon flanc saignait, et mon épaule
Ruisselait, et la sœur de Saint-Vincent de Paule,
Très jeune, pâle, et rose à travers sa pâleur,
Me veillait. Elle dit: – Sauvons-le! quel malheur!
S'il mourait, il serait damné, ce pauvre impie! –
Elle arracha sa guimpe et fit de la charpie.
Tout entière à ses soins pour le jeune inconnu,
Elle ne voyait pas que son sein était nu.
Moi, je rouvrais les yeux… – O muses de Sicile,
Dire à quoi je pensais, ce serait difficile!

The Sister of Mercy

I was twenty. I had been stabbed with bayonets.
They took me to the field hospital, pale and wet
With blood, undid my coat and laid me on the grass.
At that time I wrote verses, and thought I could pass
For a poet like Horace in love with Barinae.
Those bayonets, cutting deep into my chest,
Had pierced through my quatrains to Chloris on the way.
In the woods of Thuringia, the medics did their best,
But it was no Paris. And the patients they received!
The surgeon yelled, 'Without some linen, it's a loss,'
Then skimmed my lines and said, 'A pagan, I believe.'
The sister of mercy made the sign of the cross.
He yelled again, 'No bandages! There's nothing we can do.'
That war was great, and I prefer it to what you
Call peace. What a time that was! And I was there.
I have more ranks now and a thinner head of hair.
The ageing general thinks of that captain today
And envies him. Ah! Dawn is sweet and far away!
– As I said, I was bleeding; I had fainted no less.
I was young, wounded, dying, but alive still, oh yes,
Very much alive! The doctor said, 'He'll die soon
If no one finds some bandages to bind up the wound.
Some linen! He has at most an hour.' Nonetheless
He left me there. The raging battle, furious
With shudderings and darkness, killings, gasps of pain,
And agony, intense and scattered over the plain,
Was calling for help in the voice of every soldier.
The wounded were visited briefly, if at all.
I was alone; my side was bleeding, and my shoulder
Quivering. The sister of Saint Vincent de Paul –
Pale, very young, and turning red through her white skin –
Was watching me. She cried out, 'It would be a sin
Not to save him! The poor young man would go to hell!'
She took off her wimple and tore the cloth up well.
Fearing for the unknown young captain in her care,
She forgot to notice that her breasts were now bare.
I opened my eyes. Sicilian muses! Sacred nine!
If I could only tell you what thoughts crossed my mind!

Rome avait trop de gloire, ô dieux, vous la punîtes
Par le triomphe énorme et lâche des Samnites;
Et nous vîmes ce deuil, nous qui vivons encor.
Cela n'empêche pas l'aurore aux rayons d'or
D'éclore et d'apparaître au-dessus des collines.
Un champ de course est près des tombes Esquilines,
Et parfois, quand la foule y fourmille en tous sens,
J'y vais, l'œil vaguement fixé sur les passants.
Ce champ mène aux logis de guerre, où les cohortes
Vont et viennent ainsi que dans les villes fortes;
Avril sourit, l'oiseau chante, et, dans le lointain,
Derrière les coteaux où reluit le matin,
Où les roses des bois entr'ouvrent leur pétales,
On entend murmurer les trompettes fatales;
Et je médite, ému. J'étais aujourd'hui là.
Je ne sais pas pourquoi le soleil se voila;
Les nuages parfois dans le ciel se resserrent.
Tout à coup, à cheval et lance au poing, passèrent
Des vétérans aux fronts hâlés, aux larges mains;
Ils avaient l'ancien air des grands soldats romains;
Et les petits enfants accouraient pour les suivre;
Trois cavaliers, soufflant dans des buccins de cuivre,
Marchaient en tête, et, comme au front de l'escadron,
Chacun d'eux embouchait à son tour le clairon,
Sans couper la fanfare ils reprenaient haleine.
Ces gens de guerre étaient superbes dans la plaine;
Ils marchaient de leur pas antique et souverain.
Leurs boucliers portaient des méduses d'airain,
Et l'on voyait sur eux Gorgone et tous ses masques;
Ils défilaient, dressant les cimiers de leurs casques,
Dignes d'être éclairés par des soleils levants,
Sous des crins de lion qui se tordaient aux vents.
Que ces hommes sont beaux! disaient les jeunes filles.
Tout souriait, les fleurs embaumaient les charmilles,
Le peuple était joyeux, le ciel était doré,
Et, songeant que c'étaient des vaincus, j'ai pleuré.

After the Battle of the Caudine Forks

Rome had too much glory, and you gods punished her
With the Samnites' cowardly and monstrous massacre,
And we who lived through it are living with it still.
– None of which prevents the dawn from breaking on each hill
And appearing in the sky with its gold-orange rays.
There's a racecourse not far from the Esquiline graves,
And when I'm walking past it sometimes, I vaguely stare
At all the people who are swarming everywhere.
This course abuts a practice field where cohorts come and go
As if they were patrolling walled cities long ago;
Where April smiles, birds sing, in far-away skies
Behind all those hills, you can watch the sun rise,
Or listen to the military trumpets blare;
Where forest roses open up their petals; and where
I sit pensively – I was over there today.
I don't know why the sun showed its face and went away
Or why the clouds opened then closed the sky again.
Out of nowhere, with their lances up, a veteran
Cavalry regiment rode by; you saw the stares
Of sunburnt faces just like Roman legionnaires.
And little children ran up, trying to follow them.
Three horsemen lead the pack as if heading a squadron,
Blowing copper buccins from the back of the throat.
Each of them in turn put his lips to a bugle,
And somehow kept breathing without missing a note.
All of these warriors were imposing in the field,
Advancing with their antique, victorious paces.
A bronze medusa was imprinted on each shield;
You could see all of the contorted Gorgon faces.
They paraded, holding up their helmets so they gleamed
The way they might have shone in rising suns. Their plumes seemed
Like lions' manes twisting in the wind as they passed.
Little girls were shouting out, 'How beautiful they are!'
Everything seemed happy; scents of flowers filled the air.
The sky was gold and brilliant; people smiled; hearts leapt.
Remembering these were defeated men, I wept.

From *La Fin de Satan* (1886)

Et Nox Facta Est

Depuis quatre mille ans il tombait dans l'abîme.

Il n'avait pas encor pu saisir une cime,
Ni lever une fois son front démesuré.
Il s'enfonçait dans l'ombre et la brume, effaré,
Seul, et derrière lui, dans les nuits éternelles,
Tombaient plus lentement les plumes de ses ailes.
Il tombait foudroyé, morne, silencieux,
Triste, la bouche ouverte et les pieds vers les cieux,
L'horreur du gouffre empreinte à sa face livide.
Il cria: – Mort! – les poings tendus vers l'ombre vide.
Ce mot plus tard fut homme et s'appela Caïn.
Il tombait. Tout à coup un roc heurta sa main;
Il l'étreignit, ainsi qu'un mort étreint sa tombe,
Et s'arrêta.
            Quelqu'un, d'en haut, lui cria: – Tombe!
Les soleils s'éteindront autour de toi, maudit! –
Et la voix dans l'horreur immense se perdit.
Et, pâle, il regarda vers l'éternelle aurore.
Les soleils étaient loin, mais ils brillaient encore.
Satan dressa la tête et dit, levant le bras:
– Tu mens! – Ce mot plus tard fut l'âme de Judas.
Pareil aux dieux d'airain debout sur leurs pilastres,
Il attendit mille ans, l'œil fixé sur les astres.
Les soleils étaient loin, mais ils brillaient toujours.
La foudre alors gronda dans les cieux froids et sourds.
Satan rit, et cracha du côté du tonnerre.
L'immensité, qu'emplit l'ombre visionnaire,
Frissonna. Ce crachat fut plus tard Barabbas.
Un souffle qui passait le fit tomber plus bas.

From *The End of Satan*

Et Nox Facta Est

For four thousand years he fell into the abyss.

He hadn't yet been able to seize a precipice
To check his flight, nor lift his huge forehead even once.
He sank into the fog and the shadows, passing suns,
Plunging toward eternal night, alone and resigned.
The feathers from his wings fell more slowly behind.
He fell in silence, thunderstruck yet ready to defy,
Sad, his mouth open and his feet stretched toward the sky,
His face imprinted with the fear of the abyss.
He yelled out, 'Death!' and clenched his fists toward nothingness.
Later on that word became a man they called Cain.
Out of nowhere a rock sliced the air he was clawing.
He embraced it, like a dead man embracing his grave,
And stopped.
          A voice above cried out to him, 'Keep falling!
You are damned. Every sun around you will expire!'
The voice resounded in the horror, then was gone.
Pale, Satan looked out toward the dawn's eternal fire.
The suns were far away, but they were still shining.
Lifting his head and arms up, Satan shouted, 'Liar!'
– That word became the soul of Judas later on.
Like a bronze idol set on top of a pilaster,
He waited for a thousand years, his eyes fixed on the stars.
The suns were far away, but they were still shining.
Thunder started rumbling in the deaf and chill skies.
Satan laughed, spitting upward at the sky's loud collapses.
The vast expanses visionary shadows fill
Shuddered. Later on that spit became Barrabas.
A passing gust of wind made him fall further still.

From *Toute la Lyre* (1888)

«L'hexamètre ...»

L'hexamètre, pourvu qu'en rompant la césure,
Il montre la pensée et garde la mesure,
Vole et marche; il se tord, il rampe, il est debout.
Le vers coupé contient tous les tons, et dit tout.
C'est ce qui fait qu'Horace est si charmant à lire.
Son doigt souple à la fois touche à toute la lyre.

À Théophile Gautier

Ami, poète, esprit, tu fuis notre nuit noire.
Tu sors de nos rumeurs pour entrer dans la gloire;
Et désormais ton nom rayonne aux purs sommets.
Moi qui t'ai connu jeune et beau, moi qui t'aimais,
Moi qui, plus d'une fois, dans nos altiers coups d'aile,
Éperdu, m'appuyais sur ton âme fidèle,
Moi, blanchi par les jours sur ma tête neigeant,
Je me souviens des temps écoulés, et songeant
À ce jeune passé qui vit nos deux aurores,
À la lutte, à l'orage, aux arènes sonores,
À l'art nouveau qui s'offre, au peuple criant: oui,
J'écoute ce grand vent sublime évanoui.

*

Fils de la Grèce antique et de la jeune France,
Ton fier respect des morts fut rempli d'espérance;
Jamais tu ne fermas les yeux à l'avenir.
Mage à Thèbes, druide au pied du noir menhir,
Flamine aux bords du Tibre et brahme aux bords du Gange,
Mettant sur l'arc du dieu la flèche de l'archange,
D'Achille et de Roland hantant les deux chevets,
Forgeur mystérieux et puissant, tu savais

From *All the Lyre*

'The hexameter ...'

The hexameter, breaking with caesuras as it ought
To keep the measure better, and express a clear thought,
Soars and marches, twists or crawls along, then stands tall.
The broken line contains every tone and says it all.
That's what makes Horace so exciting to read.
His finger strikes all the lyre's strings in one sweep.

To Théophile Gautier

Friend, poet, spirit, you are fleeing from our night.
You are leaving our uproar to enter the light,
And your name is spreading out like rays from a cloud.
I who knew you young, I who loved you then as now,
I who, dismayed more than once by our proud
Wing-beaten flights, would lean on your soul for support,
I whose head and hair the passing days are snowing on,
I see the fled years, and, as I'm dreaming of what's gone,
Of our sun's rising to this height from which it falls,
Of the storm, the struggle, and the echoing halls,
Of the art, and the people shouting 'yes' to this time –
I listen to the vanished wind of the sublime.

*

Son of ancient Greece and of a much younger France,
Your respect for the dead was a hope in advance,
And you always looked to the future without fear.
Theban mage, druid at the base of a menhir,
High priest near the Tiber, Brahmin near the Ganges,
You haunted the epics of Roland and Achilles
And notched Michael's arrows in God's mighty bow.
Magical coiner, you would somehow always know

Tordre tous les rayons dans une seule flamme;
Le couchant rencontrait l'aurore dans ton âme;
Hier croisait demain dans ton fécond cerveau;
Tu sacrais le vieil art aïeul de l'art nouveau;
Tu comprenais qu'il faut, lorsqu'une âme inconnue
Parle au peuple, envolée en éclairs dans la nue,
L'écouter, l'accepter, l'aimer, ouvrir les cœurs;
Calme, tu dédaignais l'effort vil des moqueurs
Écumant sur Eschyle et bavant sur Shakspeare;
Tu savais que ce siècle a son air qu'il respire,
Et que, l'art ne marchant qu'en se transfigurant,
C'est embellir le beau que d'y joindre le grand.
Et l'on t'a vu pousser d'illustres cris de joie
Quand le Drame a saisi Paris comme une proie,
Quand l'antique hiver fut chassé par Floréal,
Quand l'astre inattendu du moderne idéal
Est venu tout à coup, dans le ciel qui s'embrase
Luire, et quand l'Hippogriffe a relayé Pégase!

*

Je te salue au seuil sévère du tombeau.
Va chercher le vrai, toi qui sus trouver le beau.
Monte l'âpre escalier. Du haut des sombres marches,
Du noir pont de l'abîme on entrevoit les arches;
Va! meurs! la dernière heure est le dernier degré.
Pars, aigle, tu vas voir des gouffres à ton gré;
Tu vas voir l'absolu, le réel, le sublime.
Tu vas sentir le vent sinistre de la cime
Et l'éblouissement du prodige éternel.
Ton olympe, tu vas le voir du haut du ciel,
Tu vas du haut du vrai voir l'humaine chimère,
Même celle de Job, même celle d'Homère,
Âme, et du haut de Dieu tu vas voir Jéhovah.
Monte, esprit! Grandis, plane, ouvre tes ailes, va!

Lorsqu'un vivant nous quitte, ému, je le contemple;
Car entrer dans la mort, c'est entrer dans le temple.
Et quand un homme meurt, je vois distinctement
Dans son ascension mon propre avènement.
Ami, je sens du sort la sombre plénitude;
J'ai commencé la mort par de la solitude,
Je vois mon profond soir vaguement s'étoiler.

How to bend all the rays into one glowing coal.
The setting sun encountered the dawn in your soul.
Yesterday blended with tomorrow in your brain.
You blessed the new art, but the old art would remain.
You understood that when an unknown spirit speaks
To the people, like lightning trailing fiery streaks,
One must listen, accept, love, and open the heart;
And you stared down the mockers (calmly standing apart)
Seething at Aeschylus and spitting on Shakespeare.
You knew that this century breathed its own air,
And that, since art progresses by transfiguring,
It is adorning beauty and combining greatness there.
And many heard your laughter that would gush out and peal
When the theatre held Paris as if it were its prey,
And when that constellation of the modern ideal
(As April drove the ancient winter away)
Suddenly appeared, and the sky shimmered at us
Like dawn, and when Hippogriff relieved Pegasus!

*

I greet you at the threshold of Death to let you be.
Discover truth as you once discovered beauty.
Climb the bitter stairway. From the height of its steps,
You will see the black arches in the pit's lower depths.
So die – the final hour is the final step's degree.
Eagle, soar: you will see depths you desire to see.
You will see the absolute, the real, the sublime.
You will feel the summit's sinister wind when you climb
And the astonishing brilliance of eternity.
You will see your Olympus from the sky's balcony;
From truth's height you'll see human dreams for what they are,
Even Job's, even Homer's, which you'll glimpse from afar,
Oh soul! And you will see Jehovah with God's eye.
So climb, grow, soar, spread your wings open, fly!

When someone departs from us, I look at him well;
For entering death is entering the temple,
And when a man dies, I begin to see again
My future there in his ascension to heaven.
Friend, I can feel the hand of destiny intrude;
I've begun to die by seeking out solitude.
I see the stars of my deep night snuff out the day.

Voici l'heure où je vais, aussi moi, m'en aller.
Mon fil trop long frissonne et touche presque au glaive;
Le vent qui t'emporta doucement me soulève,
Et je vais suivre ceux qui m'aimaient, moi banni.
Leur œil fixe m'attire au fond de l'infini.
J'y cours. Ne fermez pas la porte funéraire.

Passons; car c'est la loi; nul ne peut s'y soustraire;
Tout penche; et ce grand siècle avec tous ses rayons
Entre en cette ombre immense où pâles nous fuyons.
Oh! quel farouche bruit font dans le crépuscule
Les chênes qu'on abat pour le bûcher d'Hercule!
Les chevaux de la mort se mettent à hennir,
Et sont joyeux, car l'âge éclatant va finir;
Ce siècle altier qui sut dompter le vent contraire,
Expire … – O Gautier! toi, leur égal et leur frère,
Tu pars après Dumas, Lamartine et Musset.
L'onde antique est tarie où l'on rajeunissait;
Comme il n'est plus de Styx il n'est plus de Jouvence.
Le dur faucheur avec sa large lame avance
Pensif et pas à pas vers le reste du blé;
C'est mon tour; et la nuit emplit mon œil troublé
Qui, devinant, hélas, l'avenir des colombes,
Pleure sur des berceaux et sourit à des tombes.

Here comes the hour when I too must go away.
My life's thread quivers as if waiting for the blow;
The wind that carried you off lifts me up also
And I'm about to follow all of those who loved me.
I sense their looks from the depths of infinity.
I am running there. Don't close any of Death's gates.

Let's pass by; it's the law; no one ever escapes.
Everything leans forward; and this great century
Enters the shadow from which everyone would flee.
The twilight resounds with the crashing of the trees
Now being cut to build the pyre of Hercules!
The horses of Death nibble at their bits and neigh
At this dazzling age that is about to pass away.
This proud century that knew how to tame the gale
Expires … Oh Gautier! you, their brother and equal,
You leave after Dumas, Musset, and Lamartine.
Our source has dried up as if it had never been.
And just as there's no Styx, there's no Fountain of Youth.
The reaper advances, gathering everything in
His path, which he cuts with his blade and passes by.
It's my turn; and the night fills up my troubled eye
Which sees the fate of doves in the future that looms,
And weeps on the cradles and smiles at the tombs.

Notes

General Remarks

AS WITH MY INTRODUCTION, my notes are meant to help readers understand and enjoy Hugo's poetry, but are by no means required reading. They provide some glosses on lines and phrases, place the poems in publishing and historical context, and offer some perspective on what is left out of my selection.

All but a handful of the poems are presented in their entireties. Of those presented in a less than complete form, at least two, 'To the Column' and 'Et Nox Facta Est' are the openings of longer poems which I would like to translate more fully. Another, 'Magnitudo Parvi', is potentially of this type, except that my translation of the first section of this very long poem feels more complete, perhaps because Hugo's subject matter is 'the greatness of the small'. The opening piece of my collection, 'To My Odes', is in fact the closing stanza of a longer poem with that title. Inspired by Gide's use of this stanza in his *Anthologie de la poésie française,* I am employing the six lines as a kind of epigraph. The different pieces entitled 'Setting Suns' are at once individual poems and parts of a sequence. The only other poems not presented in full, 'The Cow' and 'Reply to an Act of Accusation', are special cases. I have translated in verse everything except each poem's closing verse-paragraph, for which I provide prose translations in the notes along with the French originals. Generally I am uncomfortable with this degree of editorial intervention, but in these instances my decisions are firm. Both poems work better without their closing commentaries in verse, not only from a modern perspective but on their own aesthetic terms. I hope concerned readers will take the opportunity to compare the poems' endings for their own satisfaction.

I have compiled and edited the French texts from several sources whose titles and publication information I provide in my bibliography. Because Hugo's texts are well established and do not vary greatly from edition to edition, my editing consisted largely of checking stanza breaks and restoring suppressed accent marks to capital letters. The order of the French texts and translations is determined first by the publication dates of the collections in which the poems originally appeared, and second by the order of the poems within each collection. (For *The Legend of the Centuries,* I have chosen the second series for purposes of dating, in part because it is the collection's middle volume and in part because the final series is relatively small.) To give the reader a sense of chronology, I have marked each division between collections with a title page, including the volume's publication date or dates. At the same time, I have silently suppressed most dates and place names attached to the poems in their published versions. Hugo sometimes assigned fictitious dates and places of composition to his poems, as if to create a poetic narrative of his life. Without a more complete selection of his poems, however, the dates and place names do not add up to much and may distract the reader. (I comment more on Hugo's dating of poems in some notes.) With the exception of the two halves of *Contemplations,* 'Former Times' and 'Today', I have also suppressed subdivisions within collections. Like dates and place names, subdivisions require a kind of critical mass of poems to make any real impact or sense.

As confident as a translator may be about inclusions, it is hard not to regret some omissions. While I feel it is important that I have resisted including poems solely for the sake of proportional representation, I can imagine adding to my selection a couple of poems from each of Hugo's collections. I do not regret my scant representations of *Odes and Ballads, The Songs of Daybreak,* and most of the posthumously published collections, for example, and I trust that no one will grieve over the absence of such late and not-so-great poems as *The Pope* and *The Highest Pity.* In contrast, I feel that I have unfortunately excluded some wonderful poems from Hugo's best finished collections, *Les Contemplations* and *The Legend of the Centuries,* even as poems from these two books comprise the bulk of my selection. Prominent in my decisions to omit were concerns about overall space and my desire to provide readers with a user-friendly introduction to Hugo's poetry. Though one of its effects may be to emphasize the lyric side of Hugo, omitting some of the longer poems should not be viewed as a slight against Hugo's philosophical and visionary poetry, as my inclusion of poems like 'The Slope of Reverie' should make clear. I would in fact have liked to include more poetry from Hugo's fragmentary epic, *The End of Satan,* but judging that, for now at least, I lack the room for a selection substantial enough to convey the sweep and power of this work, I have held back from including all but its opening, finding some solace and a precedent in Hugo's practice of keeping poems in reserve. As I present it here, my selection from *The End of Satan* is both a poem in its own right and a hint of what is to come.

Chronology of Hugo's Life and Publications

Principal Events and Publications in Hugo's Life

1802: Victor-Marie Hugo born in Besançon on February 26.

1820: *Bug-Jargal* (novel).

1821: Death of mother (*née* Sophie Trébuchet).

1822: Publication of first book of poems, *Odes et poésies diverses* (*Odes and Other Poems*). Marriage to Adèle Foucher. Hugo's brother Eugène goes insane at wedding dinner.

1823: *Han d'Islande* (novel, *Hans of Iceland*). Birth of first child, Léopold, who dies after a few months. *Odes et poésies diverses* reworked into *Odes*.

1824: Birth of daughter, Léopoldine. *Odes* reworked into *Nouvelles Odes* (*New Odes*).

1826: Birth of son, Charles. *Nouvelles Odes* reworked into *Odes et Ballades* (*Odes and Ballads*).

1827: *Cromwell* (play) published with a long preface outlining Hugo's romantic aesthetic.

1828: Death of father, General Joseph-Léopold-Sigisbert Hugo. Final version of *Odes et Ballades* (*Odes and Ballads*). Birth of son, Victor (François-Victor).

1829: *Le Dernier Jour d'un condamné à mort* (novel, *The Last Day of a Condemned Man*). Play *Hernani* premières at the Théâtre Français. *Les Orientales* (poems, *Orientalia*).

1830: Battle of *Hernani* on February 25. Birth of daughter, Adèle.

1831: *Notre-Dame de Paris* (novel, *The Hunchback of Notre Dame*). Première of play *Marion de Lorme*. Sainte-Beuve and Madame Hugo begin affair. *Feuilles d'automne* (poems, *Leaves of Autumn*).

1832: Première of play *Le Roi s'amuse* (*The King Takes His Amusement*).

1833: Première of play *Lucrèce Borgia*. Juliette Drouet becomes Hugo's mistress. Premier of play *Marie Tudor*.

1835: *Les Chants du crépuscule* (poems, *The Songs of Daybreak*).

1837: *Les Voix intérieures* (poems, *Inner Voices*).

1838: Première of play *Ruy Blas*.

1840: *Les Rayons et les ombres* (poems, *Sunbeams and Shadows*).

1841: Elected to the Académie Française on third candidature (Hugo had previously tried in 1836 and 1839).

1843: Marriage of daughter Léopoldine and Charles Vacquerie, 15 February. Drowning of the couple at Villequier, 4 September. Première of play, *Les Burgraves* (*The Burgraves*).

1844: Beginning of affair with Madame Biard.

1845: Arrested in bed with Madame Biard for adultery.

1846: Death of Juliette Drouet's daughter, Claire.

1848–51: Hugo takes an active interest in politics following the 1848 revolution. He is elected to the legislative assembly in 1849 and initially supports Louis Napoleon, then declares himself a Republican (a liberal). After Louis Napoleon's coup on 2 December 1851, Hugo flees to Belgium with the help of Juliette Drouet.

1852: *Napoléon le Petit* (political tract, *Napoleon the Little*). Hugo family moves to the island of Jersey (a British possession just off the French coast).

1853: *Les Châtiments* (*Punishments*). Madame de Giradin initiates the Hugo family into the 'turning tables' (séances).

1855: Hugo family moves to Guernsey, another Channel Island.

1856: *Contemplations* (poems).

1859: Refuses amnesty offered by Louis Napoleon. First series of *La Légende des siècles* (poems, *The Legend of the Centuries*).

1862: *Les Misérables* (novel).

1863: Daughter Adèle flees to Canada in search of an English officer with whom she is infatuated.

1864: *William Shakespeare* (essay on genius).

1865: *Les Chansons des rues et des bois* (poems, *Songs of the Streets and the Woods*).

1866: *Les Travailleurs de la mer* (novel, *The Toilers of the Sea*).

1868: Birth of grandson, Georges (George). Death of Madame Hugo.

1869: *L'Homme qui rit* (novel, *The Laughing Man*). Birth of granddaughter, Jeanne (Jeannine).

1870: Returns from nineteen-year exile following the Franco-Prussian war, the capture of Louis Napoleon at Sedan, and the proclamation of the Third Republic.

1871: Elected *député* (national representative) of Paris. Death of son, Charles.

1872: *L'Année Terrible* (*The Horrific Year*). Daughter Adèle brought back from the New World and placed in an asylum.

1873: Death of son, François-Victor.

1874: *Quatrevingt-treize* (novel, *Ninety-Three*).

1876: Elected senator of Paris.

1877: Second series of *La Légende des siècles* (poems, *The Legend of the Centuries*). *L'Art d'être grand-père* (poems, *The Art of Being a Grandfather*).

1878: *Le Pape* (long poem, *The Pope*). Hugo suffers a stroke and congestion of the brain in June. In the years following, Hugo writes little, but continues to publish by using poems and other writings he has held in reserve.

1879: *La Pitié suprême* (long poem, *The Highest Pity*).

1880: *Religions et Religion* (long poem, *Religions and Religion*). *L'Âne* (long poem, *The Ass*).

1881: *Les Quatres Vents de l'esprit* (poems, *The Four Winds of the Spirit*).

1882: *Torquemada* (play).

1883: Death of Juliette Drouet. Third series of *La Légende des siècles* (poems, *The Legend of the Centuries*). Complete edition of *La Légende des siècles*.

1885: Death of Hugo in Paris, 22 May. Hugo's casket placed for a day of viewing under the Arc de Triomphe on 1 June. 2 June declared a day of national mourning. Hugo's remains removed to the Pantheon.

Posthumously Published Collections of Poetry

1886: *La Fin de Satan* (unfinished epic, *The End of Satan*).
1888: First part of *Toute la lyre* (*The Whole Lyre*).
1891: *Dieu* (unfinished epic, *God*).
1893: Second part of *Toute la lyre* (*The Whole Lyre*).
1898: *Les Années funestes* (*The Ominous Years*).
1902: *Dernière Gerbe* (*Last Gleanings*). Expanded edition in 1941.
1942: *Océan, Tas de pierres* (*Ocean, Pile of Stones*). *Océan vers* (*Ocean verse*) in 1986.
1960: *Le Verso de la page* (*The Reverse Side of the Page*).
1964: *Œuvres d'enfance et de jeunesse, 1814–20* (*Juvenalia, 1814–20*).

Selected Bibliography

French Editions of Hugo's Poetry Consulted for this Volume

Hugo, Victor.   *Les Contemplations.* Ed. Léon Cellier. Paris: Garnier, 1969.
              Œuvres complètes. Ed. Jean Massin. 18 vols. Paris: Club français du livre, 1967–1970.
              Œuvres complètes. Ed. Jacques Seebacher and Guy Rosa. 16 vols. Paris: Laffont, 1985–1990.
              Œuvres poétiques. Ed. Pierre Albouy. 3 vols. Paris: Gallimard, Pléiade, 1964–74.
              Victor Hugo: Poésie. Ed. Bernard Leuillot. 3 vols. Paris: L'Intégrale/ Seuil, 1972.

(I also consulted the paperback editions of individual collections published by Gallimard and Garnier-Flammarion, as well as the 'Livre de Poche' and 'Classiques Larousse' books.)

Suggestions for Further Reading in English

Houston, John Porter. *Victor Hugo.* Revised edition. Boston: Twayne Publishers, 1988. Twayne's World Authors Series.
Ireson, J.C. *Victor Hugo: A Companion to His Poetry.* Oxford: Clarendon Press, 1997.
Nash, Suzanne. *'Les Contemplations' of Victor Hugo: An Allegory of the Creative Process.* Princeton, N.J.: Princeton University Press, 1976.
Robb, Graham. *Victor Hugo: A Biography.* New York & London: W.W. Norton & Company, 1997.
Porter, Laurence M. *Victor Hugo.* New York: Twayne Publishers, 1999. Twayne's World Authors Series.

Notes to the Poems

Odes and Ballads
This collection of poems, Hugo's first, was originally entitled *Odes and Other Poems,* then reworked several times between 1822 and 1828 before receiving its final title and form. Hugo tempers the conservative politics of the odes with his additions and changes. The ballads are often fable-like or fantastical, as if Hugo were deliberately moving away from topical subjects.

'To My Odes'
These six lines are final stanza of the first ode from the 'Second Book' of odes. (Hugo dates the second book '1822–23'.)

Orientalia
Influenced by literary examples such as Byron's and Goethe's poetry, as well as the Greek struggle for independence, *Orientalia* experiments with poetic forms and a vaguely Middle Eastern subject matter. The poems toward the close of the collection are less overtly concerned with Middle Eastern subjects; in their dream-like quality, they reveal something about Hugo's received ideas about 'the Orient' and suggest that, as the book ends, the poet must awake from his dream.

'The Captive'
In this poem and several others in *Orientalia*, Hugo uses an intricate stanza form at which my translation only hints. The six-syllable lines are rhymed *ababccb*. Some of Paul Valéry's poems in *Charmes,* such as the opening and closing pieces ('Aurore' and 'Palme'), owe something to Hugo's experiments here and elsewhere.

'Moonlight'
The epigraph from Virgil, 'Amidst the friendly silence of the moon', is from the second book of the *Aeneid* (line 255).

'The Djinns'
This poetic tour de force makes use of the same rhyming scheme employed in 'The Captive', but the number of syllables in the line varies with each stanza. As the djinns, or genies, approach, the syllables increase by one with each stanza, going from two syllables to eight, then jump to ten syllables at the climactic moment, before decreasing incrementally from eight to two as the djinns pass by and fly away. The epigraph is from Canto 5 of the *Inferno* (lines 46–50).

'Reverie'
The epigraph is from Canto 2 of the *Inferno* (lines 1–3): 'The day was departing, and the dark air was releasing all living creatures of the earth from their burdens.'

'Rapture'
The epigraph from the Book of Revelations is probably not meant to recall a specific line so much as a prophetic tone.

Autumn Leaves
In his introduction to this collection (dated 24 November 1831), Hugo at first apologizes for his publication of tranquil, descriptive, and visionary poems during a time of revolution. He then turns this apparent poetic short-coming into a strength, arguing that art has its own will and laws. (In some respects Hugo's discussion anticipates the 'art for art's sake' argument that Théophile Gautier will make later in the decade.) Considering that Hugo's play *Hernani* was about to cause a more than aesthetic scandal, the introduction to *Autumn Leaves* may seem evasive or self-protective, however accurately it describes the contents of the book. The first poem of the collection, 'This century was two years old!...' ('Ce siècle avait deux ans!...') is biographical and lightly historical. In the final poem, 'Friends, one last word!...' ('Amis, un dernier mot!...'), Hugo makes some references to the political situation of Europe and bids farewell to 'love, family, and childhood' as he prepares to add a bronze string ('corde d'airain') to his lyre. Virtually every poem in between avoids political subject matter.

'The Slope of Reverie'
The Latin epigraph is probably an invention of Hugo's, though Gervasius of Tilbury (a thirteenth-century English chronicler) did exist. The epigraph means roughly, 'The obscurity of the subject matter makes the words obscure'. As if to prove its truth, many lines of this poem are obscure, such as the couplet, 'Everything, like a landscape on a photographic plate,/ Was mirrored in its silky streams and ever-shifting state.' A prose translation perhaps demonstrates this line's difficulty even more: 'Everything, like a landscape in a dark room, was being reflected with its rivers of silk.' Here 'dark room' does not quite carry its modern photographic sense, but arguably alludes to the photographic experiments of Louis Daguerre – if not his daguerreotypes (with their silvery, silky surfaces), then his dioramas of land-scapes presented in dark rooms to increase their impact on the spectator.[1]

The lines describing 'cities buzzing more than trees' in 'Amazon's jungles' might be more literally translated 'cities buzzing more ... than an American forest'. I have chosen to interpret 'American' as South American, but Hugo may be referring to a North American forest. Cybele (pronounced 'SIB-uh-lee') was a goddess of nature in ancient Greece and Asia minor. The line 'Evander's Etruscan, Orpheus's antique Greek,' is more literally, 'The Pelagian of Orpheus, the Etruscan of Evander'. The Pelagians were thought to be some of the most ancient people in Greece; the Etruscans were the among the most ancient inhabitants of Italy. In the context of the line,

1   See P.A. Gadenne's note to these lines in his edition of *Les Feuilles d'Automne, Les Chants du crépuscule* (Librairie Larousse, Paris, 1958), p. 42.

Orpheus, the mythical poet, and Evander, king of Arcadia (in the *Aeneid*), represent originary figures of Greece and Rome. Irmensul was a Saxon god.

'Setting Suns (II)' and 'Settings Suns (VI)' are part of a six-poem sequence of descriptions and reflections.

The Songs of Daybreak
To some extent, this collection fulfils Hugo's promise, made at the end of *Autumn Leaves,* to add a bronze string to his lyre. The first few poems, including the ode 'To the Column', are on political and historical subjects. Still, most poems in the volume are personal or descriptive. The word 'crépuscule' in the title of the collection can refer to either 'daybreak' or 'twilight'. Apparently Hugo wished to suggest moments of doubt, reflection, or transition.

'To the Column'
I have translated the first part of a seven-part ode dated 9 October 1830. As the epigraph to the poem indicates, Hugo wrote this poem in response to the Chamber of Representatives' refusal of a request to have Napoleon's remains placed beneath the column at the *Place Vendôme*. Hugo had already written a poem to the column in *Odes and Ballads,* but in this 1830 ode one can see more clearly his blend of liberal politics and attraction to the mythology of Napoleon – a combination of 'liberty and glory', as he sometimes termed it. The column was inaugurated on 15 August 1810, but Hugo's childhood memory of a military parade is either fabricated or displaced: there was no ceremony and Napoleon spent the day in the Tuileries palace. The 'feux du polygone' ('fortress's leaping flames') refers to the fire of artillery in or around a military citadel shaped like a polygon; 'l'or de la dragonne' ('golden tassels') refers to a gold-coloured decoration hanging on the hilt of a sword. The rivers (Nile, Rhine, Tiber) and places (Austerlitz, Eylau, Wagram, Marengo, Champaubert, and Arcole) named are battles or locations where Napoleon was victorious. Enceladus was one of the titans who attempted to scale Olympus in order to take the throne of Zeus. 'Piling Pelion on Ossa' is a proverbial expression for making a superhuman effort. (Pelion and Ossa are mountains. In order to attack Olympus, the titans piled them on top of each other.) Paullus-Aemilius, or Lucus Aemilius Paullus Macedonicus, was a Roman consul and general. He received his name 'Macedonicus' because of his victory in 168 BC over Perseus, the last successor to Alexander the Great's Macedonian throne, for which he was given a triumphal procession. 'Three hundred lawyers' is a scornful reference to the Chamber of Representatives and its litigious disputes over Napoleon's remains.

Inner Voices
Hugo dedicates this book to his father, 'Joseph-Leopold-Sigisbert Count Hugo, lieutenant general', who died in 1828. Like *The Songs of Daybreak, Inner*

Voices mixes the political and the personal; as in *Autumn Leaves,* Hugo emphasizes in his introduction the poet's independence. (One point of the title is that the poet should trust his inner voices.) Left out of my selection – for reasons of space, not quality – is a long ode, 'To the Arc de Triomphe', a kind of companion piece to *The Song of Daybreak*'s 'To the Column' and to Hugo's novel *Notre-Dame de Paris* in that it refers to the arch, the column, and the cathedral as Paris's eternal triangle of monuments. Hugo's ideas on monuments are quintessentially romantic: he believes that nature completes human monuments by transforming them over time into ruins.

'To Albrecht Dürer'
Albrecht Dürer was a German artist (1471–1528) often cited by the romantics as a kind of precursor.

'The war that scoundrel wages…'
Though addressed to a 'young man', this poem might as well be self-addressed. Hugo seems to be telling himself not to worry about negative reviews of his poetry. Zoïlus is a legendary critic who disparaged Homer. Hugo may have a specific contemporary reviewer in mind. Possible candidates include Gustave Planche and Désiré Nisard, whose reviews of Hugo were particularly harsh.

'The Cow'
My translation of this poem leaves out the final verse-paragraph:

> Ainsi, Nature! abri de toute créature!
> O mère universelle! indulgente Nature!
> Ainsi, tous à la fois, mystiques et charnels,
> Cherchant l'ombre et le lait sous tes flancs éternels,
> Nous sommes là, savants, poètes, pêle-mêle,
> Pendus de toutes parts à ta forte mamelle!
> Et tandisqu'affamés, avec des cris vainqueurs,
> À tes sources sans fin désaltèrant nos cœurs,
> Pour en faire plus tard notre sang et notre âme,
> Nous aspirons à flots ta lumière et ta flamme,
> Les feuillages, les monts, les prés verts, le ciel bleu,
> Toi, sans te déranger, tu rêves à ton Dieu!

> [In the same way, o Nature! (shelter of every creature! o universal mother! indulgent Nature!) in the same way, we – all at once, mystical and in the flesh, looking for shade and milk under your eternal flanks – we are there (scientists, poets, mixed together), hanging from every part of your strong breast! And while we – famished, with victorious shouts, quenching our hearts unceasingly at your sources – while we inhale in waves your light and flame, in order to make later our blood and soul out of them (the foliage, the mountains, the green meadows, the blue sky), you, without disturbing yourself, you are dreaming of your God!]

Sunbeams and Shadows
After publishing this collection in 1840, Hugo did not publish another book of poems until 1853. Reasons for the gap in publication include his increased involvement in the theatre, his daughter's death in 1843, and the political events surrounding the 1848 revolution. Looked at in retrospect, *Sunbeams and Shadows* can be seen as the culmination of Hugo's first decade of maturity. Alternatively, and with some authority from Hugo, this collection marks the close of the first of three large stages in Hugo's development. (Hugo's career is commonly divided into poems written before, during, and after his exile.) All such divisions ought to be viewed with some scepticism. While it is true that Hugo wrote less poetry during the 1840s than in most other decades of his maturity, he was still highly productive. Many poems later published in *Les Contemplations,* for example, were written in these years.

'Written on the pane of a Flemish window'
This poem is dated Malines-Louvain, 19 August 1832.

'Olympio's Sadness'
This is perhaps Hugo's most famous pre-exile poem. 'Olympio' was one of Hugo's poetic alter-egos (the name also appears in *Inner Voices*). In one of his manuscripts, Hugo writes that there comes a time in a poet's life when he feels himself too small to keep writing in his own name. He goes on to divide his persona into four parts: Olympio (the lyre), Herman (love), Maglia (laughter), and Hierro (combat). 'Olympio's Sadness' takes up a common romantic theme, returning to a personally significant place in nature and reflecting on the passage of time. The poem's occasion is Hugo's solitary trip to a valley near Roches in 1837, a place where he and Juliette Drouet had met every day during the fall of 1834. 'Olympio's Sadness' is dated 21 October 1837.

'Oceano Nox'
The Latin title is from Virgil's *Aeneid* (Book 2, line 250): 'Vertitur interea caelum et ruit Oceano nox' ('In the meantime, the sky revolves and night rushes from the ocean'). By itself, 'Oceano nox' might be translated 'Night on the ocean'.

Punishments
Through satire and invective, Hugo castigates Louis Napoleon and his empire throughout this overtly political volume. (The French title, *Les Châtiments,* can also be translated 'Castigations' or 'Chastisements'.) *Punishments* (1853) is the first book of poems published by Hugo in exile and marks the end of a draught of poetry publications dating back to 1840.

'Memory of the Night of the Fourth'
The title refers to 4 December 1851 and a scene Hugo witnessed that night. (Louis Bonaparte staged his coup d'état on 2 December; sporadic resistance

continued over the intervening days.) Saint-Cloud is located just outside of Paris on the southwest border.

'What the poet said to himself in 1848'
Hugo wrote this poem in November, 1848. At this time, he mostly supported Louis Napoleon because he felt that the prince was mildly liberal and could help restore peace and order to France after its year of revolution. Hugo was a self-declared moderate; he had been against the June uprisings, but later 'in the heat of the assembly' advocated lenient punishments for the revolutionaries and the abolition of the death penalty.

'The Expiation'
This long poem traces France's political situation under Louis Bonaparte back to the history of the first empire, in particular to '18 Brumaire' (9 November 1799). This was the day when Napoleon Bonaparte took the necessary steps to dissolve the revolutionary directorate, thereby paving his way to become emperor. It is not until the end of the poem that 18 Brumaire is revealed as the crime that Napoleon I and France must expiate; in the meantime, 'The Expiation' describes low-points in Napoleon's life – the retreat from Russia, the defeat at Waterloo, and the exile to St Helena. None of these 'punishments' will expiate Napoleon's crime. The real punishment is Napoleon III and the Second Empire, in particular the ways in which Louis Bonaparte and his cronies use the name of Napoleon for their own ends.

The subject of part I is Napoleon's retreat from Russia. 'Ney' refers to Michel Ney, a marshal in Napoleon's army. 'Lèse-majesté' is treason; I have left the French untranslated because it is a legal term and puns on its literal meaning, 'injury against [his] Majesty.'

Part II describes Waterloo, a battle Hugo discusses at length in his novel, *Les Misérables*. Wellington is the famous British general credited with the defeat of Napoleon. Groushee (actually 'Grouchy', but the spelling suggests an unfortunate pun in English) was a French general who was not able to track down Blücher's Prussian army and prevent it from joining Wellington's forces at Waterloo. The 'garde' refers to Napoleon's elite veterans, the imperial guard, who had fought at such battles as Friedland and Rivoli.

Part III details Napoleon's exile in St Helena. Napoleon had first been exiled to Elba, but after a brief return to power (the 'One Hundred Days' ending with Waterloo) he was exiled to St Helena (pronounced 'hell-*een*-uh'), a British island off the coast of modern-day Angola, where he died in 1821. The restored powers in Europe chose this island far away from Europe because they feared a second return of Napoleon. Hugo describes Napoleon's life on St Helena as severely restricted by British soldiers like Hudson-Lowe. Marengo was one of Napoleon's first victories. In Alexander Dumas's play *Napoleon Bonaparte,* Napoleon, dying, calls for his sword and the 'mantle' he wore at the battle of Marengo. The mantle of Marengo was draped over Napoleon's casket at his funeral.

Parts IV and V discuss the sources and growth of the Napoleon legend. For Hugo, Napoleon is most glorious in his fall. The statue of Napoleon on top of the column in the *Place Vendôme* was removed in 1816 and melted in order to make a statue of Henry IV. A new statue was put on top of the column in 1833. Ulm, Eylau, and Austerlitz were victories of Napoleon. Saint-Cloud was one of Napoleon's imperial residences. Twelve years after Napoleon died (part VI), his remains were returned to France and placed in the Pantheon in Paris.

Part VII switches to topical satire in order to attack Louis Napoleon and the Second Empire.

Beauharnais is the family name of Louis Bonaparte's mother; Hugo shows his contempt for Napoleon III's pretensions by calling his empire the 'Beauharnais Circus'.

Achille Fould was Minister of Finances in the early months of the Second Empire. The brother of a rich banker, he was rumoured to have advanced money to Napoleon III in order to help him pay the debts of his mistress.

Bernard-Pierre Magnan was the general in command of the Paris garrison at the time of Louis Napoleon's coup d'état (the day of which he was named marshal).

Eugène Rouher was the Minister of Justice at the time of the Louis Bonaparte's coup; he went on to become very influential in the new government.

Esquirou de Parieu was a national representative who became a member of Louis Napoleon's cabinet in 1849 (he was appointed *ministre de l'Instruction publique,* a post Hugo had desired). Hugo calls him a chameleon ('protean' in my translation) presumably because he was, in Hugo's mind, willing to do anything to advance his career.

Marie-Dominique-Auguste Sibour was the archbishop of Paris; when asked to declare his opposition to Louis Bonaparte's coup, he replied that such a declaration would be useless.

Casemates are armoured compartments for artillery on a rampart.

Jena and Austerlitz are two of Napoleon I's greatest victories.

Cartouche was the nickname of Louis-Dominique Bourguignon, a famous eighteenth-century bandit who terrorized the region around Paris. Due to the fame of Bourguignon, 'cartouche' ('cartridge') became a synonym for 'bandit'.

Lodi was a victorious battle of Napoleon I.

Pierre Carlier was named prefect of police in 1849; he became an adviser to the state a few days after Louis Napoleon's coup.

Pierre-Marie Pietri became prefect of police in 1852.

Charelemagne-Émile Maupas, one of the leading participant's in Louis Napoleon's coup, took over as prefect of police after Carlier. He later became Minister of Police.

Poissy is a town known for, among other things, its prison.

Jacques Callot (1592–1635) was an engraver and painter, famous for his carnivalesque figures.

Raymond-Théodore Troplong became President of the Council of the State and Senate during the Second Empire. Hugo considered him an apologist for Napoleon III's usurpation of power and use of force.

Pierre-Jules Baroche held various governmental posts before and after Louis Bonaparte's coup, eventually rising to the level of minister. Hugo argued with Baroche in the national assembly over Louis Napoleon.

Like Cartouche, Louis Mandrin was a famous eighteenth-century bandit. Mandrin is one of Hugo's favourite nicknames for Napoleon III.

'All the marble victories sculpted on the door' refers to the twelve statues, representing Napoleon's twelve greatest victories, sculpted by Claire Pradier for Napoleon's tomb.

The story of Balthazar seeing 'the writing on the wall' is from the fourth chapter of Daniel.

'To the People'
This is the more famous of two poems in *Punishments* with the same title. Hugo often associates himself with the ocean and the people, sometimes distinguishing between 'the people' and 'the crowd'.

'Stella'
The Latin title means 'star'. The main conceit of the poem is that Poetry is a kind of prophet that comes before and paves the way for Liberty. According to Hugo's poetic logic, Sinai, the mountain in Egypt where the Ten Commandments were revealed to Moses is analogous to Taygetos (or Taygetus), a mountain in Greece near Sparta where Lycurgus, Sparta's legendary law-giver, can be said to have been inspired.

'Blow forever, trumpets of thought ...'
The story of the prophet blowing down the walls of Jericho with trumpet blasts is from the fourth book of Joshua. Hugo suggests that Joshua and the trumpet blasts are like Hugo and his poetry. For dramatic effect, the first line and the last line of the poem are separated from the rest, as if to suggest the power of one voice standing alone.

'It was raining that night ...'
This poem is only tangentially related to the political thrust of *Punishments,* via its final line.

Les Contemplations
This collection was published in 1856, a year after Walt Whitman's first edition of *Leaves of Grass* and a year before Charles Baudelaire's first edition of *Les Fleurs du mal.* Many readers consider it or *The Legend of the Centuries* Hugo's finest collection of poems. It is one of Hugo's most diverse volumes, containing short love lyrics and long prophetic poems, personal reminiscences and public proclamations. While less overtly political than the preceding collection, *Punishments* (1853), and containing fewer narrative poems than the collection that follows, *The Legend of the Centuries* (first series, 1859), *Contemplations* arguably best represents Hugo's range.

The two most important biographical events surrounding this collection are Hugo's exile and the death of his daughter Léopoldine. Following the coup d'état of Louis Napoleon on 2 December 1851, Hugo was forced to flee France because of his outspoken democratic sentiments. He would not return until the fall of Napoleon and the proclamation of the Third Republic in 1870. During this time Hugo had no way of knowing whether he would ever see France again, though at one point he refused the amnesty the Second Empire offered him. Hugo's exile was made more personally difficult in that he could no longer visit the grave of Léopoldine, whose death in 1843 is alluded to in the division of *Les Contemplations* into 'Former Times (1830–1843)' and 'Today (1843–1855)'. Of Hugo's children, Léopoldine was the oldest to have survived infancy, and his favourite. On 15 February 1843, at the age of eighteen, she married Charles Vacquerie, the brother of a friend of her brother. The couple drowned together in an accident at Villequier less than seven months later, on 4 September. (Vacquerie, who was an excellent swimmer and could have saved himself, stayed and drowned with his pregnant wife whom he was unable to rescue.) For a number of years after her death, Hugo made an annual pilgrimage to Léopoldine's grave in September or October.

In his introduction to *Contemplations,* Hugo writes, 'it is a soul that narrates itself in these two volumes, "Former Times, Today". An abyss separates them, the grave.' At its most fundamental level, then, the collection seems to be divided between the poems he wrote before and after the death of his daughter Léopoldine. Hugo in fact dramatizes the before and after by printing the date of his daughter's drowning and a dotted line on the page following the second poem in the second half of the book. But the architecture of *Contemplations* is somewhat more complicated. The two halves are subdivided into three books each, for a total of six subdivisions: 'Dawn', 'The Soul in Bloom', 'Struggles and Dreams', 'Pauca Meae', 'On the Move', and 'On the Shore of Infinity'. Hugo also adds an introductory poem and a postscript, 'To the One Who Stayed Behind in France'. To make matters more tricky, the poems are not arranged chronologically beyond the general division marked by the date of Léopoldine's death. And to complicate the situation still further, Hugo supplies many poems in the collection with fictitious dates. The result is a work that allows for at least three competing frameworks of interpretation: the 'narrative of the soul' outlined by the author's supplied dates, the biographical narrative suggested by the dates of composition, and the simultaneously thematic and narrative ordering of the poems within the books of the collection.

To explain more fully how Hugo's dating of the poems invites different readings would require a complete translation of *Contemplations* and a lengthy critical apparatus, but even a few general observations help. One pattern in the dating is Hugo's tendency to antedate the more light-hearted or celebratory poems to a time period before his daughter's death. Thus, 'The poem goes away into the fields …' a piece Hugo wrote perhaps two months after Léopoldine's drowning, and 'Vere Novo', a piece he wrote in exile, are presented as compositions of 1831. Hugo moreover often changes the dates of some poems about his daughter ('Oh spring! oh dawn! oh memories! …'

'At Villequier', 'Tomorrow, at dawn ...') to coincide as closely as possible with anniversaries of her death. In general, Hugo is more likely to antedate than to postdate his poems. In his edition of *Contemplations,* Léon Cellier tabulates that Hugo antedates forty-three poems and postdates only one poem in 'Former Times', and that he leaves twenty-nine poems undated and fourteen poems with the same date. In 'Today', Hugo antedates fourteen poems, postdates fifteen, keeps the same year in forty, and leaves one poem undated. The collection's final poem, 'To the One Who Stayed Behind in France', is in fact the poem composed last. Hugo finished it on 2 November 1855 and dated it 'Guernsey, 2 November 1855, All Souls' Day.' *Contemplations* was published in Paris and Brussels on 23 April 1856 – Shakespeare's birthday.

'My Two Daughters'
Hugo's daughters were Léopoldine (1824–43) and Adèle (1830–1914). 'My Two Daughters' forms a kind of pair with 'Happy the man...'

'The poet goes away ...'
Ulemas are scholars or priests trained in traditional Moslem religion and law. The mufti is a judge who interprets Moslem religious law.

'The clarity that fills ...'
In the line 'The pines next to the ponds spread their green parasol,' the French is actually not 'ombrelle' (parasol), but 'ombelle' (umbel, a flat-topped or rounded flower cluster in which the individual stalks arise from about the same point). The image of a parasol is nevertheless evoked in this description, if not through the sound play then via the shape of the umbel.

'To André Chénier'
André Chénier is an eighteenth-century poet often viewed as a precursor to the romantics. Hugo learned from Chénier some techniques for varying the rhythm of the alexandrine line and thus for rendering poetry prose-like. (See my introduction and the notes to 'Reply to an act of accusation'.) Ugolino is the damned soul in Dante's *Inferno* (Cantos 32 and 33) who chews on another sinner's skull beneath a frozen lake. Grandgousier is the wild drinker and jester of Rabelais's *Gargantua and Pantagruel.* He sires the giant Gargantua.

'Life in the Fields'
It may seem strange that 'Mercuries' appears among the list of Egyptian sphinxes, Ammon Ras, and Anubises, especially given that Hugo goes out of his way to point out that the Egyptian gods are more ancient than those of Olympus. Hugo is probably using Mercury for Thoth, the Egyptian god of the dead.

'Reply to an act of accusation'
In this poem, Hugo makes various claims about his own poetic achievement. As the title indicates, 'Reply to an act of accusation' takes the form of a public letter composed in response to a written attack. Hugo gives the poem the

date January 1834, even though he composed the poem in October 1854. It is likely that Hugo found out about the letter to which he is replying well after the fact. In one of the volumes of his *History of Dramatic Literature* (1854), Jules Janin, an influential critic and friend of Hugo, cites a letter dated January 1834 under the title 'Concerning dramatic literature: Letter to Mr. Victor Hugo': 'I accuse you, then, monsieur, of having caused, through perverse doctrines and means that you alone know how to employ, the loss of dramatic art and the ruin of French theatre.' The author of the letter was a member of the Academie Française. He goes on to assert that Hugo's overpassionate disciples 'have wanted to put [their new aesthetic] into practice... like the soldiers of Mohammed or the followers of Robespierre.' In 'Reply to an act of accusation', Hugo claims that he helped liberate literature in the same way that the French Revolution helped liberate society. Hugo was in fact widely regarded as France's leading romantic figure, especially after the controversy and triumph of his play *Hernani* on 25 February 1830, the so-called 'Battle of *Hernani*.' Hugo's most frequent target in 'Reply to an act of accusation' is Nicolas Boileau, whose *Art Poétique* was considered the bible of French classicism.

'Verse of poetry' ('ancien vers françois') might be more literally rendered 'ancient French line' or 'old French poetry'. Hugo uses an archaic spelling of 'French' to poke fun at authors who employed old spellings in their writing. In the lines that speak of trampling 'the verse of poetry' underfoot, the pun on metrical feet also exists in the French.

'Let there be darkness' is a reworking of God's 'Let there be light' in Genesis. The French language was reputed to be naturally clear, as indicated in the popular saying 'What isn't clear isn't French'.

For 'Racca' see Matthew 5:22. The word means something like 'You fool!'

The French for 'it had to be dirt' is more literally 'it was only a *grimaud*' (a lower-class schoolboy).

The Pont Neuf is a bridge in Paris.

The *Cid* is a play by Corneille; *Andromaque,* a play of Racine; *Mérope,* a play of Voltaire. The French literally reads 'the *Phèdre*s, the *Jocaste*s,' tragedies by Racine and Corneille, respectively.

Patois is a regional French dialect, generally associated with the peasantry. *Argot* refers to a specialized vocabulary or set of idioms used by a particular class or group (sailors, convicts, etc.). Here a low social class is implied.

Claude Favre, seigneur de Vaugelas, is the author of *Remarques sur la langue française* (1647), a book that attempts to fix rules for the proper usage of words.

Convicts in the *ancien régime* sometimes had a shoulder branded with a *fleur de lys*. Hugo associates the letter 'F' – the first letter of 'forçat' (convict) – with the 'F' used in certain dictionaries indicating words were 'familier' (common, too familiar). By a fortunate coincidence, the English words 'common' and 'convict' also begin with the same letter.

'And then, like a bandit, I arrived' ('Alors, brigand, je vins') alludes to a famous line from Boileau's *Art Poétique,* 'Enfin, Malherbe vint' ('Finally, Malherbe arrived') used to date the beginning of well-formed, classical verse.

Boileau's claim is that, before the arrival of the poet François de Malherbe (1555–1628), French verse was chaotic and, in a sense, uncivilized. Hugo is claiming that he has accomplished for French poetry something like the opposite.

The French Academy was, and in many ways still is, notorious for its conservative pronouncements on what counts as good French. For Hugo and other romantics, French classical poetry was overly rhetorical ('Her topes hiding under her skirt').

Alexandrine couplets are square in the sense that they are regular and measured. They resemble massed troops of soldiers in that they are relatively long lines that stretch down the page, occasionally broken by blank spaces.

'I put a red bonnet on the old lexicon' is probably the most famous line from this poem. 'Bonnet rouge' refers to the hat worn by the 1792 revolutionaries.

Syllepsis, hypallage, and litotes are all rhetorical terms. Syllepsis is related to the figure zeugma and refers to constructions in which one word (usually a verb) is used with two different words or phrases (usually direct objects), as in Alexander Pope's 'Here thou, great Anna! whom three realms obey,/ Dost sometimes counsel take – and sometimes Tea.' Hypallage occurs when a word is made to refer to some word other than the one it logically qualifies, as in Shakespeare's 'This was the most unkindest cut of all,' where the unkindness is attributed to the cut rather than the person who delivered the blow. Litotes (pronounced 'lie-*toe*-tees') refers either to understatement or to affirmation via the negative of the contrary, as in the expression 'That's not half bad'. My definitions and examples are from *The New Princeton Encyclopedia of Poetry and Poetics* (Princeton University Press, 1993).

'Aristotle's milestone' is Hugo's way of referring to the Aristotelian notion that nature is governed by fixed, immovable laws. Hugo is also comparing himself to a revolutionary orator standing on a box or a large rock to speak to a crowd.

The Dacians, the Scythians, and the Huns were barbarians.

François Guichardin and Tacitus are historians. Hugo is arguing against the notion that poems are supposed to privilege universal truths over historically specific facts and truths. Guichardin and Tacitus did not hesitate to discuss such brutal rulers as Caesar Borgia and Vitellius, so why should Hugo exclude from his poetry the details of daily life?

In the couplet 'The cow and the heifer would converse now at peace,/ The former Margoton and the latter Bérénice,' Hugo imagines a peaceful coexistence of literary words like 'heifer' and everyday words like 'cow'. Margoton is a peasant's name and Bérénice a queen's name.

For Rabelais, see the notes to 'The clarity that fills….'

Ça ira and *La Carmagnole* were songs and dances of the 1793 revolutionaries. Pindos is a mountain in Greece said to be sacred to Apollo and the Muses.

'Gongorism shivered in its Spanish frills and stole' is more literally, 'Emphasis shivered in its Spanish frills'. Hugo is alluding to the precious style of the sixteenth-century Spanish poet, Gongora. John (Jean) is a common peasant name. Myrtilette (Myrtil) is a typical name for a shepherdess in bucolic poetry. Hugo is claiming to marry the everyday with the classical.

In Hugo's play, *Hernani,* Don Carlos asks 'What time is it?' (Act II, Scene 1). In classical French drama, noble characters were not supposed to use common expressions.

Ivory, alabaster, and snow are literary adjectives for white skin.

Cyzique or Cyzicus was a town in Asia Minor where Mithradates was defeated by the Roman General Lucullus in AD 74.

'The courtesans became whores' is more literally 'The Laïses became whores'. Laïs was a Greek courtesan whose name was a euphemism for her profession in classical French poetry.

Pierre Restaut was an eighteenth-century author of a French grammar and a treatise on versification, both of which were still in use in nineteenth-century classrooms.

In the lines about wigs turning red and changing into lions' manes, Hugo is referring to the practice, common in revolutionary days, of abusing statues and busts from the age of Louis XIV. In a letter from 1837, Hugo talks of the Flemish penchant for mounting such busts above doorways as though they were sculptures of lions. Whether by means of paint or power of suggestion, the white wigs thus become red lion manes.

Charles-François Lhomond was an eighteenth-century professor who wrote a widely used French grammar. Dominique Bouhours was a seventeenth-century author of a book entitled *Doubts Regarding the French Language.* Claude Brosette was the friend and editor of Boileau; he wrote some commentaries on grammar. Charles Batteux was an eighteenth-century priest who wrote about the poetics of Aristotle, Horace, and Boileau, among others. Jean Galbert de Campistron was a disciple of Racine; his plays had some success in the late seventeenth and early eighteenth centuries.

'Make peace with syntax! Wage war on rhetoric!' plays on the revolutionary saying 'Guerre aux châteaux, paix aux chaumières!' ('War on the châteaux, peace to the cottages!'). Hugo is advocating a plain style and an end to rhetorical excess and inversions of word order.

'You could see the Athos, the ethos, and the pathos' echoes a verse in Molière's *The Learned Ladies* (*Les Femmes savantes,* Act III, Scene 5). The lines that follow contain other references to Molière, whom Hugo is presenting as a positive aesthetic model and an antidote for classical stiffness. Ethos (Greek for 'character' or 'custom') and pathos (Greek for 'emotion' or 'suffering') are rhetorical terms referring to different oratorical strategies or effects. The Athos is a mountain in Greece.

Cathos is one of Molière's 'pretentious petticoats' ('précieuses ridicules') in the play of that name. Pouceaugnac, the title character of Molière's *Monsieur de Pourceaugnac,* is an unwanted suitor of the heroine of the play. César Chesneau Dumarsais was a seventeenth-/ eighteenth-century grammarian and author of a *Treatise on Tropes.* The 'comic dancers' ('matassins') are gypsy-like dancers who typically wear bells and other jingling ornaments along with swords. They dance around and chase Pouceaugnac with syringes filled with water (loosely translated 'squirt guns'). 'Helicon's streams' refers to the river

Permessus (or Hippocrene) on Mount Helicon, which was supposed to give inspiration to all poets who drank from it.

For metrical vocabulary such as 'caesuras', see my introduction.

The dream of Athalie and Théramène's *récit* were widely quoted passages from Racine's tragedies *Athalie* and *Phèdre*. In classical French drama, a *récit* is a reported narrative of offstage action.

George-Jacques Danton and Maximilien de Robespierre were figures associated with the Terror during the French Revolution.

César-Pierre Richelet was a seventeenth-century author of a French dictionary. 'Dangeau' probably refers to the Abbé de Dangeau, the seventeenth- and eighteenth-century author of a book of essays on grammar.

Periphrasis is the rhetorical figure of circumlocution. The most famous periphrasis in French literature occurs in Racine's *Phèdre*, when Phèdre is referred to as 'the daughter of Minos and Pasiphaé'.

The lines about the tower of Babel are perhaps intentionally obscure. The tone is quasi-prophetic; the logic of the image relates to the revolutionary comparisons that precede it: Hugo's democratization of language demolishes the classical ideal of a privileged, pure speech – a kind of Tower of Babel in that it is a man-made construction aimed at perfection. With the destruction of this tower, all words are again equal. Hugo even calls into question the alphabetical order of individual letters as a kind of hierarchy.

Nicolas Beauzée was an eighteenth-century grammarian. Tristan l'Ermite was the provost of Louis XI. The combination 'Tristan and Boileau' seems to suggest the collaboration of political and literary authority. There was also a seventeenth-century poet Tristan who was seen as a precursor of Racine.

Hugo's claims about liberating the personal pronoun, the participles, and the verbs are somewhat vague. With the personal pronoun, Hugo may be referring to his increased use of the first person.

'The *reum confitentem*' is a proverbial expression meaning 'the accused [man] who confesses'. The original phrase is from Cicero's *Pro Ligario*, 'Habemus reum confitentem' translates 'Let us have the accused man who confesses'. Hugo's 'You've the *reum confitentem*' thus means something like: 'You have before you the accused man confessing what he did.'

Polyhymnia is the muse of lyric poetry; Euterpe, the muse of music; and Calliope, the muse of epic.

For 'threw off the balance of the even-weighted line' see my metrical remarks in the introduction. The 'band of twelve feathers' refers to the twelve syllables of the alexandrine. The line 'deceives the caesura by a word' is more literally 'deceives the scissors' where Hugo seems to be playing on the Latin root of caesura ('to cut' or 'to cut off'). The 'cage of mid-line' is literally 'the cage of the caesura'.

The sentence beginning 'And thanks to these bandits' can be parsed as follows: 'Thanks to these bandits and to these terrorists (Truth, Imagination, and Poetry), the muse, reappearing, leads us back and takes us in.'

For Hugo, poetry's 'triple forehead' consists of the comic, the elegiac, and the philosophical.

Plautus's comedies were popular in ancient Rome (among the plebs) just as Shakespeare's plays were popular in London (among the crowd or mob).

Job is renowned for his patience and wisdom. Horace speaks of poetic madness several times in his poetry.

My translation leaves out the poem's final verse-paragraph:

Le mouvement complète ainsi son action.
Grâce à toi, progrès saint, la Révolution
Vibre aujourd'hui dans l'air, dans la voix, dans le livre;
Dans le mot palpitant le lecteur la sent vivre;
Elle crie, elle chante, elle enseigne, elle rit.
Sa langue est déliée ainsi que son esprit.
Elle est dans le roman, parlant tout bas aux femmes.
Elle ouvre maintenant deux yeux où sont deux flammes,
L'un sur le citoyen, l'autre sur le penseur.
Elle prend par la main la Liberté, sa sœur,
Et la fait dans tout homme entrer par tous les pores.
Les préjugés, formés, comme les madrépores,
Du sombre entassement des abus sous les temps,
Se dissolvent au choc de tous les mots flottants,
Pleins de sa volonté, de son but, de son âme.
Elle est la prose, elle est le vers, elle est le drame;
Elle est l'expression, elle est le sentiment,
Lanterne dans la rue, étoile au firmament.
Elle entre aux profondeurs du langage insondable;
Elle souffle dans l'art, porte-voix formidable;
Et c'est Dieu qui le veut, après avoir rempli
De ses fiertés le peuple, effacé le vieux pli
Des fronts, et relevé la foule dégradée,
Et s'être faite droit, elle se fait idée!

[Thus the movement completes its action. Thanks to you, saintly progress, the Revolution vibrates in the air today, in voices, in books; the reader feels her living in the palpitating word; she shouts, she sings, she teaches, she laughs. Her tongue is as nimble as her spirit. She is in the novel, speaking softly to women. She is now opening two eyes where two flames are: the one on the citizen, the other on the thinker. She is taking Liberty, her sister, by the hand, and makes her enter all the pores of every man. Prejudices, formed like coral from the sombre accumulation of the elements' abuses, are dissolving due to the shock of all of the floating words filled with her will, her aim, her soul. She is prose, she is verse, she is drama; she is expression; she is emotion: a lantern in the street, a star in the firmament. She enters the depths of immeasurably deep language; like a powerful megaphone, she breathes into art; and it is God who wills this, after having filled the people with his pride, effaced the old wrinkles on foreheads, and lifted up again the degraded crowd – and having made herself a right, she makes herself an idea!]

'Vere Novo'
The Latin title means 'With the new spring' or 'With the return of spring.' It is probably borrowed from Virgil's *Georgics* (Book I, line 43).

'The Party at Thérèse's'
An early reviewer of *Contemplations* asserted that this poem sparkled like a Watteau painting. The atmosphere of The Party at Thérèse's' is very much that of a Watteau or a Fragonard, but it is difficult to pin down Hugo's tone – could he be mocking Thérèse? Critics are not sure to whom the Thérèse of the title refers, if Hugo has someone in mind at all. The two best candidates are Laura, the Duchess of Abrantès (an earlier version of the poem has Laura instead of Thérèse) and Léonie Biard, one of Hugo's mistresses who sometimes went under the pseudonym Thérèse de Blaru. It may be that Hugo is being purposely ambiguous; he often sent the same love poems to different women.

The shepherd Aminta is the hero of Tasso's pastoral play of that name. Leonore is a common name in Italian novels. For Plautus, see the notes to 'Reply to an act of accusation'.

Alcantor is a character in Molière's *The Forced Marriage*. Aberand (Arbate) is a character in Racine's *Mithradates*. Trivelin, Columbine, Scaramouche, and the rest are stock characters in Italian sixteenth- and seventeenth-century comedy (the *commedia dell'arte*). Pierrot is a clown.

'Happy the man …'
This poem is a kind of companion piece to 'My Two Daughters'.

'A Stop in the Middle of a Walk'
This is the final poem of 'Dawn', the first book of *Contemplations*. In it, Hugo mentions some of the figures whose suffering or martyrdom Hugo identified with. Dante was exiled from Florence; Socrates was condemned to death; Scipio Africanus, the Roman general, died in exile; Milton died blind, poor, and forgotten; Thomas More was beheaded; Aeschylus, according to legend, left Athens as a result of Socrates's victory in a dramatic contest; Aristides was banished from Athens by Themestocles; Jean Huss was condemned by the Council of Constance to be burnt at the stake. Caiaphas was the high priest who, fearing the influence of Jesus, helped arrange for his arrest and crucifixion. The 'stop in the middle of the walk' refers simultaneously to the poet's stop at the source and the sudden halt of the dazzled man at the end of the poem.

'The Spinning Wheel of Omphale'
Omphale was the queen of Lydia who purchased Hercules as a slave and, according to one version of the myth, made him wear women's clothes and spin wool. The spinning wheel is Hugo's embellishment and an anachronism at that: the ancients did not have spinning wheels. Atrium is also an anachronism: it is a Latin architectural term and has nothing to do with Greek homes or palaces.

Jupiter took the form of a bull and kidnapped Europa, then transported her to Crete to satisfy his sexual desires. The hydra of Lerna, the Nemean lion, Cacus, and Geryon are monsters that Hercules defeated in the course of his twelve labours. The water sprites are also presented as monsters that Hercules subdued, though the reference is vague. The 'typhons des eaux' may perhaps represent whirlpools. Hugo may also have in mind Typhon, the giant and half-brother of Geryon.

'Letter'
The woman addressed in this letter may be Juliette Drouet. 'A river that is neither the Ganges nor the Nile' is more literally 'A river that is neither the Ganges nor the Cayster.' Hugo is drawing on Virgil's *Georgics* (Book I, lines 383–4). The Cayster is a river in Asia Minor.

'Words Spoken in the Shadows'
The woman who speaks is modelled on Juliette Drouet.

'Magnitudo Parvi'
The Latin title means 'the greatness of the small'. I have translated only the first part of a very long poem in four parts. After an extended meditation on the 'different worlds' of the star and the shepherd, the poem eventually returns to the initial scene (Hugo's memory of a walk with his daughter Léopoldine). The poet concludes, among other things, that 'a soul is greater than a world'. 'Magnitudo Parvi' is the final poem of 'Former Times'.

'She was pale ...'
The two girls in this poem are Hugo's daughter's Adèle and Léopoldine.

'Veni, Vidi, Vixi'
The title reworks Julius Caesar's famous 'Veni, Vidi, Vici' (I came, I saw, I conquered) into 'I came, I saw, I lived', where 'Vixi' is tantamount to saying 'I am dead'.

'Tomorrow, at dawn ...'
This poem and 'At Villequier' (which directly follows) are among the most famous pieces in the collection. 'Tomorrow, at dawn ...' begins as though it were a poem addressed to a lover, only to turn into an elegy by the end of the second stanza. Harfleur is a small town about three kilometres from Le Harvre. Critics have debated whether Hugo imagines an itinerary going from Rouen to Villequier or from Le Havre to Villequier. In the latter case, the journey would be thirty-five miles as the crow flies, more on foot.

'At Villequier'
This elegy was immediately hailed as one of the most moving pieces in *Les Contemplations* and remains one of Hugo's most famous poems. Hugo draws on the book of Job in his lament for his daughter, but also questions the consolations of religion.

'Mors'
The title is the Latin word for death. Much of the atmosphere of this poem is drawn from the Book of Revelation.

'The Beggar'
This poem makes an interesting comparison to Wordsworth's 'Resolution and Independence'.

'Words on the Dunes'
The composition date and published date suggest that this poem was written a year after Hugo, exiled from France, arrived at Jersey.

'Mugitusque Boum'
The title is from Virgil's *Georgics* (Book II, line 470) and occurs in a passage where the poet is praising the life of farmers: 'mugitusque boum mollesque sub arbore somni' ('[They enjoy] the mooing of cows and soft sleep under the trees').

'Shepherds and Flocks'
Hugo dedicated this poem to Louise Colet, a woman perhaps best known today because of her relationship and correspondence with Flaubert. Colet helped Hugo send letters to his friends in France during his exile. At the time when he composed 'Shepherds and Flocks', Hugo was trying to promote Colet's poem 'The Servant Woman' ('La Servante').

Hugo's descriptions in this poem are drawn from his experiences of the micro-climates on the island of Jersey. At the end of the poem, Hugo's imagination transforms the promontory rock into a giant shepherd resting on his elbows and looking out at sea. The final line, 'La laine des moutons sinistres de la mer' ('The wool of all the sinister sheep of the sea'), is one of the most memorable in Hugo's œuvre. It plays on the two senses of the word 'mouton' (whitecaps and sheep) and invests the image with an eerie, threatening power.

'I gathered this flower for you...'
Hugo offered this poem to Juliette Drouet.

'Strophe of the poet ...'
In this poem, strophe (pronounced '*Stroaf*-ee') seems to mean more than a stanza: it stands in for something like poetry in general. The elaborate comparison to Proserpine (pronounced '*Pro*-sur-peen') invites and resists allegorical interpretations.

According to myth, Hades abducted and raped Proserpine, then made her queen of the underworld. Through the intervention of her mother, Demeter (the goddess of agriculture and fertility), Proserpine was eventually allowed to return to the earth for half of each year. Demeter's grief for Proserpine's absence is supposed to account for the change of the seasons. The strophe's shift from carefree poetry to elegiac verse parallels the shift in *Contemplations* between 'Former Times' and 'Today'. Apparently Hugo is equating

Léopoldine's death with Proserpine's rape.

'One day the solemn spirit …'
The 'prophet who is dreaming in Patmos' is John of the Book of Revelations. Patmos is a Greek island off the coast of Turkey where, according to one legend, John is dreaming and will continue to dream until Judgement Day. John is often portrayed in paintings with an eagle.

'Nomen, Numen, Lumen'
The Latin title means 'Name, Divinity, Light'. The lion of Androcles, whom Hugo contacted during a seance, declared: 'Omen, lumen, numen, nomen meum' ('Omen, light, divinity is my name'). The title illustrates Hugo's belief in the creative power of the language in that each word changes by one letter from the previous word. This poem bears some resemblance to 'Et Nox Facta Est' and other poems in *The End of Satan*.

'To the One Who Stayed Behind in France'
This long elegy both builds on the image of 'the shore of infinity' from Book VI of *Contemplations* and functions as a separate epilogue or dedication. The one who stayed behind in France is Léopoldine, whose grave at Villequier Hugo could no longer visit because of his exile.

'Before, when September would return with its tears' refers to the date of Léopoldine's drowning on 4 September. 'Clematis' (pronounced '*Klem*-uh-tis') is a creeping plant with flowers that have plume-like seeds. For 'Harfleur', see the notes to 'Tomorrow, at dawn …'

The lines about 'the Gaze' (end of part 4) are mysterious. The gaze appears not to be Death's but some sort of indefinite, impersonal, anonymous look.

In the line 'Jerusalem has put my Paris in eclipse', Hugo uses the word 'Solime' ('Salem') for Jerusalem. This choice seems to indicate not the literal city of Jerusalem but something like the world of spirits. Genesis 14:18 refers to Melchizedek as the king of Salem.

Hugo pairs three geographically close cities, Rouen, Villequier, and Caudebec, with the biblical place names Horeb, Cedron, and Balbeck, though he does not appear to intend a precise analogy. The French cities relate to his daughter's drowning. Horeb is a mountain in Arabia where God appeared to Moses. Cedron is the river that separates Jerusalem from the Mount of Olives. Balbeck, or Heliopolis, was the city where the false god Baal was worshipped.

Gethsemani (or Gethsemane) refers to the place where Christ experienced his 'agony in the garden'. The subject of Christ's anguish over the death he foresaw for himself was popular among French romantics. Lamartine and Nerval wrote poems about it.

The final image of the poem portrays the contemplator on the shore of infinity.

Songs of the Streets and the Woods
For the most part, this collection is deliberately light. Hugo may have been trying to emulate his friend Théophile Gautier, who had gained some fame for his book of poems composed in short quatrains, *Emaux et Camées* (*Enamels and Cameos*). Hugo divides this collection into two parts, 'Youth' ('Jeunesse') and 'Wisdom' ('Sagesse'), a typically romantic pairing.

The Horrific Year
This collection traces Hugo's experiences before, during, and after the siege of Paris in 1870–1. Hugo encouraged his fellow Parisians to withstand the Prussians' siege and did not want France to cede any territory. He did not support the Paris Commune but afterwards pleaded on behalf of the Communards for clemency. See introduction for more details.

'1 January'
Hugo is addressing his two grandchildren in this poem.

'Letter to a Woman'
The woman of the title may be Hugo's sister-in-law, Julie Chenay. Balloons filled with letters were sent out of Paris during the siege. The first such mail balloon was given the name 'Victor Hugo'.

General Isidore-Pierre Schmitz was one of the generals in charge of the army of Paris.

'It's Aesychlus translated by the eighteenth century' is more literally 'It's Aeschylus translated by Father Brumoy'. Brumoy was an eighteenth-century Jesuit priest who translated and summarized Greek tragedies. Brumoy felt that Aeschylus was too monstrous for modern taste.

George and Jeannine are Hugo's grandchildren. During the siege, zoo animals from the Jardin des Plantes were in fact eaten by the Parisians.

Hugo places an asterisk after the phrase 'Ce qui fit la beauté des Romaines antiques' ('What made all of the women of Rome especially beautiful') and cites four lines from the Latin poet Juvenal, more or less translated by Hugo in the five alexandrines starting with the asterisked verse:

> Praestabat castas humilis fortunas Latinas,
> Casulae, somnique breves, et vellere tusco
> Vexatae duraeque manus, et proximus urbis
> Annibal, et stantes Collina in turre marite.

Hugo cites line 287 and lines 289–291 from Juvenal's sixth satire In leaving out line 288 ('quondam, nec vitiis contingi parva sinebant'), Hugo had to modify some of the verse surrounding it. The original passage in Juvenal might be translated: 'In days of old, humble fortunes kept the women of Latium chaste. What kept vice from polluting their modest homes was work and short sleep, hands chafed and hardened by Tuscan fleece, Hannibal nearing the city, and their husbands standing guard at the Colline gate.' In 213 BC, Hannibal neared Rome's Colline gate.

The phrase 'Paris, the escapee' is more literally 'Paris is Latude'. Latude was a famous eighteenth-century prisoner in the Bastille who made several daring escapes.

The Art of Being a Grandfather
This deliberately light collection made Hugo's grandchildren, Jeanne and Georges (Jeannine and George in my translations), the most famous children in France.

'Open Windows'
The manuscript indicates that the poem's setting is the island of Guernsey.

'Jeannine Asleep ('She's asleep …')'
This poem is one of several with the same title. Charenton was an asylum for the insane. Some of the threats cited in the poem resemble those made against Hugo.

The Legend of the Centuries
This collection was published in three separate series during Hugo's lifetime (1859, 1877, 1883) before being joined into one large volume in 1883. Hugo called the poems in *The Legend of the Centuries* 'little epics'; taken as a whole, the collection forms one massive epic that traces the history of humankind from creation to the present and beyond. *The Legend of the Centuries* is divided into sections with titles like 'Between Giants and Gods', 'After the Gods, the Kings', and 'Between Lions and Kings'. (From this perspective, the collection's title might be translated 'The Legend of the Ages'.) The individual poems are often long narratives on mythical and historical subjects. For many readers, *The Legend of the Centuries* rivals *Contemplations* as Hugo's finest volume.

'Conscience'
This poem is from the first series of *The Legend of the Centuries*, though Hugo first considered including it in *Punishments*. (In that context, Cain would have been a figure for Louis Napoleon.) The names of the members of Cain's family and other proper names can be found in Genesis, with variant spellings. Hugo changes some details of the biblical account, such as the relative ages of the family members. I have shortened the name 'Jabel' to 'Jab'.

'Boaz Asleep'
This poem, from the first series of *The Legend of the Centuries*, is one of Hugo's most famous. The story of Ruth and Boaz is in the fourth chapter of Ruth, from which most of the details of this poem derive. The town Jerimadeth seems to be Hugo's invention. It has been suggested that Hugo may be punning on the phrase 'J'ai rime à dait' ('I made a rhyme with "dait"'). Including a hidden joke in a serious poem is not out of character for Hugo.

The phrase 'reaper of eternity' is more literally 'reaper of eternal summer'.

'Christ's First Encounter with the Tomb'
This poem is from the first series of *The Legend of the Centuries*. Hugo draws on all four gospels for details, but concentrates on John 11. Sometimes Hugo takes some liberties with his source or embellishes the facts: Bethany is relatively close to Jerusalem, for example, not a three days' march. (Perhaps Hugo wanted to call to mind the three days Christ would be in the tomb.) The 'praetor's home' at the end of the poem presumably refers to the house of Pontius Pilate, the Roman governor of Judea, but Hugo has invented the scene of priests assembling there. As with the 'three days', Hugo may have in mind a later scene associated with Christ's passion and death.

'The Hydra'
This poem is from the second series of *The Legend of the Centuries*.

'Mohammed'
This poem is from the first series of *The Legend of the Centuries*.

'The Parricide'
This poem is from the first series of *The Legend of the Centuries,* though Hugo for a time considered using it in *Punishments* (see notes to 'Cain'). Kanut the Great (also spelled 'Canut' and 'Canute') became king of Denmark in 1014 and king of England in 1015. Hugo seems to have drawn his facts about Kanut from various histories, dictionaries, and literature on Nordic myth. According to tradition, Mount Savo marks the utmost boundary of Norway.

'The Work of the Prisoners'
This poem is from the second series of *The Legend of the Centuries*. The mountain 'Galgal' ('Gesequel' in my translation) seems chosen in part because its Hebrew root means 'cavern'. The Sporades (pronounced '*Spore*-uh-deez') are all of the Greek islands in the Aegean except the Cyclades. The island Patmos is famous ('shines among the Sporades') because John is supposed to have written the Book of Revelations there.

'The Infanta's Rose'
This poem is from the first series of *The Legend of the Centuries*. An infanta is the daughter of a Portuguese or Spanish king. Hugo seems to have been inspired by a Velasquez portrait of 'Marie' Marguerite Theresa, daughter of Philip II of Spain (see introduction). Philip II was the king who sent the 'Invincible Armada' to conquer England in 1588 – ships famously wrecked by a storm before they reached their intended destination. Had she lived, Marie (1880–83) would have been eight years old at the time of the Armada. The setting of the poem seems to be the gardens at Aranjuez, the royal residence southeast of Madrid.

Spain possessed Brabant, Flanders, and Sardinia in the sixteenth century. For 'the Bible's Cain', see the notes to 'Conscience'. Iblis is the ruler of the demons according to the Koran.

'Charles was the vulture' refers to Charles V, father of Philip, a king who increased Spain's territory.

'Ourques' or 'hourques' are small, solid ramming ships.

The phrase 'from the Ganges to the Po' is more literally 'from the Ganges to Posilipo', which is Hugo's way of saying 'from India to Europe'.

'Abdallah Bei-it' and 'Bei-it Cifresil' are inventions of Hugo. Their names mean 'servant of Allah' and 'sent by Allah', respectively.

'After the Battle'
This poem is from the first series of *The Legend of the Centuries*. It is not certain whether this anecdote is based on a story Hugo's father told him.

'The Sister of Mercy'
This poem is from the third series of *The Legend of the Centuries,* in the section entitled 'Les Paroles de mon oncle' ('My Uncle's Stories' or 'In the Words of my Uncle'). Like his father, Hugo's uncle Louis served in the Napoleonic wars.

'After the Battle of the Caudine Forks'
This poem is from the second series of *The Legend of the Centuries*. Hugo describes a walk he took in the Bois de Boulogne after his return from exile, but transfers the scene to Rome. The magnificent parading soldiers are defeated veterans of the recent Franco-Prussian war.

The Samnites defeated the Romans at the Caudine Forks in 321 BC. Hugo is comparing the Germans to the Samnites and the French to the Romans. The 'Esquiline graves' were for the slaves and the poor in ancient Rome; they correspond to the Mont Valérien cemetery near Longchamps (a course for horse racing) in the Bois de Boulogne. A buccin is a military trumpet. Medusa was one of the Gorgons (mythical monsters) who gaze turned onlookers into stone. Gorgon faces were imprinted on shields in imitation of the mythic shield of Perseus to which Medusa's head was attached, as if the design made them capable of petrifying the enemy.

The End of Satan
Hugo never finished this long epic about the fall and redemption of Satan. Hugo identifies with the Satan of this epic, who is a kind of exile who eventually returns to his home. The story is complex, but one recurring theme is that Satan is a force of liberty. The culmination of the progress of liberty is the fall of the Bastille.

'Et Nox Facta Est'
This poem opens the epic. The Latin title, 'And then there was night,' reverses the famous line in Genesis signalling the dawn of creation. The power of individual words to create recalls the poem 'Nomen, Numen, Lumen' in *Contemplations* (see notes to that poem). Satan's words 'death' and 'liar', and

his spit, are the creative forces behind three of the most notorious figures in the Bible, Cain, Judas, and Barrabas.

All the Lyre

This collection was published posthumously, in 1888. It is divided into seven sections, representing the 'seven strings' of the lyre, to which Hugo attached different titles in his manuscripts. When considering the title 'Toute l'âme' ('All the soul'), for example, Hugo divided the collection into Childhood, Loves, Love, Idylls and Comedies of the Heart, Clouds (of the soul), Duty, and The Unknown. Hugo's exact intentions for this volume are hard to pin down; the selection was compiled by Hugo's friend and editor, Paul Meurice.

'The hexameter ...'

The hexameter is one of the most common metres of ancient Greek and Latin poetry, often associated with epic. Horace uses hexameters in his epistles. Hugo seems to regard the alexandrine as the French equivalent of the hexameter. Hugo's liberal use of the caesura (see introduction) arguably makes his lines like Horace's broken yet soaring verse.

'To Théophile Gautier'

This famous poem was one of Paul Valéry's favourites. Hugo included it in the *Tombeau de Théophile Gautier,* a volume published in 1873, a year after Gautier's death. (A 'Tombeau' is a collection of poetic tributes to a recently deceased poet.) Gautier was a long-time friend of Hugo and a fellow poet. He had been instrumental in Hugo's success during the Battle of *Hernani* (see introduction and note to 'Reply to an act of accusation').

'When the theatre held Paris as if it were its prey' alludes to the 1830s, especially the Battle of *Hernani* (at which Gautier sported an outrageous outfit and was one of the most boisterous members of the audience). A hippogriff is a mythological monster with the wings, claws, and head of a griffin, and the body and hindquarters of a horse. Pegasus was the winged horse that with a stroke of its hoof caused the fountain Hippocrene to spring forth from Mount Helicon. (Mount Helicon was sacred to the muses and the Hippocrene was said to be a source of poetic inspiration.) The triumph of *Hernani* and the romantic movement signals the moment 'when Hippogriff relieved Pegasus' in the sense that the hippogriff represents a 'romantic' hodge-podge of noble and common, and Pegasus represents a kind of classically inspired beauty.

The phrase 'you will see Jehovah with God's eye' implies that Jehovah is one manifestation of a more general and encompassing God.

Hugo is claiming greatness for himself and his age by evoking the 'pyre of Hercules' in his description of the immanent funeral of the century. After Hugo died, his life was commonly compared with the course of the century.

Hugo groups Gautier with Dumas, Musset, and Lamartine as one of the last of the romantics. The implication is that Hugo is the last romantic.

Index of Titles

Index of First Lines